주한미군지위협정(SOFA)

서명 및 발효 23

_____

주한미군지위협정(SOFA)

서명 및 발효 23

| 머리말

미국은 오래전부터 우리나라 외교에 있어서 가장 긴밀하고 실질적인 우호·협력관계를 맺어 온 나라다. 6·25전쟁 정전 협정이 체결된 후 북한의 재침을 막기 위한 대책으로서 1953년 11월 한미 상호방위조약이 체결되었다. 이는 미군이 한국에 주둔하는 법적 근거였고, 그렇게 주둔하게 된 미군의 시설, 구역, 사업, 용역, 출입국, 통관과 관세, 재판권 등 포괄적인 법적 지위를 규정하는 것이 바로 주한미군지위협정(SOFA)이다. 그러나 이와 관련한 협상은 계속된 난항을 겪으며 한미 상호방위조약이 체결로부터 10년이 훌쩍 넘은 1967년이 돼서야 정식 발효에 이를 수 있었다. 그럼에도 당시 미군 범죄에 대한 한국의 재판권은 심한 제약을 받았으며, 1980년대 후반 민주화 운동과 함께 미군 범죄 문제가 사회적 이슈로 떠오르자 협정을 개정해야 한다는 목소리가 커지게 되었다. 이에 1991년 2월 주한미군지위협정 1차 개정이 진행되었고, 이후에도 여러 사건이 발생하며 2001년 4월 2차 개정이 진행되어 현재에 이르고 있다.

본 총서는 외교부에서 작성하여 최근 공개한 주한미군지위협정(SOFA) 관련 자료를 담고 있다. 1953년 한미 상호방위조약 체결 이후부터 1967년 발효가 이뤄지기까지의 자료와 더불어, 이후 한미 합동위원회을 비롯해 민·형사재판권, 시설, 노무, 교통 등 각 분과위원회의 회의록과 운영 자료, 한국인 고용인 문제와 관련한 자료, 기타 관련 분쟁 자료 등을 포함해 총 42권으로 구성되었다. 전체 분량은 약 2만 2천여 쪽에 이른다.

2024년 3월
한국학술정보(주)

| 일러두기

- 본 총서에 실린 자료는 2022년 4월과 2023년 4월에 각각 공개한 외교문서 4,827권, 76만 여 쪽 가운데 일부를 발췌한 것이다.

- 각 권의 제목과 순서는 공개된 원본을 최대한 반영하였으나, 주제에 따라 일부는 적절히 변경하였다.

- 원본 자료는 A4 판형에 맞게 축소하거나 원본 비율을 유지한 채 A4 페이지 안에 삽입하였다. 또한 현재 시점에선 공개되지 않아 '공란'이란 표기만 있는 페이지 역시 그대로 실었다.

- 외교부가 공개한 문서 각 권의 첫 페이지에는 '정리 보존 문서 목록'이란 이름으로 기록물 종류, 일자, 명칭, 간단한 내용 등의 정보가 수록되어 있으며, 이를 기준으로 0001번부터 번호가 매겨져 있다. 이는 삭제하지 않고 총서에 그대로 수록하였다.

- 보고서 내용에 관한 더 자세한 정보가 필요하다면, 외교부가 온라인상에 제공하는 『대한민국 외교사료요약집』1991년과 1992년 자료를 참조할 수 있다.

| 차례

기록물종류	문서-일반공문서철	등록번호	26048 9626	등록일자	2006-07-27
분류번호	741.12	국가코드	US	주제	

문서철명	한.미국 간의 상호방위조약 제4조에 의한 시설과 구역 및 한국에서의 미국군대의 지위에 관한 협정 (SOFA) 전59권. 1966.7.9 서울에서 서명 : 1967.2.9 발효 (조약 232호) *원본

생산과	미주과/조약과	생산년도	1952 - 1967	보존기간	영구

담당과(그룹)	조약	조약	서가번호	--

참조분류	

권차명	V.55 비세출자금기관 관계자료, 1964-66

내용목차	* 비세출자금기관 (PX) 사용자의 범위 결정문제 포함
	* UNCURK 대표단 및 사무직원에 대한 특권 인정문제 포함
	* UN개발사업처 직원 및 UN전문기구에서 파견한 각종 기술자의 주한미군 시설 계속 사용 요청(1966) 포함
	
	* 일지 :
	1953.8.7 이승만 대통령-Dulles 미국 국무장관 공동성명
	           - 상호방위조약 발효 후 군대지위협정 교섭 약속
	1954.12.2 정부, 주한 UN군의 관세업무협정 체결 제의
	1955.1월, 5월 미국, 제의 거절
	1955.4.28 정부, 군대지위협정 제의 (한국측 초안 제시)
	1957.9.10 Hurter 미국 국무차관 방한 시 각서 수교 (한국측 제의 수락 요구)
	1957.11.13. 26 정부, 개별 협정의 단계적 체결 제의
	1958.9.18 Dawling 주한미국대사, 형사재판관할권 협정 제외 조건으로 행정협정 체결 의사 전달
	1960.3.10 정부, 토지, 시설협정의 우선적 체결 강력 요구
	1961.4.10 장면 국무총리-McConaughy 주한미국대사 공동성명으로 교섭 개시 합의
	1961.4.15, 4.25 제1. 2차 한.미국 교섭회의 (서울)
	1962.3.12 정부, 교섭 재개 촉구.공한 송부
	1962.5.14 Burger 주한미국대사, 최규하 장관 면담 시 형사재판관할권 문제 제기 않는 조건으로
	           교섭 재개 통고
	1962.9.6 한.미국 간 공동성명 발표 (9월 중 교섭 재개 합의)
	1962.9.20~ 제1-81차 실무 교섭회의 (서울)
	  1965.6.7
	1966.7.8 제82차 실무 교섭회의 (서울)
	1966.7.9 서명
	1967.2.9 발효 (조약 232호)

마/이/크/로/필/름/사/항

촬영연도	*롤 번호	화일 번호	후레임 번호	보관함 번호
2006-11-24	I-06-0072	08	1-184	

0001

64. 1. 11. 11:00A.M.

1433

기 안 용 지

자체 통제		기안처	미주과 이근팔	전화번호 8— 3052	근거서류접수일자
과장	국장	차관	장관		
	전결		1/10		
관계관 서명	교 통 부				
기안 년월일	1964. 1. 10.	시행 년월일	64.1.11	보존 년한	정서 / 기장
분류 기호	외구미 722.2	전체 통제		종결	
경유 수신 참조	교 통 부 장 관	발 신	장 관		
제 목	미 주둔군지위 협정 체결교섭 자료 요청				

1. 미 주둔군지위 협정 체결을 위한 한.미간 교섭상 필요하오니 귀부 산하 관광공사에서 운영하고 있는 Foreigner's Commissary에 관하여 아래 사항을 ~~조사~~ 회보 하여 주시기 바랍니다.

조사 사항

1) 판매소 개수 및 주소
2) 사용 대상자 구분
3) 등록된 대상자별 세대 수 및 인원 총수
4) 사용 신청 및 허가 절차
5) 1인당 판매 한도액 및 월간 판매실적
6) 판매 제한 한도액과 판매실적액과의 차의의 원인
7) 1963 년도의 총 판매실적
8) 취급 품목

발송 No. 14 1964. 1. 10 외무부

승인양식 1—1—3 (1112—040—016—018) (190mm×260mm16절지)

0002

9) 미군 경영 피·엑스 취급 품목과의 가격 차의

10) 사용자의 증가를 예상한 전망 및 개선책

(1) 경영 면:

(2) 가격 면: 끝

2. 1966년 1월 17일에 계획된 제39차 건명
회의에서는 주한 외교사절 단 및 유엔
기관 원들에 대한 미군 비세출기간 시응
특전부여 문제도 토의키로 되여 있는바
상기 항목에 관한 실태 및 전망에
의거한 해문제에 대한 귀부 입장도
아울러 회시하여 주시기 바랍니다

보통문서로 재분류 (1966. 12. 31)

한·미국 간의 상호방위조약 제4조에 의한 시설과 구역 및 한국에서의 미국군대의 지위에 관한 협정(SOFA)
전59권. 1966.7.9 서울에서 서명 : 1967.2.9 발효(조약 232호) (V.55 비세출자금기관 관계자료, 1964-66)

9

1964. 1. 14

특정외래품 판매소 현황

고동부 관광국

0004

현   황

1, 판매소의 개수및 주소, 시설개요
   서울특별시 용산구 한강로 3 ─ 40 (1개소)
   판매장및 창고   108평
   상깁보관창고   248평 (임대차계약)
   냉장고 3대 야외냉장고 1대 설치

2, 이용대상자구분
        미군 px 를 이용할수 있는 일반외국인및 일시외래관광객이
   대상자으로 되어 있으며 선고사, 실업가, 기술자, 교육자, 신문기자
   등임 (약 65%가 선고사)

3, 대상자 등록상황
        (따로 붙임)

4, 등록신청및 허가절차
   판매소에서 발행하는 구매회원가입을 신청을 필한후 구매회원카드틀
   교부 받음으로써 자격이 부여됨.
   (외화예치는 상업은행에서 취급)

5, 1인당 판매한도액 및 월간판매실긱
          대인   월   75 ˢ
          소인   월   50
          판매실적   (따로붙임)

6, 판매재한 한도액과 판매실적액과의 차이의원인
   가, 외화및 기타 자물사정으로 정기에   상깁공급이 원활하지
       못하고 있음.
   나, 고객들이 원하는 품목의 구색을 갖우지 못하고 있음.
   다, 한국에 장기간 기주하여 식생활이 한국화된 사람이 비고적
       많음. (선고사 등)

0005

한·미국 간의 상호방위조약 제4조에 의한 시설과 구역 및 한국에서의 미국군대의 지위에 관한 협정(SOFA) 11
전59권. 1966.7.9 서울에서 서명 : 1967.2.9 발효(조약 232호) (V.55 비세출자금기관 관계자료, 1964-66)

7, 판매실적

　　대인　　　월　　　/ 75$

　　소인　　　"　　　50

　　판매실적　　(따토불입)

8, 취급품목

　　외래품　　　식료품, 조미료, 육류, 가정용품, 냉동품

　　　　　　　주류, 연초(주류, 연초는 월품 판매량을 제한)

　　국산품　　　야채, 구실, 휴지, 기타 기타식료품.

9, 미군 취급품목과의 가격차이

　　미군　　　상품원가　25%　　(원가에는 수출세 면제

　　　　　　　　　　　　　　　　　수송비 불포함)

　　판매소　　　　　25%

10, 이용자의 증가를 예상한 전망밑 개선책

　　가, 경영면

　　　(1) 구매회원 대표들도 구성된 자문위원회와 긴밀한 협조.

　　　(2) 지방회원에 대한 정기적인 속달과 배달 제도의 적극추진

　　　(3) 우량국산품 판매의 확대화

　　　(4) 써비스의 향상

　　나, 가격면

　　박리다매 주의를 원칙으로하고 현관리 운영비 25%를 인하하도

　록 재검토

　　다, 시설면

　　냉장고, 진열대 계산기등 기타 시설을 개선함.

0006

당부의 의견

1, 군사 산하 사업소에서 (운수사업소 판매소)
   획득한 외화로 특별계정을 설치하여 구매회전 자금제도가
   인급함.(재무, 상공부)

2, 1964년도 소요외화중 1월에 우선20만$의 배정이 시급함.
   (재무부)

3, 현재 상공부령 76호에 의거 규제된 취급상품의 일부확대조치가
   필요함(상공, 재무)

4, 신규 대상자 약300세대에 의하여는 상품발주 시설개선등 준비가간
   을 참작하여 5월초부터는 취급이 가능하다고 사료됨.

상 품 판 매 전 망

구매인원	최고판매액	최저판매액	평균판매액
현인원 2000명	일인당 월50불 $1,200,000	일인당 월20불 $480,000	1인당 월30불 $720,000
외고관및 기타회원 300세대	세대당 월 $150 $546,000	세대당 월100불 $360,000	세대당 125불 $450,000
계	$1,746,000	$840,000	$1,170,000
필요한 발주기금 20의 경우	$1,396,800	$672,000	$936,000

외상거래 250,000.$

한·미국 간의 상호방위조약 제4조에 의한 시설과 구역 및 한국에서의 미국군대의 지위에 관한 협정(SOFA)
전59권. 1966.7.9 서울에서 서명 : 1967.2.9 발효(조약 232호) (V.55 비세출자금기관 관계자료, 1964-66)   13

구 매 미 원 사 항

1, 국적별 구매세대(1963.12.31 현재)

구분 / 국적별	지역별 세대수					직원수		
	서울	지방	임시	단체	계	성인	20세미만	계
미 국	413	213	13	5	644	903	472	1,375
서 독	45	8	2		55	96	9	105
영 국	31	7			38	58	17	75
카 나 다	18	7			25	37	19	56
아 이 런 드	19	55			74	75		75
오스트랄리아	11	6	1		19	25	11	36
뉴 질 런 드	4				4	5		5
이 스 라 엘	4				4	6	1	7
화 란	3		1		4	5	2	7
노 위 이	3				3	4	2	6
벨 지 움	2				2	2		2
서 서	7	3			10	14		14
오 스 트 리 아	2	3			5	6	2	8
불 란 서	3	3	1		7	10	4	14
자 유 중 국	8		2		10	13	2	15
이 태 리	3				3	3		3
스 페 인	2				2	2		2
알 젠 틴	1				1	1		1
일 논	56	3	42		101	106	5	111
비 율 빈	5		1		6	9	3	12
던 마 크	1				1	1		1
마 레 이	1				1	2		2
계	641	308	63	5	1,017	1,383	549	1,932

0008

상 품 관 세 미 정 산 표

품명					1963년도		
1	936,726.00	1,179,726.80	221,038.00	116,377.00	87,296.00	77,920.00	33,895.00	2,672,972.80
2	1,295,507.00	894,876.00	284,352.00	101,460.00	190,682.00	301,823.00	31,392.00	3,096,956.00
3	1,080,394.00	1,044,950.00	263,076.00	104,345.00	170,648.00	251,179.00	46,704.00	2,962,754.00
4	1,110,590.00	836,532.00	210,439.00	97,140.00	204,238.00	188,123.00	55,891.00	2,856,353.00
5	1,204,361.00	1,553,036.00	327,356.00	106,228.00	319,036.00	245,508.00	162,532.00	3,836,079.00
6	1,265,275.00	995,358.00	319,443.00	66,545.00	313,511.00	220,717.00	154,203.00	3,333,049.00
7	1,011,082.00	1,313,005.00	284,543.00	11,676.00	308,633.00	376,011.00	139,412.00	3,535,162.00
8	790,068.00	1,166,747.00	314,974.00	12,975.00	321,267.00	232,811.00	106,351.00	2,943,217.00
9	732,917.00	1,215,310.00	411,056.00	11,145.00	308,098.00	154,197.00	93,575.00	3,056,338.00
10	901,059.00	873,656.00	297,640.00	12,569.00	410,565.00	139,837.00	83,531.00	2,318,467.00
11	396,601.00	1,013,282.00	291,036.00	8,612.00	327,134.00	116,726.00	100,913.00	2,250,564.00
12	1,277,756.00	2,310,762.00	444,556.00	34,003.00	328,064.00	291,095.00	156,315.00	4,637,559.00
계	11,603,777.00	14,446,000.80	3,748,956.00	677,224.00	3,463,728.00	2,629,265.00	1,106,714.00	
	30.7	33.4	10	1.8	9.2	7.0	7.9	100

대한민국 외무부

발신전보

번호: WTH-0113
번호: WUK-0114
일시: 131720

긴급

외 신 과
전 수 암 호

수신인: ___주태대사, 주영대사___

주둔군 지위협정 체결교섭에 참고하고저 아래사항을 문의하오니
조속히 내사하여 보고하시기 바람:

1. 귀주재국에 주둔하고 있는 미국군대 PX 의 사용이 허가된자의
   범위

2. 통상 PX 사용이 허용되고 있는 군대 구성원, 군속 및 그들의
   가족외에도 관례적으로 PX 사용이 허용된자가 있다면 어떠한
   자들인지 구체적으로 알려주시기 바람. (외구미) 끝

장 관

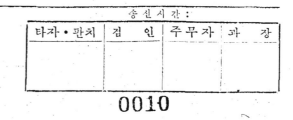

미주과	앙고재	일 월 일	담 당	과 장	국 장	특별보좌관	차 관	장 관
			②⑤					

공재관		자체	외구가북란	기안처		송신시간:			
		통제	손일동			타자·판치	검 인	주무자	과 장
긴 제									

필 요 ☐   보안관폐

0010

대 한 민 국 외 무 부

발 신 전 보

긴 급

번 호: WJA-01092
일 시: 131720

외 신 과
| 접 수 | 암 호 |

수 신 인: ___주 일 대 사___

주둔군지위협정 체결교섭에 참고하고저 아래사항을 문의하오니

조속히 내사하여 보고하시기 바람:

1. 미일협정 제15조에 관한 합의의사록에 의하면 PX 사용은 "통상해외에서
   그러한 특권이 부여된 미국정부 관리 및 인원"도 이용할수 있도록
   규제되고 있는바 이범주속에 어떠한 사람들이 포함되는지 구체적인
   내용

2. 그들의 가족들의 PX 사용 허용 여부

3. 협정상 PX 사용이 허용된 군대 구성원, 군속 및 그들의 가족과
   전기 (1)항에 속하는자 외에 (미국외의 타국 외교관등) 관례적으로
   PX 사용이 허가되고 있는자의 유무 (외구미) 끝

장 관

미주과	양고재	일월오일	담 당	과 장	국 장	특별보좌관	차 관	장 관
			김					

송신시간 :

타자·판치	검 인	주무자	과 장

동 제 관		자체 동제	외채(?)관 기안처			
긴 제						

필 요 ☐   보안불필요 ☐

0011

대한민국 외무부

착신전보

ORD.
종   별

수신인 : 장관

발신인 : 주영대사

대WUK 0114

대통지시에 대하여 하기와같이 보고함.

1. 영국에 주둔하고있는 미국군 대PX 사용이 허가된자는 미국

육, 해공군 소속군인뿐이라함.

2. 영국 주재미국 대사관 직원들은 특별대우로 동PX 를 사용할수

있다함. (외구미)

1964 JAN 15 PM 7 11

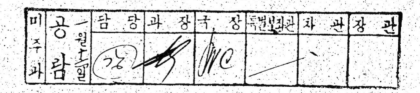

미주과	공람	일원十일	담당	과장	국장	특별보좌관	차관	장관

구미

외신과

접인

수신시간 :

강

0012

대한민국 외무부

착신전보

URGENT
종 별

번 호: THW-0121
일 시: 170900

수신인: 장관

발신인: 주태국대사

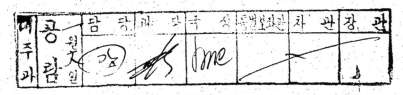

참조: 구미국장

대 WTH -0113

1. 당지 미국PX 의 사용이 허가된자의 범위는 다음과같음.

A. ALL U. S. MILITARY PERSONNEL AND THEIR DEPENDENTS

B. CIVIL SERVICE PERSONNEL OF U. S. EMBASSY AND THEIR DEPENDENTS

C. CIVIL SERVICE PERSONNEL OF USIS, USOM AND OICC COFFICER IN
CHARGE OF CONSTRUCTION AND THE DEPENDENTS

D. RADIO TEMPORARY DUTY PERSONNEL AND THEIR DEPENDENT

E. MEMBERS OF US MEDICAL UNITS ATTACHED TO US EMBASSY AND
THEIR DEPENDENTS

F. US MEDICAL MISSION ATTACHED TO 7TH DAY ADVENTIST HOSPITAL
AND THEIR DEPENDENTS

전기c 항 OICC 는 실질적으로는 미군정보기관이다고함.

2. 따라서 공무로 당지에 파견되어있는 모든 미국인은 P X 의 사용이 허가
되고있는것으로 보임.

1964 JAN 17 AM 11 37

수신시간:

비서	통상	증정	재무
정무 ○	문서	기기	조달
정보	의전	국방	농림
외교	총무	상공	

검 인

0013

외 신 과

관리
번호 1550

상　　　공　　　부

상역상 1311.13

1964.　1.　17.

수　신　외무부 장관

참　조　정무국 미주과장

제　목　P.X에 관한 질의

　　　1964. 1. 14.자 P.X이용에 관한 귀부주관 회의에서 논의된바에 의하여 당부소관사항을 정책자료에 자하고저 하오니, 하기사항에 대하여 시급히 귀부의견을 회시하여 주시기 바랍니다.

기

　　　1. P.X의 본래의 정의(定義)와 목적(目的)은 무엇이며, 그 이용한계는 어디까지 인것이 원칙인가,

　　　2. 국제적으로 P.X를 이용하고 있는 범위는 어디까지인가

　　　3. 협정안중 c.d.e.f 각항별로 주한외국인의 수는 얼마인가(추정 수라도 좋음). "끝"

보통문서로 재분류 (1966. 12. 31.)

1964년 9월 17일 미주과장 직권으로 0시2분 도재분류

상　공　부　장　관　　　이　　　병　　　호

0014

기 안 용 지

<table>
<tr><td rowspan="2">자통
체계</td><td rowspan="2">의우사우란
손일동</td><td rowspan="2">기안처</td><td rowspan="2">미주과
이근팔</td><td>전화번호</td><td>근거서류접수일자</td></tr>
<tr><td colspan="2"></td></tr>
<tr><td colspan="2"></td><td>과장</td><td>국장</td><td>차관</td><td>장관</td><td></td></tr>
<tr><td colspan="2"></td><td></td><td>정</td><td></td><td></td><td></td></tr>
<tr><td>관계관
서 명</td><td colspan="5"></td></tr>
<tr><td>기안
년월일</td><td>1964. 1. 30.</td><td>시행
년월일</td><td colspan="2">1964</td><td>보존
년한</td></tr>
<tr><td>분류
기호</td><td>외구미 722.2</td><td>전체
통체</td><td colspan="2"></td><td>정서 기 장</td></tr>
<tr><td>경수
참조</td><td>유신</td><td colspan="2">내무부장관</td><td>발신</td><td>장 관</td></tr>
<tr><td>제 목</td><td colspan="5">미주둔군지위협정 체결교섭 자료 요청</td></tr>
</table>

1. 미주둔군지위협정 체결을 위하여 한.미 실무자교섭회의
에서는 미군 피엑스를 포함한 비세출자금기관조항을 검토 중
인바 동 조항 심의에 참고코저 하오니 귀부에서 특정외태품
거태 단속 결과 미군 피엑스로 부터 유출된 물자취체 실적에
관하여 아태 사항에 대한 가능한 구체적인 자료를 당부에
제공하여 주시기 바랍니다.

    가. 취체 물품 동록

    나. 건수.

    다. 액수.

    라. 관련자 수(한국인 및 민국인 별)

    마. 기타

2. 1964. 1. 30 자 The Korean Republic 지 4 페지에 있는
PX 관계 기사 내용의 확실성 여부도 아울러 회보 해주시기 바랍니다.

승인양식 1-1-3　　(1112-040-016-018)　　　　(190mm×260mm16절지)

0015

협 조 전	응 신 기 일

문서번호 외미전 710-19   제 목 외인판매소 운영에 대한 건의

수 신: 구미국장 발 신:의견실장 년 월 일 1964.2.4. 제 1 의견

외국특저단체 한국연합회 로부터 별첨 운영에 관하여 건의
서한을 송부하여 왔으므로 **동**사본을 송부하오니 참고하시기
바랍니다.

의 견 실 장   정   도   순

KOREA ASSOCIATION OF VOLUNTARY AGENCIES

K A V A

1-1 1Ka, Myung-dong
Chong-Ku, Seoul
(Seoul 1.P.O. Box 1641)

APO 301
San Francisco, Calfifornia
(letter Mail   Only)

January 20, 1964

Gen. Il Kwon Chung
Minister of Foreign Affairs
Republic of Korea

Dear Gen. Chung:

On behalf of the seventy (70) foreign voluntary agency
members of KAVA, I should like to bring to your attention
a matter of great importance to us. The matter of concern
to us is the Foreigners' Commissary, which is operated
under the Korea Tourist Bureau of the Ministry of Transportation.

The supply of food in the Foreigners' Commissary has
been insufficient to meet the needs of the 2,000 foreign
customers who are authorized to purchase at the Foreigners'
Commissary. The primary cause of an inadequate stock of
food has been the lack of money on the part of the Foreigners'
Commissary to stock what is required.

What may meet this problem of enough money to maintain an
adequate stock of food is a revolving fund to enable the
Foreigners' Commissary to maintain a regular supply of food.

The purchasing power of the foreing community might be
roughly estimated from $720,000 to $1,000,000 per year.
Properly stocked and operated, the Foreigners' Commissary
would provide a source of foreign exchange for Korea. An
increase in the present number of foreign customers for the
Commissary can be reasonalby expected in 1964. Your action
now to provide a revolving fund for the Foreigners'
Commissary will be a constructive step in obtaining an
increasing foreign exchange for Korea.

KAVA is anxious to do what it can to bring about a Commissary
that is properly stocked and efficiently operated. Please call
upon me, on behalf of KAVA for any information and help you
may require in connection with providing for a bigger and
better Foreigners' Commissary that will benefit Korea and
the foreign community.

Please accept this letter as a formal request on the part of
KAVA and its member agencies for your action in this very
important matter.

Sincerely,

0017

Frank W. Ryan
Chairman of KAVA

기 안 용 지

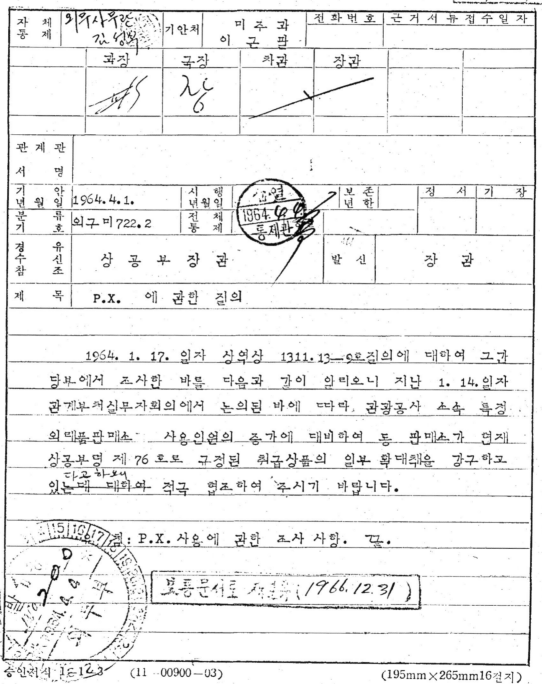

관리번호 1434

자동통체제	외무사무관 김성부	기안처	미주과 이군팔		전화번호	근거서류접수일자
	과장	국장		차관	장관	

관계관서명					
기안년월일	1964. 4. 1.	시행년월일	1964. 통제관	보존년한	정서기장
분류기호	외구미 722.2	전통체제			
경수참조	유신조	상공부장관		발신	장관
제목	P.X. 에 관한 질의				

    1964. 1. 17. 일자 상역상 1311. 13─9호질의에 대하여 그간
당부에서 조사한 바를 다음과 같이 알리오니 지난 1. 14.일자
관계부처실무자회의에서 논의된 바에 따라 관광공사 소속 특정
의때품판매소 사용인원의 증가에 대비하여 동 판매소가 현재
상공부령 제 76 호로 규정된 취급상품의 일부 확대책을 강구하고
다고하오니
있는데 대하여 적극 협조하여 주시기 바랍니다.

    첨 : P.X. 사용에 관한 조사 사항. 끝.

보통문서로 재분류 (1966. 12. 31)

승인처식 1─123   (11─00900─03)   (195mm×265mm16절지)

0018

1. **P.X.** 의 정의와 목적 및 이용한계:

    가. **P.X.** 의 정의 및 목적:

        적당한 일반 판매시설이 없거나 또는 적당한 가격으로 필요한 품품을 공급하지 못 하는 지역에서 미군인, 군속, 기타 인정된 자에 대하여 일상 필수품을 판매함을 그 목적으로 한다.

    나. 이용 한계:

        (1) 미군대 구성원

        (2) 미국방성 군속

        (3) 미군 주둔지역에서 복무하는 U.S.O.관계 직원.

        (4) 국방성 계약자를 통하여 고용된 미국민간인 기술자.

        (5) 국방성 계약자

        (6) 국방성 보조기관 직원

        (7) 주한 유엔군대 구성원

        (8) 국방성 이외의 미행정부 직원.

        (9) 유엔관계 대표, 직원,

        (10) 미군에 복무중인 미 **Red Cross** 직원.

        (11) 미군표 사용이 허가된 유엔군 종군기자.

        (12) **AID** (USOM)의 직접 고용 직원 및 계약상 **P.X.** 사용이 허가된 **AID** 관계 계약자.

        (13) 예비역 군인으로서 현역 훈련을 받고 있는 자.

        (14) 퇴역 미군인.

        (15) 외국 외교단원.

        (16) 저명인사 및 공무여행중인 미군인과 동반가족.

        (17) 미 8군 사령관이 인정하는 자.

        (18) 상기 각항 해당자의 가족.

        이상 열거한 바와 같이 **P.X.** 사용 대상자의 범위는 상당히 광범위한 것임.

2. 국제적인 **P.X.** 이용 범위:

    가. 영국: 미군대 구성원 및 미대사관 직원.

0019

나. 태국: 미군대 구성원, 군속 및 그들의 가족, 미대사관직원 및 동 가족, USIS 관계 직원 및 가족, 7th Day Adventist Hospital 소속 U.S. Medical Mission 관계 직원. 등 공무로 태국에 파견되어 있는 모든 미국인임.

3. 협정초안 각항별 수: C,D,E, 각항별 인원 수는 확실치 않으나 논의의 대상이 되고 있는 (F)항 해당자 만드 약 300 세대로 추산하고 있음. 끝.

(1966.12.31)

0020

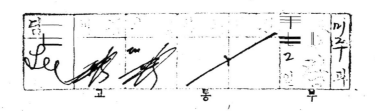

고   통   부

고관업 1535,6 — 나817   1964, 5,1.

수신 외무부장관

제목 특정외래품 판매소 운영

　　　1, 특정외래품판매소는 그 영업의 성질상 국내 유일의 외국
인 생활필수품의 공급소로서 이들이 필요로 하는 물품을 동판매
소에서 구입할수 있도록 상품을 항상 보유하고 있어야 하나
그간 정부외환 사정상 동판매소에서 필요로하는 상품 구입비에
대한 외환의 부족으로 영업이 부진 상태에 있든바

　　　2, 금번 재무부에서 동사업의 필요성을 감안하여 FY 64에
필요한 외환 $840,000을 배정조치하여 제1차로 1/4기분 $200,000
에 상당한 물품을 도입 추진중에 있으며

　　　3, 상품 취급 품목도 대폭 확대 계획중에 있으므로

　　　4, 동판매소의 운영을 매우 호전될 것으로 기대하오니 귀
부에서 추진중이던 주한외교사절단원및 가족(약300세대)에 대한
동판매소 이용을 적극 추진하여 주시기 바랍니다. 끝

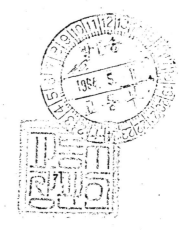

　　　　　　　고통부장관　　　　　김　　　　　　운

0021

특정 외래품 판매소 운영개선 ~~방안~~ 현황및 전망

0022

1, 외국인(구매좌원) 이용 현황

　가, 구매좌원 심수포 ;

　　1) 전체인원　　　　세대수 : 1,005

　　　　　　　　　　　가족수 : 1,902

　　2) 지익범분포　　　세대인원　서울　624(1,237명)

　　　　　　　　　　　　　　　　지방　309(592 명)

　　3) 국 적 별

국 적 별	세 대 수	가 족 수	국 적 별	세 대 수	가 족 수
미 국	632	1,344	스 위 스	10	14
서 독	53	103	오스드리아	5	8
영 국	40	77	붉 란 서	8	14
카 나 다	25	56	중 국	10	15
아 일 랜 드	74	75	이 대 리	4	4
오스드라리아	17	36	스 페 인	2	2
뉴 지 랜 드	4	5	아 르 젠 틴	1	1
외스라엘	4	7	일 본	104	111
홀 랜 드	4	7	필 립 핀	6	12
놈 웨 이	3	6	덴 마 드	1	1
벨 지 움	2	2	마 래 이	1	2

　나, 구매직원 직업별 통계　　(1963, 12, 31 현재)

지역\직업	기술자	상업	선교사	교육자	기 자	의 사	기 타	계
서울	62	189	257	54	13	15	34	624
지방	35	17	230	12		8	7	309
계	87	206	487	66	13	23	113	1,005

0023

FY63

다, 년간 이용인원

년 이용 수	세대수	인원
	10,983	14,419 명
월 평 균	915	1,202 명

라. 품종별 판매실적

품종 \ 구분	판 매 액		판매비율
식 료 품	₩11,603,777,00	$ 89,259,83	30,7 %
음 료	14,496,080,80	111,508,31	33,4 %
과 자	3,748,956,00	28,838,12	10 %
냉 동	677,224,00	5,209,41	1,8 %
담 배	3,463,728,00	26,644,06	9,2 %
가 정 용 품	2,629,965,00	20,230,50	7 %
위 탁 품	1,106,714,00	8,513,18	7,9 %
계	37,726,444,80	290,203,42	100 %

0024

2 타기구와의 경영현황

구분 업체	보유상품 종류	월평균 판매액	1인당월구 매한도액	1인당월평 균구매액	회원수
공사	평균500종	$24,184	대인 $75 소인 $50	$20,12 (이용자기준)	1,010세대 (1907명)
미8군 카미사리	3,000종	$60,000	$50	$50	1,200세대
미대사관 카미사리	800종	$12,000	무제한	$60	300세대

0025

3.64년도 사업전망 및 소요외화

가. 상품판매전망

월	현 회 원 (2000명)	포섭예상회원 (300세대)	월간판매예상액	상하반기 판매예상
1—6월	$15×2,000명		$30,000	$180,000
7—12월	$50×2,000명	$150×300세대	$145,000	$870,000

년간 판매예상총액 $1,050,000

(주) 1—6월까지 상품재고 확보및 회원확대 포섭을 대비하든
준비기간으로 하고 판매전망을 63년도의 실적에 기준을둠.
7—12월까지는 상품의 원활한 공급과 회원확대 포섭이 실현
될것을 예상하고 전망한것임.

나. 소요외화 (상품 구매용)

판매예상액	상품 구매소요외화	외화 수입(이윤)
$1,050,000	$840,000	$210,000

(주) 소요외화 산출내역

$$1,050,000 \times \frac{100}{125} = \$840,000$$

판매가격 = CIF (수입가격) × 125

0026

다, 외화 사용 계획

(1) 분기별 사용계획

1/4 분기	2/4 분기	3/4 분기	4/4 분기	계
$200,000	$ 240,000	$ 200,000	$ 220,000	840,000

(2) 품종별 상품 구매 계획(년간)

구 분	발 주 액	비 율	취급상품 종류
식 료	$336,000	40 %	450 종
음 료	$252,000	30 %	150 종
과자류	$ 42,000	5 %	100 종
냉동물	$ 42,000	5 %	20 종
담 배	$ 42,000	5 %	20 종
가정용품	$ 84,000	10 %	150 종
기 타	$ 42,000	5 %	110 종
계	$840,000	100 %	1,000 종

0027

현 재 취 급 품 목

1, 양주류
2, 선과(과입에 한한다)
3, 건과("   "   )
4, 각종다류
5, 청량음료수류(코카콜라 오렌지 소다수, 및 진제일에 한한다
6, 쥬우스류
7, 양식 요리용 각종식료품
8, 양식요리용 육류(냉동육 또는 관입에 한한다, 양식요리용 야채
   류 관입에 한단다)
   양식 요리용 어개류 (관입에 한단다)
   양식 요리용 조미료(관입에 한한다)
   양식 요리용 양신료 (관입에 한한다)
   제과재료(조코렛 푸딩및 바니라푸딩에 한한다)
   연유분류(관입에 한한다)
   낫드류("   )
   푸른스 ("   )
   시럽스 ("   )
   면제류 (   )
            (지대임)
   설탕 (각 사탕, 그립정탕 및 색소설탕에 한한다)
   낙동물 (바터 및 치스에 한한다)
9, 빠다
10, 치스및 우유제품
11, 우유분
12, 관입우유
13, 우육
14, 계류
15, 오드밀

0028

16, 야 채(건조품, 관입및 생야채)

17, 관입 및 건조과실

18, 향료및 조미료

19 설 당

20 조리용 및 사다타유

21, 혼합과자 및 특수 소맥분

22, 비누및 청쟁제

23, 변소용 약품류

24, 과 자 류

25, 가정필수품

26, 연 초 류

27, 주정음료, 강심주, 합성주

28, 빌 감속

29, 각종 제관물

30, 차, 커피, 코코아

0029

⊙ 추가 취급 품목

1, 각종 화장품

2, 사진 재료(필림, 인화지, 투태쉬구)

3, 문방구(만년필 사ー프 잉크)

4, 가정용품(각종파리슈 및 웹스, 취사용품 식탁용품, 세척제, 면도용품)

5, 위생용품(반찬소, 붕대, 닳지면, 앨폼(약웅) 액체 암도니어, 비타민
   등 영양제)

0030

협 조 전	응 신 기 일

분 류 기 호	제목 문서이첩

수 신 미주과장　　　　　　발신일자 64. 5. 25.　　　（협조제의）

별첨 교통부로부터의 공한은 귀과 소관으로 사료되여

이첩 합니다.

유첩 : 교관업 1535,6 - 4845

（발신명의）　　통상진흥과장　김영승

（제1의견）

（제2의견）

교　　통　　부

교관업 1535,6— 484

1964,5,1

수신 외무부장관

제목 미 군용물품중 식료 일부분양 추천

　　　　국제관광공사 총재토부터 별첨과 같이 동사 산하 특정외래품
판매소 소요물품의 도입지연으로 앞으로 동 판매소 이용 외국인에
대한 물품의 적기 공급이 불가능함으로 이를 해결위 위한 잠정적인
대책으로 미군용 물품중 식료품 일부를 분양 판매코저 계획하고 있
는바 동 물품의 일부분양 가능 여부와 수속절차를 주한 미국 대사
관과 협의하여 주시고 그결과를 회보하여 주기 바랍니다.

유첨　국제관광공사 총재가 보내온 공문사본. 끝

교 통 부 장 관　　　　김　　　윤

1964. 5. 25. 통상국으로 과외결재

0032

국 제 관 광 공 사

국관업238   1964,4,14
수신 교통부장관
참조
제목 미군용 물품중 식료일부분양 추천의뢰

    1. 당공사 산하 외래품 판매소는 *FY* 64에 소요될 외화로서
총 $840,000 을 정부로 부터 1964,3,31 배정받었으나 배정날자가 이
와 같이 지연되어 제1차 발주를 1964,4 월중순에 하게 되드라도 동 물
품이 8월초순에야 도착 판매될 예정이므로 1964,5월부터 8월7까지 약
3개월간은 공백기가 생기게 되어 외국인의 일상생활에 지장을 초래하
게된 실정입니다.

    2. 따라서 상기 공백기간중 외국인의 일상생활에 대한 편의를
제공하고저 외래품 판매소 자물위원인 *FRANK. W. RYAN* 씨를 통
하여 미군용 물품중 일상식료분양에 대하여 미 8군과 비공식으로 교섭
한바 분양할 의사가 있으나 한국정부 기관의 미 대사에 대한 분양 요
청서에 의거하여 미국대사가 8군 사령관에게 분양을 지시하여야 된다
합니다.

    3. 이상 내용을 검토하시와 교통부 장관께서 외무부장관 경유
미국대사에게 분양요청을 하여 주시기 바랍니다. 끝

            국 제 관 광 공 사
                    총 재 오 재 경

                                              0033

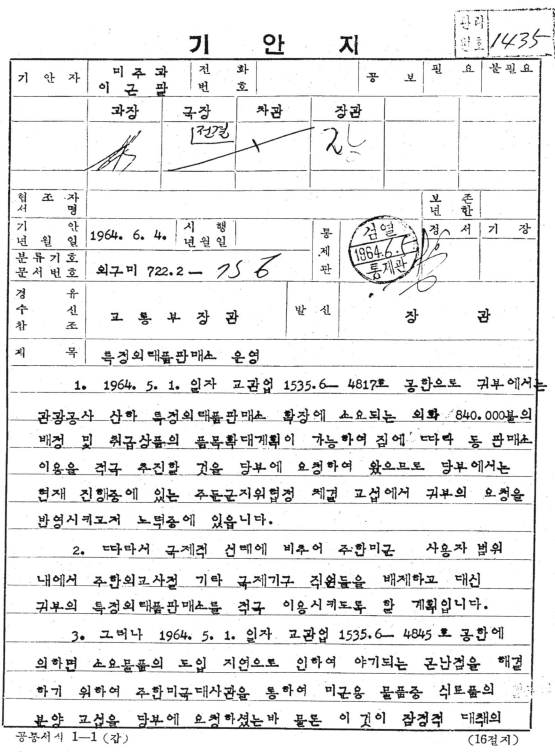

기 안 지

관리
번호 /435

기 안 자	미주과 이 근 팔	전 화 번 호			공 보	필 요	불필요

	과장	국장	차관	장관			
		[전결]		2L			

협 조 서 명 자			보 존 년 한

기 안 년 월 일	1964. 6. 4.	시 행 년 월 일	통 제 관	검열 1964.6. 통제관	정 서	기 장

| 분 류 기 호
문 서 번 호 | 외구미 722.2 — 156 | | | | | |

경 유 수 신 참 조	교 통 부 장 관	발 신	장 관

제 목	특정외태품판매소 운영

   1. 1964. 5. 1. 일자 교관업 1535.6— 4817호 공한으로 귀부에서는

관광공사 산하 특정외태품판매소 확장에 소요되는 외화 840.000불의

배정 및 취급상품의 품목확대계획이 가능하여 짐에 따라 동 판매소

이용을 적극 추진할 것을 당부에 요청하여 왔으므로 당부에서는

현재 진행중에 있는 주둔군지위협정 체결 교섭에서 귀부의 요청을

반영시키고저 노력중에 있읍니다.

   2. 따라서 국제적 선례에 비추어 주한미군 사용자 범위

내에서 주한외교사절 기타 국제기구 직원들을 배제하고 대신

귀부의 특정외태품판매소를 적극 이용시키도록 할 계획입니다.

   3. 그러나 1964. 5. 1. 일자 교관업 1535.6— 4845 호 공한에

의하면 소요물품의 도입 지연으로 인하여 야기되는 곤난점을 해결

하기 위하여 주한미국대사관을 통하여 미군용 물품중 식료품의

분양 교섭을 당부에 요청하셨는바 물론 이 것이 잠정적 대책의

공통서식 1—1 (갑)

(16절지)

하나라고 사려되기는 하나 주둔군지위협정 체결 교섭에 임하는

우리측의 입장에 지장을 초래할 우려가 있아오니 이 점 양찰

하시어 운영면에 최선을 다하여 주시기 바랍니다. 특히 여사한

문제가 있을 경우에는 미 8군 혹은 미대사관측에 교섭하기

전에 당부와 협의토록 배려하시기 바랍니다. 끝.

보통문서로 재분류 (1966. 12. 31.)

협 조 전

응 신 기

문서번호 외구미 722.2 ― 23   제 목 주둔군지위협정 체결 교섭

수 신: 의전실장   발 신: 구미국장   년 월 일 1964. 6. 11 제 1 의견

　　한·미 간 주둔군지위협정 체결 교섭에서 논의되고 있는
비세출자금기관(P.X.) 사용자의 범위 결정에 관하여 우리
측은 별첨과 같은 입장을 취하려 하오니 이에 대한
귀견을 회시하여 주시기 바랍니다.

　　유 첨: 비세출자금기관 사용자의 범위 결정.　　끝

보통문서로 재분류 (1966. 12. 31.)

구 미 국 장   장 상 문

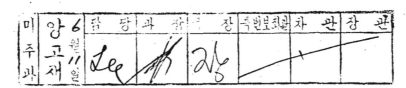

미주과	양고재	6월 11일	담 당	과 장	국 장	특번보좌관	차 관	장 관
			Lee		26			

비세출자금기관 사용자의 범위 결정

1. 미측이 제안한 사용자의 범위

미측은 제 37 차 주둔군지위협정 체결 교섭 실무자회의에서 미군 P.X.사용자의 범위를 별첨과 같이 결정할 것을 제안하여 온바 그 범위는 상당히 광범위한 것이며 특히 문제가 되는 것은 (f)항의 규정으로서 이에 해당하는 사용자는 주한미대사관직원을 제외한 주한 외교단원 전원, UNCURK, UNTAB, Scandinavian Medical Mission, AKF, 및 International Lutheran Mission 등 각기관의 직원들로서 한국 정부의 명시적 합의에 의하여서 미군이 사용을 허가하는 것으로 되어 있음.

2. 우리측의 입장

우리측은 국내산업의 보호육성 및 국제적관례등 제점을 고려하여 미측이 제안하여 온 사용자의 범위를 가능한한 축소하기 위하여 주한 미군당국이 한국정부의 명시적 합의에 의하여 상기 각 기관의 직원 들 에게 P.X. 사용을 허가할 수 있는 (f)항의 규정을 삭제할 것을 제의코저 함.

(1) 미군당국이 관세면제의 특전 하에 수입하는 P.X. 물품이 국내 시장에 유출됨으로서 시장을 교란시키고 국내산업을 위축시키는 결과를 초래하고 있는 실정에 감하여 국내산업의 보호를 위하여 서는 P.X. 물품의 시장유출을 봉쇄할 것이 요망되며 따라서 현 사용자의 범위를 가능한한 축소할 것이 필요함.

(2) P.X. 사용에 관한 국제적 선례를 보면 영국에서는 미군대구성원 및 미대사관 직원이 사용하고 있으며 태국에서는 미군대구성원 군속 및 그들의 가족 미대사관직원 및 가족 USIS 직원 및 가족 7th Day Adventist Hospital 소속 U.S. Medical Mission 직원등 공무로 태국에 파견되어 있는 미국인들이 사용하고 있으나 우리 나바에서와 같이 광범위하게 사용하고 있는 예는 볼수 없음.

0037

(3) 사용자의 범위를 축소하기 위하여서는 우선 해당자들이
P.X.를 사용하지 못하게 되여도 그들의 일상생활에 있어서
별로 지장이 없도록 하기 위하여 교통부 산하 관광공사에서
경영하고 있는 특정외래품판매소를 대체 사용케 하고저 그간
관계부처와 접촉하여 온 결과 동 판매소가 사용자의 증가를
예상하여 금년도에 필요로 하는 외화 840,000 불을 배정
받고 취급품목도 확대할 수 있게 됨에 따라 (f)항 해당자
들에게 동 판매소를 이용시킬 수 있는 준비태세가 이루어
지고 있음.

3. 귀실에 대한 문의 사항

(1) 미측안 (f)항 해당자들은 그 대부분이 주한외교단원을 위시하여
UNCURK 직원등 외교특권을 향유하고 있으며 귀실과의 접촉이
빈번한 자들로서 이러한 자들에 대하여 미군 PX 사용을 배제하려는
우리측 입장에 대한 귀실의 의견.

(2) 상기자들은 P.X.를 사용할 수 없게 될 경우 귀실을 통하여
일상필수품을 수입하려 할 가능성도 있는바 이에 수반되는
귀실의 사무 취급상의 문제점이 있으면 그에 대한 의견.   끝

0038

AGREED MINUTE

The United States Armed Forces may grant the use of the organizations referred to in paragraph 1 of Article to: (a) other officers or personnel of the United States Government ordinarily accorded such privileges; (b) those other non-Korean Armed Forces in Korea under the Unified Command which receive logistical support from the United States Armed Forces, and their members; (c) those non-Korean persons whose presence in the Republic of Korea is solely for the purpose of providing contract services financed by the United States Government; (d) those organizations which are present in the Republic of Korea primarily for the benefit and service of the United States Armed Forces, such as the American Red Cross and the United Service Organizations, and their non-Korean personnel; (e) dependents of the foregoing; and (f) other persons and organizations with the express consent of the Government of the Republic of Korea

0039

협　조　전	응　신　기 ∨ 일

문서번호의의전 _710.110_　　　제 목　주둔군지위협정 체결 교섭

수　신 : 구미국장　　발　신 : 의전실장　　년 월 일 1964. 6. 18제 1 의견

　　외구미 722.2-23 호로 문의하신 주한 외교공관원의 피. 엑스

사용에 대한 문의 사항에 대하여 아래와같이 회신합니다.

　　　　　　　　　　　　기

1. (F) 항해당자에 대한 P.X 사용권은 당연히 배제하여야

함.

2. 전기인들에 대한 P. X 상용이 배제될경우 당실은 주한

외교공관원 (국제기구포함) 의 일상물품수입을 위산 사무취급준비가

이미되어있읍니다.

　　　　의　전　실　장　정　도

제 목: 특정외래품 판매소 운영

특정외래품판매소 운영에 관하여 1964.7.2. 동 소장과 대화한 내용은 다음과 같음.

1. 특정외래품판매소에서 판매하는 물품의 가격 결정은 원가에 관리비, 임차료, 파손율, 순이익등 제점을 고려하여 결정하되 미국인도 포함된 자문위원회의 의견도 참작하며 결정권은 소장의 권한에 속하고 있음.

2. 가격 구성 제 요소는 다음과 같음.
   인천 씨.아이.에프 원가에 종태는 25 퍼센트를 가하여왔는 바 그 내역은 다음과 같음.

   (1) 원가   100 푸로
   (2) 관리비   15 푸로
   (3) 건물임차료   5 푸로
   (4) 물품 파손   2 푸로
   (5) 순 이익   3 푸로

3. 상기와 같이 원가에 25 푸로를 가하여 운영하여 온 결과 결손을 보게 되는 실정임으로 지금은 원가에 50 푸로를 가산하여 판매하고 있음.

4. 물품에 대한 과세(관세, 국내물품세)등 제 문제는 현재의 대상자가 특권 향유자가 않인 만큼 재고려할 필요가 있음.

5. 현재의 가격선을 인하 할 수 있느냐의 문제에 관하여서는 앞으로 사용인원 수가 증가되고 판매물품의 수량이 증가하면 운영면에서 합리화를 기하여 가격의 재조정을 할 수 있는 가능성이 있음.

6. 피.엑스에서 취급하는 물품의 주문 수입은 외교관을 위하여서는 가능한 문제임.

0041

주한 공관·대표기관

Country	공관장 대사 M	F	관원 M	F	계	Country	공관장 대사 M	F	관원 M	F	계
Australia	1	1	4	3	9	Turkey	1	.	2	1	4
x Austria	1	1	2	2	6	U. K.	1	1	5	3	10.
x Belgium	1	1	2	2	6	~~U. S.~~					
x Brazil	1	1	4	2	8	x Upper Volta	1	1	1	.	3
China	1	1	20	19	41 ㉒	Viet Nam	1	1	2	2	6 ㉑
x Denmark	1	1	2	1	5	~~UNCURK~~	26	25	85		209
x Ecuador	1	1	.	.	2						
France	1	1	5	3	10						
Germany	1	1	4	4	10						
x Greece	1	1	3	2	7	UNCURK	10	9	5	③	27.
Holy See	1	.	2		3	UNMCK.	1	1	2	2	6
x Israel	1	1	1	1 ㉓	4	UNTAB	1	1	1	.	3
Italy	1	1	3	2	7	UNICEF	1	.	.	.	1
Malaysia	1	1.	2	.	4	~~FAO~~	1	1	.		2
x Netherland	1	1	4	4	10	NMC					
New Zealand	1	1	5	4	11 ㉓						
x Norway	1	1	1	1	4						
Panama	1	1	.	-	2						
Philippines	1	1	3	3	8						
x Spain	1	1	3	2	7	0042					
x Sweden	1	1	2	1	5						
Thailand	1	1	3	2	7						

RESTRICTED

A/AC.39/SR. 491

27 February 1964

~~ORIGINAL : ENGLISH~~

UNITED NATIONS COMMISSION FOR THE
UNIFICATION AND REHABILITATION OF KOREA

SUMMARY RECORD OF THE
FOUR HUNDRED AND NINETY FIRST MEETING OF UNCURK
Held at Commission Headquarters, 47 Okin Dong, Chongno Ku, Seoul, on
Saturday, 12 October 1963, at 10.00 a.m.

CONTENTS:

PRESENT:

Chairman:	Mr. BRADY	— Australia
Members:	Mr. DE VOOGD	— Netherlands
	Mr. SHEIKH	— Pakistan
	Mr. BUENO	— Philippines
	Mr. BAJA	— Philippines (Alternate)
	Mr. ANSUCHOTE	— Thailand
	Mr. BAYKAN	— Turkey
Also Present:	Mr. G. NUTTER	— Australian Observer
	Mr. W.F. PELT	— Netherlands Observer
Secretariat:	Mr. KHALIDI	— Principal Secretary
	Mr. OZBUDUN	— Political Affairs Officer
	Mr. Sawhney	— Secretary

0043

1.   Prior to the adoption of the agenda, the CHAIRMAN (Australia), the members of the Committee and the Principal Secretary welcomed the members of the Commission residing in Tokyo. They also extended welcome to Mr. G. NUTTER of the Australian Embassy in Tokyo, and Mr. W.F. PELT of the Netherlands Embassy in Tokyo, who had come to participate in the observation of the Presidential election.

I   ADOPTION OF THE AGENDA

2.   <u>The agenda was adopted.</u>

II   CURRENT DEVELOPMENTS IN
THE REPUBLIC OF KOREA

3.   The members discussed political developments in the Republic of Korea since the previous session of the Commission.

III   OBSERVATION OF THE PRESIDENTIAL ELECTION

4.   The Commission took note of the invitation of Republic of Korea to UNCURK to observe the forthcoming Presidential election, and <u>decided</u> to conduct an observation.

5.   <u>The attached resolution was adopted.</u>

6.   The members exchanged views on various procedures relating to the election. Methods to be employed by the observation teams were also discussed.

7.   Mr. DE VOOGD (Netherlands) brought up the question of the newspapermen who were expected to approach team leaders for comments during their observation of the election. <u>It was unanimously agreed</u> that the reporters should be informed that the teams were in the field on behalf of the Commission, which conducted observation of the election in pursuance of its mandate from the General Assembly. The Commission was therefore responsible to submit its report to the General Assembly and team leaders were thus unable to give any comments individually.

8.   The meeting adjourned for a 10-minute recess and resumed to discuss "Other Business" at 11.55 a.m. (Mr. NUTTER and Mr. PELT had withdrawn).

0044

IV   OTHER BUSINESS

United Nations Command Logistical Support

9.   Mr. BAYKAN (Turkey) summarized the negotiations undertaken by the Committee subsequent to the withdrawal of banking facilities by the United Nations Command (UNC), including the meeting of the Committee with the Commander-in-Chief of the UNC, and individual contacts with the United States Embassy.

10.   Mr. KHALIDI (Principal Secretary) stated that he had been informed by Mr. HABIB, the Counselor at the United States Embassy, that the matter was under consideration and he expected a favourable reply would be forthcoming in a few days.

11.   Mr. ANSUCHOTE (Thailand) stated that he had a talk with the Foreign Minister, who assured him that the ROK Government had great regard for UNCURK and that it would fully endorse all facilities including those pertaining to banking and other logistical support for UNCURK.

12.   Mr. OZBUDUN (Political Affairs Officer) stated that in pursuance of the instructions of the Committee, particularly the CHAIRMAN (Thailand) and Mr. BAYKAN (Turkey), he had called on the Director of the Political Affairs Bureau and the Chief of Protocol of the ROK Ministry of Foreign Affairs, and conveyed to them the views of the Commission that the logistical support received by the Commission from the United Nations Command was an integral whole and should not be subjected to any division. The Director said that he had been instructed by the Foreign Minister to convey to the American Embassy that the ROK Government was in full agreement with the logistical support and other facilities ? accorded to UNCURK, which were in accordance with the Privileges and Immunities Agreement which the Government had signed with the United Nations in 1951. The Director had further stated that during negotiations on the Status of Forces Agreement, the U.S. representative had handed over to the ROK representative a list, which was neither discussed nor commented upon. Thus an alleged rumour that the curtailment of banking facilities for UNCURK was based on a demand by the ROK Government was thoroughly unfounded. The Director had assured him that they would contact the American Embassy and would also send them a letter stating their position.

13.   It was agreed that this question would be taken up again at the next meeting to be held on Friday, 18 October 1963.

The meeting rose at 1.10 p.m.

0045

UNITED NATIONS COMMISSION FOR THE
UNIFICATION AND REHABILITATION OF KOREA

A/AC.39/SR.491   12 October 1963

Resolution of the United Nations Commission for the Unification
and Rehabilitation of Korea, adopted in Seoul on 12 October 1963

The United Nations Commission for the Unification and
Rehabilitation of Korea:

Having taken note of the assurances of the Government of the
Republic of Korea in a letter dated 18 September 1963 addressed to
it by the Minister of Foreign Affairs expressing his Government's
readiness to extend the UNCURK full co-operation and all appropriate
facilities required for the successful observation of the presidential
election;

Taking further note of a letter dated 18 September 1963 addressed
to it by the Chairman of the Central Election Management
Committee inviting the Commission to observe the whole processes of
the forthcoming presidential election;

Welcoming the initiatives taken by the Government and the
Central Election Management Committee of the Republic of Korea extending
UNCURK for the first time an invitation to observe an election of
national scope;

Mindful of the fact that the Commission shall "represent the
United Nations in bringing about the establishment of a unified,
independent and democratic government of all Korea";

Recalling that the mandate accorded by the General Assembly to
UNCURK includes, inter alia, its availability "for observation and
consultation throughout Korea in the continuing development of
representative government based on the freely-expressed will of the
people, including elections of national scope", and that the mandate
authorizes the Commission "to travel, consult and observe throughout
Korea";

Considering that the General Assembly has called "upon all States
and authorities to facilitate this activity on the part of the Commission"
and that it has been the recipient of the continued assurances of the
Government of the Republic of Korea unequivocally to accept the competence
and authority of the United Nations to deal with the Korean question;

Considering further that the forthcoming Presidential Election of
Republic of Korea indeed represents a major step in the pledge of the
military Government to restore civilian representative government by
the end of the year;

Resolves to observe the said Presidential Election.

0046

2. RESOLUTION 195 (III) OF 12 DECEMBER 1948 DECLARING THAT "THERE HAS BEEN ESTABLISHED A LAWFUL GOVERNMENT (THE GOVERNMENT OF THE REPUBLIC OF KOREA)...." AND ESTABLISHING THE UNITED NATIONS COMMISSION ON KOREA

<u>The General Assembly</u>

<u>Having regard</u> to its resolution 122(II) of 14 November 1947 concerning the problem of the independence of Korea,

1/

<u>Having considered</u> the report of the United Nations Temporary Commission on Korea (hereinafter referred to as the "Temporary Commission"); and the report 2/ of the Interim Committee of the General Assembly regarding its consultation with the Temporary Commission,

<u>Mindful</u> of the fact that, due to difficulties referred to in the report of the Temporary Commission, the objectives set forth in the resolution of 14 November 1947 have not been accomplished, and in particular that unification of Korea has not yet been achieved,

1. <u>Approves</u> the conclusions of the reports of the Temporary Commission;

2. <u>Declares</u> that there has been established a lawful government (the Government of the Republic of Korea) having effective control and jurisdiction over that part of Korea where the Temporary Commission was able to observe and consult and in which the great majority of the people of all Korea reside; that this Government is based on elections which were a valid expression of the free will of the electorate of that part of Korea and which were observed by the Temporary Commission; and that this is the only such Government in Korea;

3. <u>Recommends</u> that the occupying Powers should withdraw their occupation forces from Korea as early as practicable;

4. <u>Resolves</u> that, as a means to the full accomplishment of the objectives set forth in the resolution of 14 November 1947, a Commission on Korea consisting of Australia, China, El Salvador, France, India, the Philippines and Syria, shall be established to continue the work of the Temporary Commission and carry out the provisions of the present resolution, having in mind the status of the Government of Korea as herein defined, and in particular to:

(a) Lend its good offices to bring about the unification of Korea and the integration of all Korean security forces in accordance with the principles laid down by the General Assembly in the resolution of 14 November 1947;

(b) Seek to facilitate the removal of barriers to economic, social and other friendly intercourse caused by the division of Korea;

(c) Be available for observation and consultation in the further development of representative government based on the freely expressed will of the people;

1/ See <u>Official Records of the third session of the General Assembly</u>, Supplement No. 9.
2/ Ibid., Supplement No. 10, pages 18 to 21.

0047

(d) Observe the actual withdrawal of the occupying forces and verify the fact of withdrawal when such has occurred; and for this purpose, if it so desires, request the assistance of military experts of the two occupying Powers;

5. Decides that the Commission:

(a) Shall, within thirty days of the adoption of the present resolution, proceed to Korea, where it shall maintain its seat;

(b) Shall be regarded as having superseded the Temporary Commission established by the resolution of 14 November 1947;

(c) Is authorized to travel, consult and observe throughout Korea;

(d) Shall determine its own procedures;

(e) May consult with the Interim Committee with respect to the discharge of its duties in the light of developments, and within the terms of the present resolution;

(f) Shall render a report to the next regular session of the General Assembly and to any prior special session which might be called to consider the subject matter of the present resolution, and shall render such interim reports as it may deem appropriate to the Secretary-General for distribution to Members;

6. Requests that the Secretary-General shall provide the Commission with adequate staff and facilities, including technical advisers as required; and authorizes the Secretary-General to pay the expenses and per diem of a representative and an alternate from each of the States members of the Commission;

7. Calls upon Member States concerned, the Government of the Republic of Korea, and all Koreans to afford every assistance and facility to the Commission in the fulfillment of its responsibilities;

8. Calls upon Member States to refrain from any acts derogatory to the results achieved and to be achieved by the United Nations in bringing about the complete independence and unity of Korea;

9. Recommends that Member States and other nations, in establishing their relations with the Government of the Republic of Korea, take into consideration the facts set out in paragraph 2 of the present resolution.

0048

APPENDIX "A"

PRESIDENT PARK CHUNG-HEE'S SPEECH ON 14th ANNIVERSARY OF THE OUTBREAK OF THE KOREAN WAR IN JUNE 1950

/Official translation obtained from the Office of the Mayor,
Special City of Seoul/

My Dear Brethren:

Today we observe the fourteenth anniversary of the unprecedented suffering of this nation:

With utmost indignation and emotion, we recall the barbarous bloodshed touched off by the Communists in betrayal of the Fatherland. Because of their bloodshed and destructive aggression, our territory was scorched, many of our brethren underwent cruel death, and our vanguards of national defense and numbers of anti-Communist comrades-in-arms from our allies lost their lives.

Today I, with all the people, recall and denounce the barbarous deeds of the Communists, and piously pray for the 100,000 souls of fallen officers and men of Korea and her allies.

Fourteen years have passed since that time. But the Communists are still awaiting another chance for invasion across the 155-mile De-Militarized Zone. They are threatening the world peace and freedom through persistent schemes for aggression.

I therefore emphasize that the recollection today of the Korean war will not only remind the Korean people of their past sufferings from the Communists but also provide an opportunity for all other free people to strengthen their vigilance toward the Communist enemy.

Especially, in view of the bellicose Chinese Communists' movement in Southeast Asia to expand their power, we should more cautiously beware of their aggressive ambition than ever before, and should be determined to immediately fight back against aggression they may launch in the future.

We should do our best in avoiding such acts as thoughtless instigation, destruction which may give advantage to the Communists or creation of confusion or unrest, and must make more efforts to achieve stability and development of our politics, economy and society. Through strengthened ties with the U.S. and other allies, we should be effectively prepared for national defense in collective security.

My Dear Citizens !

Today we should also renew our determination to accomplish our most important home task — territorial unification. On this occasion, I restate the Government's basic policy to achieve our territorial unification under the U.N. resolution.

0049   ..../

Despite the strenuous efforts of the United Nations which have lasted for 16 years, the national tragedy of territorial division still continues, because the North Korean puppet regime, which was established coercively by the Soviet occupation forces in defiance of the Korean people, ignores the authority and competence of the United Nations and refuses to accept the U.N. resolution.

Ever since the Republic of Korea government was inaugurated, we have faithfully observed the U.N. Charter, accepted and sincerely honored all U.N. resolutions and measures. I hereby reaffirm that we shall continue to support the U.N. resolution on Korea's territorial unification based on democracy and justice.

We shall render full cooperation to the U.N. Commission for the Unification and Rehabilitation of Korea (UNCURK) in performing its mission. We hope that the U.N. Forces, which protected the independence and freedom of this nation from Communist aggression, will continue to perform their mission in the future in view of the mounting Communist threat.

My dear citizens !

Faced with many domestic and foreign difficulties, we should make this anniversary a turning point for our renewed determination and redoubled efforts.

I reaffirm our paramount national policy of anti-Communism and firmly pledge with all the people to march toward the accomplishment of the impending national tasks of production increase and construction under the slogan of defeating Communism for territorial unification.

Thank you very much.

June 25, 1964

Park Chung-Hee
President
Republic of Korea

0050

AFFECT OF POSSIBLE CANCELLATION OF LOGISTICAL SUPPORT PROVIDED THROUGH THE UNITED NATIONS COMMAND TO UNCURK AND UNMCK

1. Possible cancellation of logistical support from the Eighth United States Army in Korea by non-inclusion of UNCURK and UNMCK in the Status of Forces Agreement might result in the loss of the following facilities and privileges now authorized by the United Nations Command:

   a. Commission Support:

      (1) APO Privileges
      (2) Billets (In field and Pusan)
      (3) Army Exchange Privileges (PX) (for spare parts and equipment)
      (4) Banking Facilities (official transactions)
      (5) Military Payment Certificates (MPC)
      (6) Class I Bulk Issue (Purchase of items for operation of a Mess)
      (7) Class II and IV Support (Motor Transport parts and repairs)
      (8) Class III - POL (Petrol, Oil and Lubricants)
      (9) Equipment Maintenance
     (10) Potable Water (UNMCK only)
     (11) Transportation (Rail and Air)
     (12) Repair and Utilities (UNMCK only)
     (13) Signal Support (Telephones, etc.)
     (14) Self Service Supply Centre (Located in Pusan but serving UNCURK and UNMCK)

   b. Mission Support:
      (UNCURK & UNMCK)

      (1) Army Exchange Privileges (PX)
      (2) Commissary Privileges
      (3) Banking Facilities
      (4) Field Ration Mess Privileges
      (5) Medical Care
      (6) Medical Care of Dependents
      (7) Dependents School Facilities
      (8) Embassy Commissary Facilities
      (9) Housing - UNMCK personnel, Pusan (Personnel live in Army Compound and would therefore experience considerable difficulties if without support from EUSA)

0051

한·미국 간의 상호방위조약 제4조에 의한 시설과 구역 및 한국에서의 미국군대의 지위에 관한 협정(SOFA)
전59권. 1966.7.9 서울에서 서명 : 1967.2.9 발효(조약 232호) (V.55 비세출자금기관 관계자료, 1964-66)

협 조 전	응 신 기 일

문서번호 외구미 722.2— 748 제 목 주둔군지위협정 체결 교섭

수 신: 총무과장 발 신: 구미국장 년 월 일 1964. 6. 30.제 1 의견

　　　주둔군지위협정 체결 교섭 실무자회의에서 논의되고 있는
비세출자금기관(P.X.)의 사용자 범위 결정 문제를 오는
7월 2일 개최되는 당부 국장회의에서 검토코저 하오니 상정
토록 조치하여 주시기 바랍니다.

구 미 국 장   장 상 문

협 조 전

문서번호 외구미 722.2 — 749. 제 목 주둔군지위협정 체결 교섭

수 신 : 배부처 참조 발 신 : 구미국장 년 월 일 1964.6.30. 제 1 의견

주둔군지위협정 체결 교섭 실무자회의에서 논의되고 있는
비세출자금기관(P.X.)의 사용자 범위 결정 문제를 오는 7월
2 일 개최되는 국장회의에 상정코저 관계자료를 별첨 송부
하오니 이를 검토하여 주시기 바랍니다.

유 첨 : 비세출자금기관 사용자 범위 결정문제 1부. 끝.

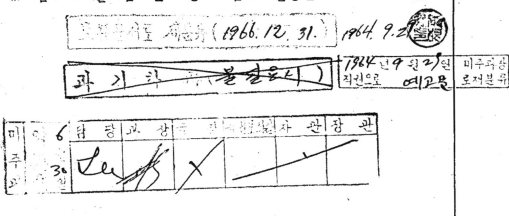

구 미 국 장 장 상 문

배부처 참조 : ~~장관~~, 차관, 기획관리실장, 의전실장, 아주국장, 통상국장,
방교국장, 정보문화국장, 외무공무원교육원장, 총무과장.

승인서식 1—34 (11—13330—01)   (195mm×265mm16절지)

0053

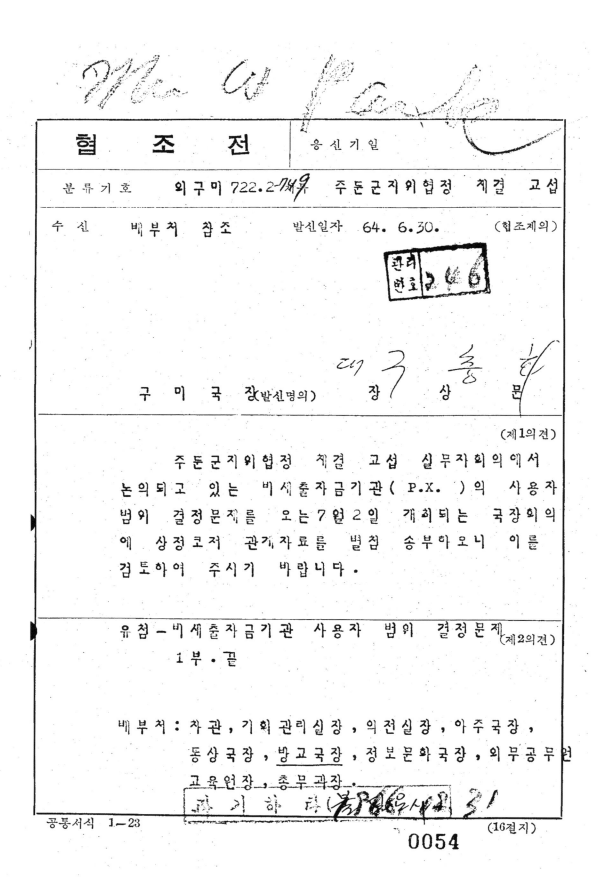

협 조 전	응신기일

분류기호 외구미 722.2-749 주둔군지위협정 체결 고섭

수신 배부처 참조 발신일자 64. 6.30. (협조제의)

관리번호 246

구 미 국 장(발신명의) 장 상 문

(제1의견)

　　주둔군지위협정 체결 고섭 실무자회의에서
논의되고 있는 비세출자금기관(P.X.)의 사용자
범위 결정문제를 오는 7월 2일 개최되는 국장회의
에 상정코저 관기자료를 별첨 송부하오니 이를
검토하여 주시기 바랍니다.

유첨 - 비세출자금기관 사용자 범위 결정문제 (제2의견)
　　　1부. 끝

배부처 : 차관, 기획관리실장, 의전실장, 아주국장,
　　　　동상국장, 방교국장, 정보문화국장, 외무공무원
　　　　고육원장, 총무과장.

관 기 하 당

공통서식 1-23

0054

(16절지)

주둔군지위협정 체결 고섭
비세출자금기관 사용자의 범위 결정

가. 고섭 경위

1. 미측 입장

   (1) 미측은 제 37 차 주둔군지위협정 체결 교섭 실무자회의에서
   주한미군이 경영하고 있는 비세출자금기관(이하 P.X.라 칭함)의
   사용자의 범위를 별첨과 같이 결정할 것을 우리측에 제안
   하여 온바 그중 특히 문제가 되는 것은 (f)항의 규정
   으로서 한·미 양국정부가 명시적으로 합의하는 기관 또는
   개인에게 P.X. 사용을 허가하기도 되어 있다.

   (2) 미측이 제 37 차 회의에서 밝힌 바에 의하면 현재 P.X.를
   사용하고 있는 (f)항 해당자는 UNCURK , 주한미대사관직원
   (사용자 범위의 제 (a)항 해당자임)을 제외한 주한외교단원
   전원, UNTAB, Scandinavian Medical Mission, AKF,
   International Lutheran Mission 등 각 기관의 직원들
   이락 한다.

2. 우리측 입장

   (1) 우리측은 다음과 같은 제점을 고려하여 미측이 제안하여 온
   사용자의 범위를 최소한도로 축소하기 위하여 미측초안
   (f)항의 규정을 삭제 또는 수정할 것을 미측에 제안코저
   한다.

   (ㄱ) 미군당국이 관세 면제의 특전 하에 수입하는 P.X.물품이
   국내시장에 유출됨으로서 시장을 교란시키고 국내산업을
   위축시키는 결과를 초래하고 있는 실정에 감하여 P.X.
   물품의 유출을 봉쇄할 것이 요망되며 따라서 현사용자의
   범위를 가능한한 축소할 필요가 있다.

   (ㄴ) 국제적 선례를 보면 영국에서는 미군대구성원 및 미대사관
   직원이 사용하고 있을 정도이며 태국에서는 미군대구성원
   군속 및 그들의 가족 미대사관직원 USIS 직원,

0055

Seventh Day Adventist Hospital 　소속 U.S.Medical
Mission 　직원 및 가족등 공무로 태국에 파견되어
있는 미국인들이 사용하고 있으며 우리 나라에 있어서와
같이 광범위하게 사용하고 있는 선례는 볼 수 없다.

(2) 사용자의 범위를 축소하기 위하여서는 우선 해당자들이 미군
P.X. 를 사용하지 못 하게 되어도 그들의 일상생활에 있어서
별로 지장이 없도록 하기 위하여 교통부 산하 특정의태품
판매소를 이에 대체 사용케 하고저 그간 관계부처와 접촉
하여 온 결과 동 판매소가 금년도 소요 외화 840,000불을 배정
받고 취급품목도 확대할 수 있게 됨에 따라 준비태세가
순조롭게 진행되고 있다.

나. 문제점

(1) (f)항 해당자의 P.X. 사용을 전격으로 배제하게 되면 현재
사용하고 있는 UNCURK 및 주한외교사절단원들로 부터 강력한
반대가 있을 것이다.

(2) 특히 UNCURK 대표단으로 부터의 반대는 우리 나라의 대유엔
활동에 적지 않은 영향을 미칠 가능성이 있다. 이 점은 주한
미대사관 당국자도 우려하고 있는 점으로서 한국정부가 사용
대상자의 제한을 검토함에 있어서 신중히 고려할 것을 요망
하고 있다.

(3) UNCURK 대표단은 그 대부분이 주한 각국 외교사절의 공관장
또는 관원의 자격을 겸임하고 있는 형편임으로 그들에게
P.X. 사용을 인정하게 되면 기타 각국 외교사절의 공관장이
같은 자격을 이유로 동일한 대우를 요구할 가능성이 있다.

(4) UNCURK 대표단 및 동 사무국 직원들에게 사용을 허가하게
되면 UNTAB/UNSF,UNMCK,UNICEF 등 각 기관은 물론 UN 의
Specialized Agencies 직원들에 대한 동일대우문제가 야기될
것이다.

0056

다. 해결시안

    상기 여러 문제점을 고려에 넣어 P.X. 사용자의 범위 결정문제를 해결할수 있는 시안을 열거하면 다음과 같다.

    제 1 시안 : (f)항의 규정을 삭제하여 동 항 해당자의 범위를 전격으로 배제한다.

    제 2 시안 : UNCURK 정대표 및 그들의 가족 만 사용할수 있게 한다.

    제 3 시안 : UNCURK 정대표 및 주한 각국 외교사절의 공관장 및 그들의 가족에게 사용을 허가한다.

    제 4 시안 : UNCURK 대표단 및 사무국 직원 전원, 외교관대우를 받는 기타 UN 관계 기관 직원, 주한외교사절의 공관장 및 그들의 가족에게 사용을 허가한다. 끝

0057

AGREED MINUTE

The United States Amred Forces may grant the use
of the organizations referred to in paragraph 1 of
Article   to: (a) other officers or personnel of the
United States Government ordinarily accorded such privileges;
(b) those other non-Korean Armed Forces in Korea under
the Unified Command which receive logistical support from
the United States Armed Forces, and their members; (c)
those non-Korean persons whose presence in the Republic
of Korea is solely for the purpose of providing contract
services financed by the United States Government; (d)
those organizations which are present in the Republic of
Korea primarily for the benefit and service of the United
States Armed Forces, such as the American Red Cross and
the United Service Organizations, and their non-Korean
personnel; (e) dependents of the foregoing; and (f)
other persons and organizations with the express consent
of the Government of the Republic of Korea.

미축에서 밝힌 각항 해당자는 다음과 같음:

(a): U.S.Embassy, USOM,USIS,Military Attache,MAG Personnel.

(b): Turkish and Thailand Components of UNC.

(c): USOM Contractors.

(d): American Red Cross, U.S.O.

(e): Dependents.

(f): UNCURK,UNTAB,D.P.Corps,Scandinavian Meidcal Mission,
     International Lutheran Mission, AKF.

0058

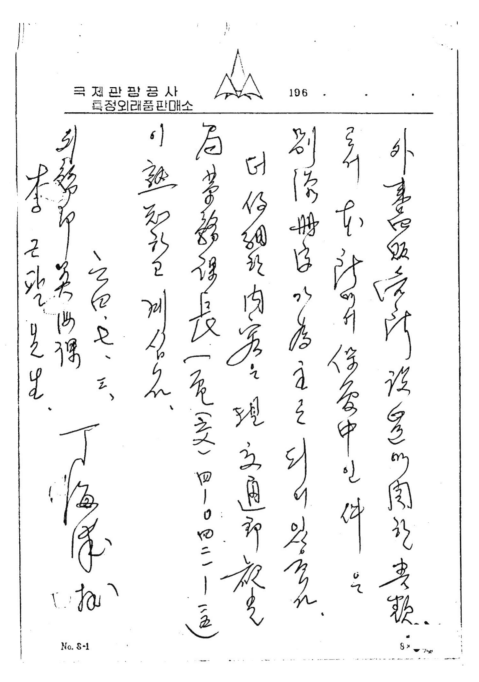

外事課로부터 送을게 關한書類...

本 件에 保管中인 件은

別添冊子에 依하고 되어있읍

더 仔細한 內容은 理文通郵課長

局文書係課長 (局(文) 四一〇四三二一三)

이 題로 하고 계십시오.

의장님 英世漏

李 주관 보사.

六.八.三

丁海彰

한·미국 간의 상호방위조약 제4조에 의한 시설과 구역 및 한국에서의 미국군대의 지위에 관한 협정(SOFA) 전59권. 1966.7.9 서울에서 서명 : 1967.2.9 발효(조약 232호) (V.55 비세출자금기관 관계자료, 1964-66)　65

第 98回 閣議
(61. 11. 28.)

交通令99号
61. 12. 19.

外國人을 爲한 特定外來品
販賣組合設置에 關한 件

經 濟 企 劃 院

1969. 7.6일 접수 K.Lee

一　議決主文

特定外來品取賣禁止法　施行에따라　駐
韓一般外國人도　그들의　日常必須品인
特定食料品및　雜貨의　購得이　不可能
함으로　이를　救濟하는　措置로써　現
行諸法規의範疇内에서　外國人에　必要
한　特定品目을　取扱하는　取賣組合을
政府機關에依하여　設置運營도록하며
同特定物資에對하여는　免税措置를　取
하는等　一連의措置를　採擇함으로써
駐韓一般外國人의　日常生活에있어서
安定과　福祉가　保障되도록한다

~/~

二. 提案理由

　特定外來品販賣禁止措置에따라　韓國에
居住　또는　一時滯在하는　一般外國人
이　그들의　日常必須品인　特定食料品
및　雜貨를　販賣購得하지　못함으로
駐韓美國大使館으로부터　이의　救濟方
途로써　外國人을　爲한　販賣組合의
設置를　提議해왔음으로　特定外來品販
賣禁止法의　立法趣旨에　背馳됨이　없
는　適宜한　對策을　檢討한　結果　그
結論으로써　議決主文과같은　一連의對
策으로써　政府가　企圖하는　特定外來
品販賣禁止法의　立法精神과　趣旨의

~2~

0062

範疇內에서 駐韓一般外國人의 日常生

活上의 安定과 福祉를 保障함에 있음

1. 問 題

駐韓一般外國人이 그들의 日常生活

에 있어서 必須品인 特定物資를 購

得使用토록 하기 爲하여 外國人自體

에 依하여 販賣組合을 設置運營토록

하되 政府가 이를 監督乃至 事後

管理토록하며 同物資에 對하여는

關稅引下措置를 取하여 줄것인가

그렇지않으면 韓國政府機關에 依하

여 同販賣組合을 設置運營토록하고

~3~   0063

現行関税法에 依據 免税措置토록 할것
인가 特定外來品取賣禁止法을 施行하
고 있는 이마당에 政府로서 早速히
決定하여야함

Ⅱ 問題와 関聯된 事項

(1) 現在 駐韓一般外国人은 美軍 PX
에서 流出되는 物資를 購得使用하
고 있음.

(2) 美大使舘에서 合法的인 特定品의
取賣購得을 爲한 時急한 對策을
要請하고 있음

(3) 関係各部處 (經濟企劃院 外務部
~4~

0064

內務部、財務部、商工部〉実務者會議

에서는 前記 議決主文과 같은 原

則에 合意하였음

(4) 美大使舘側에서도 前記 実務者會

議의 合意內容에 賛同하고 있음

(5) 実務者會議合意事項을 關係各部長

官에게 確認同意要請을 하였든바

外國人에게 販賣組合을 設置運營토

록함이 좋겠다고 囬翰을 한 商工

部를 除外한 其他部處에서는 이에

同意하였음

Ⅱ 討 議

~5~   0065

(1) 韓國政府機關에 依하여 設置運営
게하는데 따르는 長短点

가、 非営利的인 政府機關에 依하여

設置運営게 함으로써 外國人에게

所要物品을 低廉하게 提供할수있

다

나 物品販賣에 直接関與함에 따라

外貨獲得을 할수있다

다 政府機關에 依하여 運営됨으로

해서 物品의 暗流出을 防止하고

外換管理의 徹底를 期할수있다

라 販賣組合의 運営에따라 若干이

나마 雇傭增加를 招來한다

～6～

0066

마　交通部가　運營함으로써　觀光事
業과　關聯하는　旣存施設을　利用
할수있고　國産品에對한　宣傳效果
도　期할수있다

바　外國人이　必須品을　購得함에
있어서　그居住地와　販賣組合의
立地的條件이　不便하다　（特히
釜山.大邱等地가）

사　特定販賣物資의　貯藏및　保管을
爲하며　特殊施設의　新設이　必要
하다

아　外國人의　撰好物資供給을　爲하
여　外國人과　臨時로　協議하는

~7~

0067

節次가 必要하다

자. 官需購買節次를 取함으로해서
　導入에 長期間이 所要됨으로
　適期導入및 需要迎合에 相當한
　難点이 介在된다

(2) 外國人自体에 依하여 設置運営
케하는데 따르는 長短곳
가. 外貨導入이 本格化됨에 따라
　增加되는 多數의 駐韓一般外國
　人의 需要를 合理的으로 充足
시킬수 있다.

나. 韓國側에서 取貨組合運営에
따른 実際上의 隘路가 解消된다

~8~

0068

다. 販賣組合을 通하여 物品이 暗
流出될 憂慮가 많으며 이에 對한
監督 及로 事後管理가 実地로는
萬全을 期하기 困難하다

라. 이러한 待尺外來品 販賣禁止法
에 對한 特例를 認定함으로써 外
國人에 依한 特例認定要請의 處理
가 問題된다

마. 販賣組合이 契機가 되어 外胃人
에 依하여 國內에 있어서 公々然한
商去來로 發展할 危險이 많다

~9~   0069

Ⅳ 結論

　　以上 長短点을 比較判斷할때 外國
人自体에 販賣組合의 設置및 運營을
받기는것보다 諸法規의 改正節次跡이
現行法規範疇內에서 政府機關에 依하
여 設置運營도록 함이 合理的이고
合目的的이다

Ⅴ 建議

　(1) 販賣組合의 設置및 運營을 交通
部가 担當한다

　　　責任機關; 交通部、 商工部

　(2) 販賣組合을 通하여 販賣되는 外

～10～　　　　0070

來物品에 對한 關稅는 이 去來로 因한 外貨가 國庫收入이 確認되는限 免稅措置한다

責任機關 ; 財務部、韓國銀行

(3) 外國人이 外貨로서 購買함에 있어 外換管理法에 依한 運營問題는 關係部處가 協議措置한다

責任機關 ; 財務部、交通部、韓國銀行

(4) 販賣組合의 運營資金을 爲하여 이에 所要되는 年間 約 400,000弗의 政府保有弗使用에 關한 資金

~11~

0071

한·미국 간의 상호방위조약 제4조에 의한 시설과 구역 및 한국에서의 미국군대의 지위에 관한 협정(SOFA) 전59권. 1966.7.9 서울에서 서명 : 1967.2.9 발효(조약 232호) (V.55 비세출자금기관 관계자료, 1964-66)

措置를 한다

　責任機關; 財務部、 文通部、 韓國

銀行

『

參 考 事 項

1. 關係法規拔萃

(1) 外國人에 依하여 設置運營도록
한 境遇 (抵觸規定)

特定外來品販禁法 第五條 一項 但書에
關한 施行令 第三條 三號 <u>外國人에게
特定外來品을 販賣하고저 함에 있어
서 適當하다고 認定되는 施設을</u>
갖춘者로서 大韓民國의 國籍을 가

~2~　　　　　　0072

진유

(2) 免稅措置關係

關稅法第三十三條

다음의 各號의 一에 該當하는 物品에 對하여서는 閣令의 定하는 바에 依하여 그 關稅의 全部또는 一部를 免除한다

全九號 外貨로 販賣할 物品과 輸出할 또는 外貨로 販賣할 物品의 製造原料(工事를包含한다)

(3) 韓美友好通商航海條約

第十四條五號

一方締約國의 國民과 會社는 輸

~13~

0073

出 및   輸入에 關하 모든 事項에   關

하여   他方條約國으로부터   內國民

待遇와 最惠國民待遇를 받는다

2. 其他

販賣組合이 取扱할 特定外來品目

別添表와 같음

-

^14^   0074

販賣組合이 取扱할 特定外來品目

國內需要物資	輸入物資
1. 쌀	1. 빠다
2. 小麥粉 (製빵용)	2. 치一즈및 牛乳製品
3. 鷄卵	3. 牛乳粉
4. 사과、배、복숭아、딸기 銀杏	4. 罐入牛乳
5. 生鮮 (生貝및 罐貝)	5. 牛肉
6. 牛肉 (季節的)	6. 鷄類
7. 鷄類및 獵物	7. 오一토밀
8. 野菜	8. 野菜 (乾燥品、罐入및生野菜)
9. 砂糖	9. 罐入및 乾燥果實
10. 菓子類	10. 砂糖
11. 酒精飮料및 飮料類	11. 香料및 調味料
12. 煙草類	12. 調理用및 사라다油
13. 牛乳 (生乳)	13. 混合菓子및 特殊小麥粉
14. 조미료	14. 비누 및 淸淨劑
	15. 便所用藥品類

~15~

0075

한·미국 간의 상호방위조약 제4조에 의한 시설과 구역 및 한국에서의 미국군대의 지위에 관한 협정(SOFA)
전59권. 1966.7.9 서울에서 서명 : 1967.2.9 발효(조약 232호) (V.55 비세출자금기관 관계자료, 1964-66)

國內需要物資	輸入物資
	16 菓子類
	17 家庭必須品
	18 煙草類
	19 酒精飲料. 强心酒. 合成酒
	20 蜜柑屬
	21 各種製罐物
	22 茶、코-피、코코아

~16~

0076

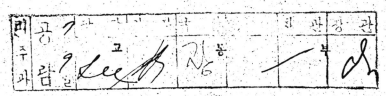

고관닙 1537,5-0897   1964,7,7.

수신 수신처참조

제목 특정외래품 판매소 운영대책 위원회 위원위촉

　　　1964,7,　 결재 각료회의에　의거 특정외래품 판매소의　운영
탑비되는 기아여 외국인의 일상생활에 편의를 제공하고 외화획득
을 도모코자 동 위원회를 구성하고　군민공장　를 위원으로
위촉 하였사오니 적극 협력도록 하여 주시기 바랍니다.

　　　1, 회의소집일시　　　　　　　1964,7,15(화)　14:00

　　　2, 회의장소　　　　　　　　　조선호텔 Rose Room

유첨 위원명단 1부. 끝

　　　고동부장관　　　　　　　　　　김　　　은

수신처
　　　가10,15,17,18,19,23,25,　정1.

0077

위원회 명단

위원장	교통부	차관
위원	경제기획원	경제기획국장
	외무부	구미국장
	재무부	외환국장
	재무부	세관국장
	상공부	상역국장
	보사부	보건국장
	농림부	양정국장
	조달청	외자국장
	전매청	업무국장
	교통부	관광국장
	국제관광공사	업무이사
간사	교통부 관광국	업무과장

0078

외무부

교 통 부

교관업1537.5 ─ 7ll   1964. 7. 10

수신   수신처 참조

제목   특정외래품 판매소 운영대책운영위원회 소집일자 변경

     교관업1537.5(64.7.7)로 통보한바있는 동위원회 소집일자를
사정에 의하여 다음과 같이 변경하였아오니 필히 참석토록하여주
시기 바랍니다.

    1. 일시   1964.7.15(수) 14.00
    2. 장소   조선호텔

접수 No. 13837
1964 7. 11
외 무 부

            교 통 부 장 관   안   경   모

        수신처 가 10.15.17.18.19.23.25.27, 정 1

                                            0079

1964. 7. 15

特定外來品販賣所

運 營 現 況

通商局長

國 際 観 光 公 社

0080

1. 設置目的

韓國에 常住 또는 一時 滯在하는 外國人으로서 美軍PX나 其他 販賣 機構 및 <u>美大使舘 販賣所</u>를 利用못 하는 外國人에게 生活必需品을 販賣

2. 沿革

    61. 12. 19   販賣所設置 (交通部)

    62. 4. 2   營業開始   (交通部)

    62. 11. 1   國際觀光公社 引受

3. 購買會員數

    가. 現會員數   2,063名 (1,097世帶)

        大人   1,538名

        小人   525名

~1~

한·미국 간의 상호방위조약 제4조에 의한 시설과 구역 및 한국에서의 미국군대의 지위에 관한 협정(SOFA)
전59권. 1966.7.9 서울에서 서명 : 1967.2.9 발효(조약 232호) (V.55 비세출자금기관 관계자료, 1964-66)

나. 將來增加予想會員　　　３００世帶

（駐韓外交使節団員 및 家族）

다. 職業別世帶

職業	서울	地方	計	備考
	세대	세대	세대	
宣教師	266	237	503	
實業家	197	20	217	
技術者	70	35	105	
教育者	57	14	71	
医師	17	9	26	
記者	15	0	15	
無職	28	7	35	
其他	4	121	125	
（一時滯在者）				
合計	654	443	1,097	

－２－

0082

4. 會員購買限度額

       大人   月 ＄75.⁰⁰

       小人   月 ＄50,⁰⁰

5. 63年度販賣實績

가. 總販賣額   ₩ 37,726,444

                        （＄ 290.203）

     호텔 分讓   ₩ 2,071,604

     純外貨販賣額   ₩ 35,654,840

                        （＄ 274,268）

     外資材料費   ₩ 23,964,684

                        （＄ 184,343）

     外貨獲得額   ₩ 11,690,156

                        （＄ 89,925）

~3~

0083

4. 年間延利用人員数

　1 4, 4 1 9 名（月 1. 2 0 1 名（日 4 0 名）

　利用客 1 人當 購買額　　　　₩ 2. 4 7 3

　　　　　　　　　　　　　　（$ 1 9.⁰⁰ ）

　1 世帶當　年間平均購買額

　　　　年 ₩ 3 2, 5 0 0 （月 ₩ 2. 7 0 8 ）

　　　　年 （$ 2 5 0.⁰⁰ ）（月 $ 2 0. 8 3 ）

　會員 1 人當 年間平均購買額

　　　　年 ₩ 1 7, 2 8 3 （月 ₩ 1. 4 4 0 ）

　　　　年 （$ 1 3 3.⁰⁰ ）（月 $ 1 1.⁰⁰ ）

~4~

0084

다. 品種別 販賣實績

種 類	販 賣 額	比 率	弗 貨 販 賣 額
食 料	₩ 11,603,777 (₩ 89,260)	30.7 %	₩ 87,952
飮 料	14,496,080 (111,508)	38.4	96,887
菓 子	3,748,956 (28,838)	10.0	28,838
煙 草	3,463,728 (26,644)	9.2	26,644
家庭用品	2,629,965 (20,231)	7.0	20,231

~5~

0085

한·미국 간의 상호방위조약 제4조에 의한 시설과 구역 및 한국에서의 미국군대의 지위에 관한 협정(SOFA)
전59권. 1966.7.9 서울에서 서명 : 1967.2.9 발효(조약 232호) (V.55 비세출자금기관 관계자료, 1964-66)

種 類	販 賣 額	比 率	弗 貨 販 賣 額
冷 凍 物	677.224 (5,209)	1.8	5,209
委 託 品 (國産品 및 自進 申告品)	1,106,714 (8,513)	2.9	8,507
計	37,726,444 ($ 290,203)	100.0	$ 274,268

～6～

0086

라. 發注品目實績 (FY 63)

食料　　　　$ 40,646.00

飲料　　　　$ 18,880.00

酒類　　　　$ 4,490.00

家庭用品　　$ 4,593.00

冷凍物　　　$ 3,307.00

菓子　　　　$ 338.00

計　　　　$ 72,257.00

~7~

0087

6. 64年度実績 （FY64. 1～6）

가 總販賣額　　　　　　　　₩ 23.916.279

　　　호텔分讓　　　　　　₩ 1.618.274

　　　純外貨販賣額　　　　₩ 22.298.005

　　　　　　　　　　　　　（ $ 131.858 ）

　　　外買材料費　　　　　₩ 12.854.085

　　　　　　　　　　　　　（ $ 98.877 ）

　　　外貨獲得額　　　　　₩ 9.443.920

　　　　　　　　　　　　　（ $ 32.981 ）

나. 延利用人員数 （FY 64. 1～6 ）

　　6.060名 （月 1.010名.　日 33名）

　　利用客 1 人當購買額　₩ 3.754

$$\left(\begin{array}{l} 130 : 1 \ 換算時 \quad \$ 29.\tfrac{00} \\ 255 : 1 \quad \textit{"} \quad \$ 15.\tfrac{00} \end{array} \right)$$

～8～

0088

1 世帶當 6 個月間 平均 購買額

                              ₩ 20.737 (月 ₩ 3.456)

                        (130:1 換算時 $ 159.⁰⁰(月 $ 26.⁵⁰)

                        (255:1   ″ $ 81.⁰⁰(月 $ 13.⁵⁰)

會員 1 人當 6 個月間 平均 購買額

                        年 ₩ 11.026 (月 ₩ 1.837)

                        (130:1 換算時 $ 85.⁰⁰(月 $ 14.¹⁶

                        (255:1   ″ $ 43.⁰⁰(月 $ 7.¹⁶

다. 品種別 販賣實績

品 種	販 賣 額	比 率	弗 質 收 入
食 料	₩ 8.7.78.208	36.7%	$ 50,546
飮 料	7.665.891	32.1	45.718
家庭用品	1.753.484	7.3	12.095
煙 草	1.075.623	4.5	7.719

~9~

品　　種	販　賣　額	比　率	弗　貨　收　入
菓　　子	948,402	4.0	6.567
冷　凍　物	743,140	3.1	4.674
分　　讓	1,618,274	6.8	
委　託　品	1,333,254	5.5	4,536
計	23,916,279	100.0	131,858

-10-

0090

라. 商品在庫 및 未着商品

　　6.30 現在商品在庫　　　₩ 6,465,406

　　　　　　　　　　　　　（$ 25,355）

　　　　　　食料　　　　₩ 1,656,694

　　　　　　飲料　　　　　3,415,266

　　　　　　家庭用品　　　　843,518

　　　　　　菓子　　　　　　252,526

　　　　　　煙草　　　　　　169,956

　　　　　　冷凍物　　　　　127,444

　　6.30 現在未着商品　　₩ 50,986,963

　　　　　　　　　　　　（$ 199,949）

　　　　　　總計　　　　₩ 57,452,369

　　　　　　　　　　　　（$ 225,304）

　　　　　　　　～11～

0091

7. 13 現在到着商品内訳

仁川 到着分 約＄110,000.-

7. FY 64 外換使用計劃

1/4分期実績	2/4分期実績	3/4分期推定	4/4分期推定	計
0	＄ 193,754	＄ 400,000	＄ 246,246	＄ 840,000

~12~

0092

8. FY 64 收支展望

가. 收支

收　　　入		支　　　出	
特外販收益 ₩168,368,900		營業費 ₩143,354,800	
主食料	上半期 $ 69,443	材料費 ₩ 137,719,800	
	下半期 $ 228,706	($ 567,079)	
飲料	上 〃 $ 26,041		
	下 〃 $ 85,765	人件費 ₩ 2,840,400	
酒類	上 〃 $ 34,721	経費 ₩ 2,794,600	
	下 〃 $ 114,353		
冷凍食料	上 〃 $ 8,680		
	下 〃 $ 28,588		
其他	上 〃 $ 34,721		
	下 〃 $ 114,353		

－13～

0093

한·미국 간의 상호방위조약 제4조에 의한 시설과 구역 및 한국에서의 미국군대의 지위에 관한 협정(SOFA)
전59권. 1966.7.9 서울에서 서명 : 1967.2.9 발효(조약 232호) (V.55 비세출자금기관 관계자료, 1964-66)

收　　　入	支　　　出
受託販賣收益　　　₩ 262,300	
上半期　　₩　　1.325	
下半期　　₩　　　353	
	利益金　　₩ 25.276,400
	（＄100,000）
總　計　₩ 168.631,200	總　計　₩ 168,631,200
（＄　748.727）	

−14−

0094

ㄴ.　　年間 1 世帶當購買額　　　₩ 153,480
　　　　　　　　　　　　　　　　（$ 601）

ㄷ,　　會員 1 人當購買額　　　　₩ 81,613
　　　　　　　　　　　　　　　　（$ 320）

9.　物品需給所要日數比較

行政節次	請達廳		自體購買
	通常購買	緊急購買	
購買委任	日	日	15 日
輸入合議	7~8	7~8	6~8
外換配定申請	10~12	10~12	12~14
公告準備期間	10~19	3	3~4
公告期間	40~43	10~25	10~25
開札및競落者選定	6~8	6~8	6~8
隨意契約承認申請	-	-	2
外換使用許可申請	5~7	3	8~10

-15-

0095

行政節次	調達厅		自体購買
	通常購買	緊急購買	
信用狀開設	5~7	3	3
船積, 輸送, 通関	68~88	68~88	68~88
總所要日數	151~192	110~150	133~177

가. 食飲料는 種類가 많을뿐만 아니
라 規格이 一定하지 않음으로 調
達廳에서 購買할때에는 規格及種
類에 있어 相異点이 發生할 境遇
文書로서 當公社의 同意를 받아야
하므로 必要以上의 時間을 浪費하
게됨.

나. 調達廳에서 購買할 境遇 當公社

-16-

0096

가 輸入合議. 外資配定및 使用許可 通關手院은 繼續取하여야 될 節次로 삼게되며 單只 購買委任 入 札行爲 信用狀開設만이 簡素化됨

다. 當公社 資金事情으로 "유산스 베이스" 購買를 함에 必要한 對金 融機關手續節次를 調達廳보다 當 公社가 行함이 有利함

―17―

10, 隘路及建議事項

가. 商工部輸入合意

隘　　　　　路	建　　　　　議
1. 品目及 數量만 表示하 輸入合意를 얻어 財務部에 外貨配定 申請	1. 年間所要量全体에 対한 品名만을 表示한 一括 輸入合意
2. 入札后 品名, 規格, 額量, 金額을 表示하여 旣히 輸入合意된 内容에 対한 事項變更 承認	1. 貿易施鈴 (大使鈴令) 改乙제 件이 現在 上申中이며 通過되면 解代可. (内容) 購買業務를)油遠行에 委任 하는것.

-18-

0098

나. 　調達廳購買委任

隘　　　　路	建　　　　議
1.　件別購買委任承 認을 得하는데 ~~要하는~~ 不必要한 時日을 要함	1.　年間所要量에 対하 여 一括購買委任 長期分의 得捷로 軍納 店을 비目標만 세워는 設定, 倒처로 隨意要 統을운다. （設定이要하는 品目, 規格, 數量, 価格 을 提示하라）

다.　　財務部外貨配定및 使用許可

1.　　輸入合意后外貨 配定을 받아야하며入 札后 品名. 規格. 數量. 金 額을 明示한 外貨使 用許可를 받는데要하는 不 必要한 時日.	1.　　政府投資機關外貨 需給計劃에 策定된 配 定額을 超過하지 않는 範 囲内에서 再外貨配定 을 省略할수 있는 措置 ~~与向~~ 二回로 分化通知로 하겠다. 用意중이다

-19-

斗. 通關商品 証紙添付問題

隘　路	建　議
1. 通關時 全体物品에 對한 個別的 証紙添付 作業으로 混雜, 破損, 紛失憂慮와 時間의 浪費가 莫甚함	1. 証紙添付制度를 廃止하여 줄것 (本問題에 対하여는 稅關局과 代案檢討中)

(마) 領事送狀発給 (外務部) ──→ 通關局에 通報

| 1. 領事送狀発給의 遲延으로 因한 通關遅延. | 1. 迅速히 発給 2. 케이블에 依한 通報. 音信 ─通0 3月 2~4 か까지) Cable로 Invoice No. Amount 電知 S.ア. H.K. M.T. |

-20-

0100

바. 外国産煙草購入委任

隘　　路	建　　議
1. 專賣法의 抵触을 받어 當公社가 外国産 製造煙草를 直輸入販賣不可能.	1. 直輸入販賣할수있 는法的措置 (손글씨 메모) 庫入原價로 專賣에서 引受販 (싸게함) 商役法

사. 國産煙草外貨販賣

| 1. 財務部令336号2 項에 販賣所는 除外 되어있음 | 1. 販賣할수있는部令補 完,
 補完을해주겠다
 10月경으로 |

-21-

0101

아. 調達厅 受託品 取路 拡大 (自進申告品分)

五~되原豆. 車輌附属品, 라듸오, 萬年筆, 電
气用品等

隘　　路	建　　議
政府 및　国営企業 体에 限하여　取路가 制限되어　取路不進 으로　많은 物品이 滯 貨되어 時日이　經過 됨에 따라　老朽되어 廃品化 憂慮.	取路를 拡大하여 実需要 者에게 販賣할수 있는 措置가　時急함. (現在 拡大方案이 政府에 서 撿討中임.) 宮內部 意内 同意

~22~

0102

자. FY65 所要外貨適期配定

隘　路	建　議
1. FY64 外貨配定이 遲延되어 (3/31 配定) 商品需給이 遲延되었으며 이로 因하여 販賣所運營에 莫大한 支障을 超來케 하였음	1. FY65 所要外貨를 1月中에 配定하여 주도록 할것.

아. 유산스 베이스 (180日) 購買承認

1. 政府支拂保証에 依하여 ⅃/C를 開設하면	1. 180日間의 유산스 베이스에 依하여 購買하면

-23-

0103

隘　　　路	建　　　議
商品到着과 同時에 代金決濟를 하게되므로 現公社의 運營資金上 到底히 一時代金決濟가 困難한 實情임.	商品을 賣却하여 代金決濟할수있는 時間의 餘裕가 있으므로 自體運營資金難이 많이 解消됨.

-24-

0104

협 조 전	응 신 기 일

문서번호 외구미 722.2 — 773   제 목 특정외래품판매소 운영

수 신: 통상국장 발 신: 구미국장 년 월 일 1964.7.20. 제 1 의견

　　　지난 7월 15일 교통부 주최로 개최된 특정외래품판매소운영
대책위원회에서는 동 판매소 운영에 관한 각종 애로 및 건의사항이
논의된 바 그 중 당부 해당사항은 다음과 같음으로 알리오니 선처
하여 주시기 바랍니다.

당부에 대한 요망사항: <u>영사송장 발급의 신속화</u>

1. 현재 주홍콩 및 주미각공관의 영사송장 발급의 지연으로
　　인하여 동 판매소 앞으로 송부되는 물품의 국내 도입
　　수속이 지연되는 사례가 있는바 앞으로 동 판매소 앞으로
　　송부되는 물품에 대한 영사송장 발급에 한하여 수시
　　신속히 처리하기 바람.

2. 영사송장을 발급하면 즉시 발급사실 및 영사송장번호,
　　액수등을 ~~본부를 동하여~~ <u>전보로 사전에</u> 통지하여 주시기 바람.

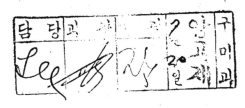

　　　　　구 미 국 장 장 상 문

승인서식 1-34 (11-13330-01)
(195mm×265mm16절지)

0105

한·미국 간의 상호방위조약 제4조에 의한 시설과 구역 및 한국에서의 미국군대의 지위에 관한 협정(SOFA)
전59권. 1966.7.9 서울에서 서명 : 1967.2.9 발효(조약 232호) (V.55 비세출자금기관 관계자료, 1964-66) 111

미국대사관 Habib 참사관과
구미국장 회담 내용

건명 : UNCURK 의 PX 사용권
일시 : 1964.7.21 , 오후 3시 30분부터 동 4시 30분까지
장소 : 구미국장실
참석자 : 미국측 - Habib 참사관
　　　　　　　Fleck 1등서기관 배석
　　　　한국측 - 구미국장
　　　　　　　　구미주과장 배석

내용 :

　　　Habib 참사관 발언 요지

　　　UNCURK 각국대표들은 PX 사용에 관하여 지대한
관심을 가지고 있음. 미국대사관으로서는 한국에는 두가지
성격의 유엔기관이 주재하고 있는 것으로 본다. 즉,
하나는 UNC 로서 군사적 목적으로 주둔하고 있는 군대를
말하며 또하나는 UNCURK 로서 정치적 성격을 띠고 있는
기관을 말한다. 따라서 UNC 에게 PX 사용권을 부여한다면
자연 UNCURK 에 대한 사용도 고려되어야 할것으로 생각
한다. 그러므로 UNCURK 의 PX 사용에 대하여는 특별히
다음사정을 참작하여 PX 조항에 관한 미국측안 A.H. #5 (f)
상 (한국정부의 동의 표시를 빌어 합의하여 PX 사용을
허용한다는 것)을 한국측이 수락하여 주기를 바란다.

　　　1. UNCURK 는 한국에 대하여 정치적으로 많은
영향을 미치고 있으며 특히 유엔에 제출하는 연차보고
기타 유엔사무총장에게 보내는 보고등에서 한국정부의
비협조적인 태도를 비난하는 내용을 표시할 가능성이 있으며
동시에 한국정부에 대한 불쾌감을 갖일것이 우려됨.

0106

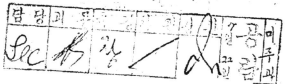

2. UNCURK 는 유엔 Resolution 에 의해서
한국에 파견된 기관으로서 모든 특권과 면제를 향유할
것을 주장하고 있음. 따라서 미국측으로서는 UNCURK
대표 또는 Principal Secretary Khalidi 와 같은
직원이 미국대사관을 방문할 경우 한국정부에서 반대한다는
뜻을 명백히 말하여도 좋은지 문의하는 것임.

장국장 발언요지

미국측의 설명은 충분히 납득하는 바이나, 한국측
으로서는 행정협정에서 미국군대구성원, 군속 및 가족
또는 군계약자 등과 같은 한미 SOFA 대상에 국한하여
PX 사용여부를 도의할 생각이며, 기타 UNCURK 와 같은
기관에 대해서는 일체 SOFA 교섭에서는 언급하지 않기를
바라며, 동시에 이내용을 미국측에서 UNCURK 대표에게
표시하여도 무방함. 또한 UNCURK 대표 또는 직원이
외무부를 방문하여도 우리로서는 동일한 입장을 표시할 것임.

건의 :

이상의 회담내용으로 보아 UNCURK 대표 또는 Principal
Secretary Khalidi 가 장·차관을 방문할 가능성
이 있는바, 동문제에 대한 답변요지를 다음과 같이 건의함:
한미간에 교섭중인 SOFA 는 미국의 군대구성원, 군속 및
가족 또는 군계약자등이 대상으로 되어 있는바 UNCURK
는 이협정에서 언급할 대상이 아님.

또한 일반 외교사절도 일체 SOFA 와는 관련이 없으
므로 제외되는 것임. 따라서 이분들은 모두 외교특권을
향유하고 있으므로 수입해오는 필요한 물품에 대해서는
외무부로서 충분히 면세등과 기타 편리를 제공할 것임.

0107

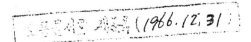

대한민국 외무부

WPM-0715
번 호: WCH-0730
일 시: 231450

발 신 전 보

종 별

수 신 인: 주미대사, 주중대사

외신과
접수암호

하기 사항을 조속히 조사 회보바람.
1. 귀 주재국에 UN Agency 가 있는지 여부, 있다면
  그 기구명.
2. 동기구 및 직원이 미주둔군의 PX 사용권을
  가지고 있는지 여부. (외구미)

장   관

통재관		자체통제		기안처		타자·판치	검 인	주무자	과 장
결 재									

필 요 □   보안불필요 □

0108

대한민국 외무부

URGENT

종별

번호: CHW-0744
일시: 250950

수신인: 장관

발신인: 주중대사

대: WCH-0730

1. 당지에있는 UN AGENCY

1) ILO 사무소   2) UNESCO EXPERT   사무소

3) UNICEF 연락사무소   4) WHO 서북 태평양대표사무소

2. 유엔기구에서 파견된 자의 PX 사용은 중국 외교부의 추천명단에따라 허용되고있으며 현재 전원 허용되고있음. 다만 중국 국적을 가진자는 인정이 않되어있다함.

3. 그밖에 미국인을 제외한 이곳 PX 사용자는 다음과같으니 참고하시기바람.

1) 외교단: 공관의장, 차석, 참사관, 수석무관.

2) 미국정부 기관요원 (예: AID)

3) 외국인으로서 미국정부기관과의 계약에의하여 당지에와있는자 특히 원조관계 공사를위하여 와있는 계약자는 중국정부와 협정체결시 PX 사용허용조항을 포함시켜 사용케하고있다함.

4) 영국 총영사관원은 현미관 RECIPROCAL BASE 의 관례에의하여 전원 허용받고있음. 인이나 중국 국적을가지고있는자는 원칙적으로 제외되어있다고함.

비서	통상	증정	재무
정무	문서	경기	조달
정보	의전 ✓	국방	농림
방교	총무	상공	

점인:

수신시간:
1964 JUL 31 PM 12 2
0109

외신과

4. 이상 PX 이용에관하여는 이곳외교부와 미대사관에서 어떤 규정이있는것이 아니라 당지에 PX 가설치된 당시부터 미대사관, 대만경비사령부, MAAG 및 중국정부간에 양해된 정책으로 관력가된것이라함. 끝.

외 신 과

0110

공 문 서

고군번 1537;4 - 8765   1964. 7.28

수 신   수신처참조

제 목   휴전지대내 판매소 운영제재 처리결과 회의결과 통보

제1차 휴전지대내 판매소 운영대책위원회에서 검토한 사항
을 통보하니 그 소관사항에 대하여 참구 참조하여 추기 바랍
니다.

주 : 본 회의 결과를 경제장관회의에 보고할것임.
유첨   회의결과 보고서 1부. 끝

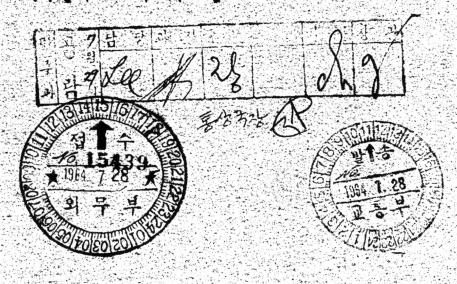

고용부장관   민 경 로

수신처
    가 10,15,17,18,19,23,25,27 끝 1.

0111

特定外來品販賣所運營對策委員會第1次會議

1. 會議日時   1964. 7. 15 14:20 ~ 17.30

2. 〃 場所   조선호텔

3. 參席者

　　　　委員長   交通部次官 代 觀光局長

　　　　委　員   經濟企劃院 經濟企劃局長 代 鄭事務官

　　　　　〃   外務部歐美局長 代 美洲課長

　　　　　〃   財務部外換局長 代 郭事務官

　　　　　〃   〃 稅關局長 代 金子峰
　　　　　〃   商工部 商易局長 代
　　　　　〃   保社部 保健局長 不參

　　　　　〃   農林部 糧政局長

　　　　　〃   調達廳外貿局長 代 外資課長

　　　　　〃   專賣廳業務局長

　　　　　〃   觀光公社 業務理事 經理理事

　　　　幹　事   交通部觀光局業務課長

4. 會議內容   特定外來品販賣所現況 및 隘路事項. 建議事項

5. 會議進行

　　交通部觀光局長의 會議趣旨說明에 이어 公社營業課長

　　現況 및 隘路事項說明이 있은后 建議事項에 對한 對策

　　討議가 있었음

　　　　別添. 建議事項에 對한 合意內容

　　　　　　　　~/~

0112

建議事項에 對한 合意內容

1. 商工部 輸入合意

建議事項、年間所要量에 對한 品目만을 表示한 一括輸入合意

貿易法 施行令 改正案이 商工部長官의 決裁를 得한 后 現在 法制處에서 審議中이므로 同 施行令이 公布되면 此件은 調達廳에서 購買業務와 同一取扱하게 되므로 同輸入合意業務는 簡素化될것이며 輸入合意는 上下半期로 나누어 取扱할것이라 함으로 業務의 迅速을 期하게 됨

2. 調達廳 購買委任

建議事項 年間所要量에 對한 一括購買委任

調達廳에서는 購買의 循期 所要判斷 在庫把握을 하여 調達廳에 購買要求하면 調達廳에서 長期契約에 依한 單價契約을 締結하고 公社에서는 所要數量만 請求하면 臨時 購入할수 있으므로 購買委任의 必要性이 要하지 않음

3. 財務部 外貨配定 및 使用許可

建議事項 一括外貨配定要求

財務部에서는 外換需給計劃에 依據 一括配定은 困難하나 上下半期로 區分配定하여 줄것에 同意하겠음

4. 財務部 通關商品 證紙添付問題

建議事項 證紙添付制度를 廢止하여줄것

此件 旣代案으로 通關地 稅關으로부터 職員이 販賣所에 出張하여 印章으로 檢印하게 되였으므로 此件은 再論하지 않었음

0113

—

5. 領事送狀 發給

建議事項 迅速한 發給 케이블에 依한 通報

　外務部에서는 輸入物品 原産地 領事舘으로 하여금

迅速 取扱하도록 協助할 것에 同意하였음

6. 外國産 煙草購入委任

建議事項 直輸入 販賣할수 있는 法的措置

　專売方에서는 煙草輸入을 爲한 外貨가 配定되어 있지

않기 때문에 公社로 하여금 所要數量의 煙草를 調達

方으로부터 購買委任받어 輸入하든 調運方에서 輸入하

던 間에 輸入된 物品을 專賣方에서는 이를 買入하여

外來品 販賣所를 煙草販賣小賣商으로 指定하여 販売도

록 한다는데 合意보았음 (販賣價格은 未合意)

7. 國産煙草 外貨販賣

建議事項 販賣할수 있는 部令補完

　專賣方에서는 販賣所에서 免税煙草를 流出시키지 않고

取扱할수 있는 流出防止策만 講究된다면 販賣가 制限

되있는 部令(財務部令 33 6 号)을 改定하여 販売許可

할것에 同意하였음

8. 調運方 受託品 販路擴大(自進申告品分)

建議事項 販路를 擴大하여 呆需要者에게 販賣할수 있는

　　　　措置가 時急함

　去 7, 10日 調運方에 開催된 特定外來品審査委員会에

서 同物品을 商工部傘下 企業体를 비롯하여 政府投與

國営企業体 및 觀光호텔에 販賣할수 있도록 議決되어

次官会議를 거처 國務会議에 上程키로 決定되었음으로

此件은 再論하지 않었음.

~3~

0114

~4~

9. FY 65 所要外貨 適期配定

建議事項 FY 65 所要外貨를 1月中에 配定하여줄것

財務部에서 FY 65 外換需給計劃이 U.S.O.M 側과

協議되는대로 可及的 年初에 配定하는데 同意하였음

10. 유산스 베이스 (180日) 購買承認

建議事項 180日間의 유산스 베이스에 依하여 購買
하면 商品을 賣却하여 代金決濟할수 있는
時間의 餘裕가 있으므로 自体運営困難이 많
이 解消됨

此件에 對하여 旣히 公社 經理理事가 商工部長次官
의 同意를 얻었으며 商易局長과도 合意를 得하였다
하므로 이는 公社에서 解決하도록 하였음

11. 其他事項

가. 現在 美軍 P.X를 利用하고 있는 外交使節団 300
世帯 (美國除外)가 韓美行政協定締結後 同 販売所를
利用하게 되므로 이들이 必要로 하는 商品의 確保
와

나. 外交官에 對하여는 一般外國人과 区別되는 特惠措
置가 있어야 한다는 것으로

다. 此件에 對하여는 研究検討키로 하였음.

0115

협 조 전	응신기일

분류기호외구미	제목 참고자료 송부

수신 의전과장　　　　발신일자 64.6.1.　　　　（협조제의）

　　미군 PX 사용에 관한 주비대사관으로 부터의
별첨 회신 사본을 보내오니 사무상 참고로 하시기
바랍니다.

　　미 주 과 장　　（발신명의）　　구　　충　　회

（제1의견）

유첨 — 주비대사의 전문 사본 1통 · 끝

（제2의견）

공통서식 1—23　　　　　　　　　　　　　　0116　　（16절지）

대 한 민 국 외 무 부

착 신 전 보

ORD
종 별

번 호: PHW-0724
281130

일 시: _____

수 신 인: 장 관

발 신 인: 주 비 대 사

대: WPH-0715

1. 당지에는 유엔 기관으로 다음과같은 것이 있음.

가. UN INFORMATION CENTER FOR THE PHILIPPINES.

나. UN TECHNICAL ASSISTANCE BOARD.

다. UN ICEF COUNTRY OFFICE.

라. WHO, REGIONAL OFFICE FOR WESTERN PACIFIC (전문 기구)

2. 외무성 및 미대사관 당국자들 말에 의하면 PX 의 사용권은 유엔 관계 기관 또는 그 직원에게는 없다 함.

(외구미)

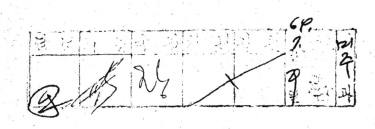

비서	통상	중정	재무
경무	문서	경기	조달
정보	의전	국방	농림
방교	총무	상공	

외 신 과

수신시간:

검 인 _____ 1964 JUL 28 PM 5 08

0117

대한민국 외무부

발신전보

민호: WTH-0811
인시: 041345

종 번

수 신 인: ___ 주 태 대 사 ___

외 신 과
접 수 암 호
1竹 X

대: THW — 0121(1964. 1. 17.)

1. 태국 주재 미군 P.X. 사용이 허가된 자의 범위에 태국 주재
   및기타국제기구
   UN 관계 기관의 직원이 포함되어 있는지 여부를 긴밤할 있다면 조속 조사
   보고 바람.

2. 만일 UN 관계직원이 미군 P.X.를 사용하고 있다면 소속 UN
   기관명 및 직위등 구체적으로 알려주시기 바람.(외구미) 끝.

미주과	양고재 8월4일	담 당	교 상	국 장 전결	특번보차점	차 신	장 관 강

장 관

0118

공세관 검 제	자체 농제	기안처	송신시간: 타자·판치	검 인	주무자	과 장

필 요 ☐   보안불필요 ☐

대한민국 외무부

착신전보

ORD
종 별

번 호: THW-0817

일 시: 061400

수신인: 장 관

발신인: 주태대사 대미

대: WTH-0811

태국주재 미군 PX 사용 허가자의 범위에는 태국 주재 유엔 관계 기관 및 기타

국제기구의 직원이 포함되어있지않음을 보고함.

당지 미군 PX 는 공용으로 당지에주재하는 미국인에게 만 사용이허가

되어있음을 첨언함.

(외구.미)

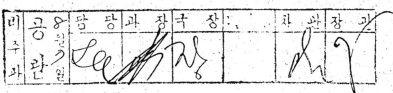

0119

비시	통상	중정	재무
정무	문서	경기	조달
정보	의전	국방	농림
방교	총무	상공	주 ㅇ

검 인

수신시간:

1964 AUG 6 PM 6 12

이근찰

외 신 과

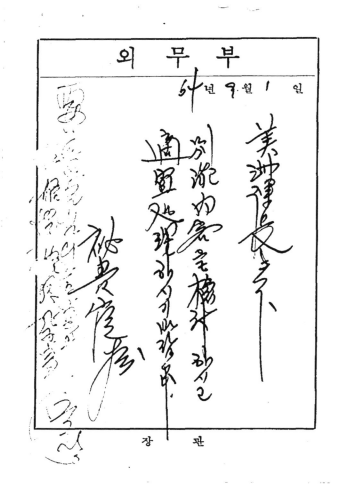

외 무 부

64년 9월 1일

장 관

0120

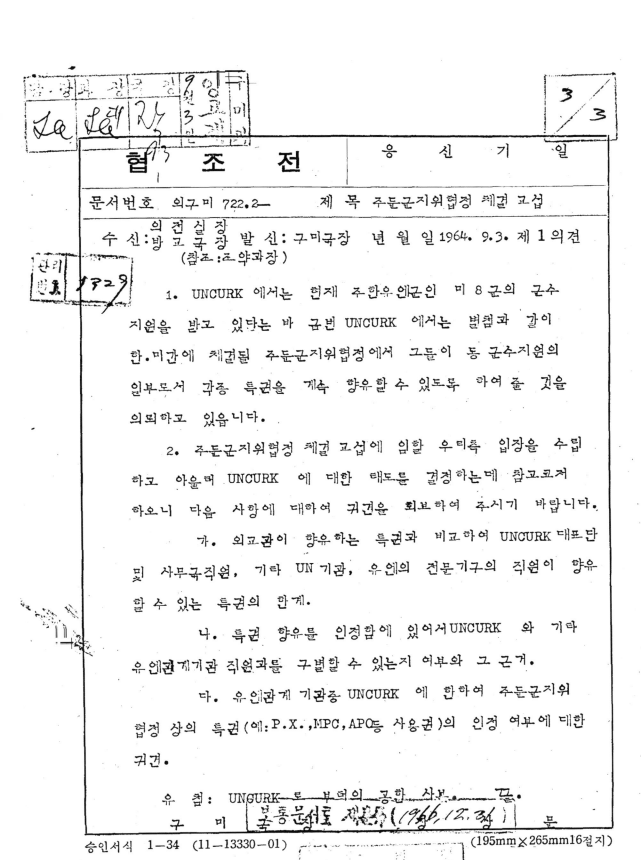

협 조 전

응 신 기 일

문서번호 외구미 722.2—   제 목 주둔군지위협정 체결 교섭

수 신 : 방교국장 발 신 : 구미국장   년 월 일 1964. 9. 3. 제 1 의견
의전실장
(참조 : 조약과장)

관리
1329

　　1. UNCURK 에서는 헌재 주한유엔군인 미 8군의 군수
지원을 받고 있다는 바 금번 UNCURK 에서는 별첨과 같이
한·미간에 체결될 주둔군지위협정에서 그들이 동 군수지원의
일부로서 각종 특권을 계속 향유할 수 있도록 하여 줄 것을
의뢰하고 있읍니다.

　　2. 주둔군지위협정 체결 교섭에 임할 우리측 입장을 수립
하고 아울러 UNCURK 에 대한 태도를 결정하는데 참고코저
하오니 다음 사항에 대하여 귀견을 회보하여 주시기 바랍니다.

　　가. 외교관이 향유하는 특권과 비교하여 UNCURK 대표단
및 사무국직원, 기타 UN 기관, 유엔의 전문기구의 직원이 향유
할 수 있는 특권의 한계.

　　나. 특권 향유를 인정함에 있어서 UNCURK 와 기타
유엔관계기관 직원과를 구별할 수 있는지 여부와 그 근거.

　　다. 유엔관계 기관중 UNCURK 에 한하여 주둔군지위
협정 상의 특권(예 : P.X., MPC, APO등 사용권)의 인정 여부에 대한
귀견.

　　유 첨 : UNCURK 토 부여의 공한 사본. 끝.

구 미   보통문서로 재분류(1966. 12. 31)   문

승인서식 1-34 (11-13330-01)   (195mm×265mm16절지)

0121

협 조 전

응신기일

분류기호 외구미 722.2 제목 주둔군지위협정 체결 교섭

수신 의견신간   발신일자 64. 9. 3.   (협조제의)

✓방교국장 (조약과장)

구 미 국 장 (발신명의)   장 상 문

(제1 의견)

　　1. UNCURK 에서는 현재 주한유엔군인 미 8 군
의 군수지원을 받고 있다는바 금번 UNCURK
에서는 별첨과 같이 한·미간에 체결될 주둔군
지위협정에서 그들이 동군수지원의 일부로서 각종
특권을 계속 향유할수 있도록 하여줄것을 의뢰
하고 있습니다.

　　2. 주둔군지위협정 체결 교섭에 임할 우리측
입장을 수립하고 아울러 UNCURK 에 대한(제2 의견)
태도를 결정하는데 참고코저 하오니 다음 사항에
대하여 귀견을 회보하여 주시기 바랍니다.

　　가. 외교관이 향유하는 특권과 비고하여
UNCURK 대표단 및 사무국직원, 기타 UN 기관,
유엔의 전문기구의 직원이 향유할수 있는 특권의
한계.

공통서식 1—23

(16절 지)

0122

나. 특권 향유를 인정함에 있어서 UNCURK
와 기타 유엔관계기관 직원과를 구별할수 있는지
여부와 그 근거.

다. 유엔관계 기관중 UNCURK 에 한하여
주둔군지위협정상의 특권 (예.P.X., MPC, APO 등
사용건)의 인정 여부에 대한 의견.

유첩 - UNCURK 로 부터 공한사본·끝

0123

Seoul — Korea

27 August 1964

Dear Mr. Chairman,

At a meeting of the Committee of UNCURK, held on 31 July 1964, some concern was expressed that, as a result of the negotiations on the impending "Status of Forces Agreement" between the Republic of Korea and the United States Embassy in Seoul, UNCURK might be deprived of the logistical support provided to it by the Eighth United States Army.

The Committee requested me to contact the Foreign Minister of the Republic of Korea to verify the accuracy of this information.

I called on the Republic of Korea Foreign Minister, Mr. Lee Tong Won, at the Foreign Ministry on the morning of 1 August 1964 and presented some of the pertinent facts involved in the matter. I requested that UNCURK be retained among those organizations that would continue to receive logistical support subsequent to the signing of the "Status of Forces Agreement." The Foreign Minister of the Republic of Korea was requested that UNCURK be kindly accorded every opportunity to retain such logistical support since the loss of this connection would heavily affect the functions as specified by the mandate accorded to it by the United Nations General Assembly. I did not ask for an immediate reply.

Subsequently, on 18 August 1964, I called on the Foreign Minister of the Republic of Korea who gave me assurances that there was no need for anxiety as he would ensure that UNCURK would enjoy continued backing from the ROK Government as far as possible though there might be some changes. UNCURK would, however, be consulted before any decisions would be taken on the issue.

It was also agreed that I should convey the assurances of the Foreign Minister to the United Nations Commission for the Unification and Rehabilitation of Korea.

Yours sincerely,

Major General

Chan Ansuchote
(Ambassador of Thailand)
UNCURK

Dr. Muammer Baykan
Representative of Turkey on
UNCURK and Chairman of the
Commission

0124

UNITED NATIONS 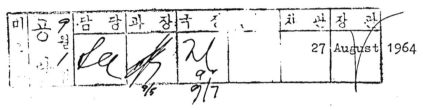 NATIONS UNIES

UNITED NATIONS COMMISSION FOR THE UNIFICATION AND REHABILITATION OF KOREA

Seoul – Korea

27 August 1964

Excellency,

At the request of the Commission I am attaching, for your information, a letter confirming discussions held between yourself and H.E. Ambassador Chan Ansuchote concerning the continuance of logistical support by the United States Eighth Army to the United Nations Commission for the Unification and Rehabilitation of Korea. The Commission is happy to receive the assurance of your kind co-operation and backing as outlined in the attached letter.

Please accept, Excellency, the renewed assurances of my highest consideration.

Muammer Baykan
Representative of Turkey
and Chairman of the Commission

His Excellency Lee Tong Won
Foreign Minister
Ministry of Foreign Affairs
Seoul

0125

AFFECT OF POSSIBLE CANCELLATION OF LOGISTICAL
SUPPORT PROVIDED THROUGH THE UNITED NATIONS
COMMAND TO UNCURK AND UNMCK

1.   Possible cancellation of logistical support from the
Eighth United States Army in Korea by non-inclusion of
UNCURK and UNMCK in the Status of Forces Agreement might
result in the loss of the following facilities and
privileges now authorized by the United Nations Command:

   a.   Commission Support:

        (1) APO Privileges
        (2) Billets (In field and Pusan)
        (3) Army Exchange Privileges (PX) (for spare parts
            and equipment)
        (4) Banking Facilities (official transactions)
        (5) Military Payment Certificates (MPC)
        (6) Class I bulk Issue (Purchase of items for opera--
            tion of a Mess)
        (7) Class II and IV Support (Motor Transport parts
            and repairs)
        (8) Class III - POL (Petrol, Oil and Lubricants)
        (9) Equipment Maintenance
        (10)Potable Water (UNMCK only)
        (11) Transportation (Rail and Air)
        (12) Repair and Utilities (UNMCK only)
        (13) Signal Support (Telephones, etc.)
        (14) Self Service Supply Centre (Located in Pusan
             but serving UNCURK and UNMCK)

   b. Mission Support:
      (UNCURK & UNMCK)
        (1) Army Exchange Privileges (PX)
        (2) Commissary Privileges
        (3) Banking Facilities
        (4) Field Ration Mess Privileges
        (5) Medical Care
        (6) Medical Care of Dependents
        (7) Dependents School Facilities
        (8) Embassy Commissary Facilities
        (9) Housing - UNMCK personnel, Pusan (Personnel live
            in Army Compound and would therefore experience
            considerable difficulties if without support
            from EUSA)

0126

협 조 전

응신기일

분류기호 710.174   제목 주둔군 지위협정 체결교섭

수신 구미국장   발신일자 64.9.7   (협조제의)

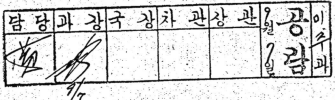

담당과	장국	장차	관	상	관	월	공	이
						일	람	과

의견실장   (발신명의)   경 도 순

외구미 722.2호로 문의하신 주둔군지위협정 체결교섭중   (제1의견)

언커크 대표 및 사무국직원의 특권인정문제에 관한 당심의 의견

을 아래와같이 회신합니다.

가) 언커크대표단 및 동사무국직원, 기타유엔기관직원, 유엔전문

기구의 직원이 향유하는 특권에 대하여는 || 대한민국과 국제연합

간의 특권및 면제에 관한 협정 || 제4조에 명백히 규정되어있는바

(제2의견)

와같이 주한외교공관의 동급의 외교관과 동등한 특권을

부여하도록 되어있읍니다.

나) 전기법정제4조 4항에 언커크대표, 언커크사무국직원,

기타국제연합의 직원, 국제연합전문기구의 직원은 외교특권을 향유

하도록규정되어있고 동5항에 전기기구등의 전문가에 대하여 응분의

공통서식 1—23   0127   (16절지)

특권을 부여하도록 되어있으며 어데까지나 동등한 대우를 하여야한다고
사료됩니다.

다) 따라서 만일 언커크대표 및 동사무국직원에 대하여만
주둔군지위협정에 어떠한 특권을 인정할경우에는 기타 유엔기관으로
부터 강력한 항의가 예상되며, 나아가서는 전기법정 제5조4항 및 5
항에 해당되는 유엔관계직원에게 상기한 특권을 인정할수밖에 없을
것으로 생각되므로 이점을 충분히 참작하여 결정하시기 바랍니다.

0128

부 전 지

제 목
요 약

　　　1964. 9. 8일 국장회의에서 미주둔군
지위협정 체결 문제에 관련된 주한미군
의 PX 사용권자의 범위에 UNCURK 각국
대표와 주한외국공관의 공관장급을 포함
할 것에 합의하였음.

　　　　　　　　　　　　9/8

각계부처

협조처

전화번호 주부

발 신

　양식 1-24 (1112-040-032-023) (130mm×190mm 32절기)

0129

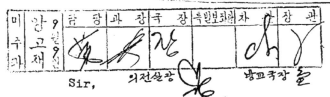

September 9, 1964

Seoul

Sir,

I have the honour to acknowledge the receipt of your note dated August 27, 1964, regarding the use by the UNCURK of the certain facilities of the United States Armed Forces.

The question has been discussed between the negotiators of the Republic of Korea and the United States at the negotiating table of the Status of Forces Agreement. I believe the concern of the Commission as expressed by H.E. Ambassador Chan Ansuchote over the question will be taken into account to the maximum extent possible at the negotiation and the UNCURK will be informed of the result of the negotiation.

In this connection, I assure you that whatever decisions may be made by the current negotiation on the Status of Forces Agreement between the Republic of Korea and the United States, the representatives of member states and officials of the UNCURK will enjoy such privileges and immunities, exemptions and facilities as are granted to diplomatic envoys of similar rank in accordance with the provisions of the Agreement Relating to Privileges and Immunities to be Enjoyed by the United Nations in Korea, effected September 21, 1951,

I avail myself of this opportunity to renew to you the assurances of my highest consideration.

Lee Tong Won
Foreign Minister

Dr. Muammer Baykan
    Representative of Turkey
    UNCURK

0130

September 9, 1964

Seoul

Sir,

I have the honour to acknowledge the receipt of your note dated August 27, 1964, regarding the use by the UNCURK of the certain facilities of the United States Armed Forces.

The question has been discussed between the negotiators of the Republic of Korea and the United States at the negotiating table of the Status of Forces Agreement. I believe the concern of the Commission as expressed by H.E. Ambassador Chan Ansuchote over the question will be taken into account to the maximum extent possible at the negotiation.

In this connection, I assure you that whatever decisions may be made by the current negotiation on the Status of Forces Agreement between the Republic of Korea and the United States, the representatives of member states and officials of the UNCURK will, in accordance with the provisions of the Agreement Relating to Privileges and Immunities to be Enjoyed by the United Nations in Korea, effected September 21, 1951, enjoy such privileges and immunities, exemptions and facilities as are granted to diplomatic envoys of similar rank.

I avail myself of this opportunity to renew to you the assurances of my highest consideration.

Lee, Tong Won
Foreign Minister

Dr. Muammer Baykan
Representative of Turkey
UNCURK

0131

협 조 전

응산기일

분류기호 외미1와 제목 서한 이송

수신 구미국장 발신일자 1965. 6. 7. (협조제의)

Sofa. Ex. Article (f12.Ex.에 노출하는
것는 回本國 및 U.N. organs. 에해가능 改府의
approval 問題를 檢討하고. approve
기어야할 agencies 및 person 들에대한
간여서도 sofa 發效前에 交涉接受
曼을 取하도록 (발신명의) 의전실장 윤 호 군

曼 뿔돌라 협힘하시음. (제1의견)
한국주재 UNICEF 및 UNTAB 부의 법첩과

여한 서한을 접수하였는 바 이는 귀국 소관으로 사료되어

이송하오니 적의 조치하여주시기 바랍니다.

법 첩: UNICEF 및 UNTAB 으로 부터의 서한 사본 6 蹯

(제2의견)

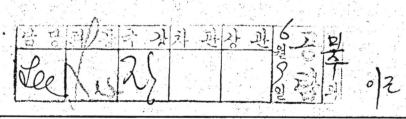

공통서식 1—23

KO/GEN/1041   Seoul, 3 June 1965

Sir,

        I have the honour to invite your attention respectfully to
a statement published in to-day's edition of the "Korea Times"
in regard to the subject of the early conclusion of a Status of
Forces Agreement between your Government and the Government of
the United States. It is stated inter alia that your Ministry
has said that the privilege of the use of the PX facilities
(which have been made available to the Representative of UNICEF)
would continue to be extended to the members of UNCURK.

        In that the UNICEF Representative in Korea is a United Nations
official, employed on a similar standing and basis to officials
and Representatives of other United Nations bodies and the
Specialised Agencies, and the entitlement of all such officials
and Representatives to privileges and immunities, exemptions and
facilities from the Host Government is embodied in the Agreement
between the Government of Korea and the United Nations signed
at Pusan on 21st. September 1951, may we presume, if the
reported statement is correct, that your Ministry will include
the Representative of UNICEF in any arrangements which may be
made to continue the abailability of the PX facility to other
United Nations staff?

        I would respectfully invite your attention in this
connection, to the fact that the Basic Agreement with UNICEF is
one of the earliest Treaties to have been concluded with a United
Nations organisation, having been signed on 25th March, 1950,
and that it remains in force at the present time. In addition,
your Government has welcomed the establishment of the Office of
a UNICEF Representative to Korea, for the purpose of furthering
relations between your Government and this United Nations
Organisation.

        It is consequently hoped that a facility which has enabled
the UNICEF Representative to obtain essential imported official and
personal commodities food and supplies may be continued in the
future on the same basis as in the past.

        I am at your disposal for discussion of the above urgent
considerations at your convenience.

        I have the honour to be, Sir,

                                        Yours sincerely,

                                        ALAN E. McBAIN
                                        UNICEF Representative in Kore

Mr. In Han Paik
Chief of Protocol   0133
Ministry of Foreign Affairs

UNITED NATIONS NATIONS UNIES

Telephone
74-8503
74-8504

TECHNICAL ASSISTANCE BOARD AND SPECIAL FUND

17-1 CHANGSUNG-DONG, CHONGNO-KU
C. P. O. BOX 143
SEOUL, KOREA

Cable Address:
"TECABOARD SEOUL"

REF: 3-1-1   4 June 1965

Dear Mr. Yoon,

We have seen the report in the Korea Times of 4 June 1965 that special arrangements will be made concerning access of the United Nations Commission for the Unification and Rehabilitation of Korea (UNCURK) to the United States Army PX Facilities when the Status of Forces Agreement is concluded between the Government of Korea and the United States of America.

On the assumption that you would wish to treat all United Nations personnel in Korea on the same basis of equality of treatment we wish to invite your attention to the possibilities of including all United Nations personnel in any special provisions of the Status of Forces Agreement.

With my respects,

Yours sincerely,

W. Roy Lucas
Resident Representative and
Director of Special Fund
Programmes in Korea

Mr. Yoon, Hogan
Director of Protocol
Ministry of Foreign Affairs
Seoul, Korea

0134

협 조 전

응신기일

분류기호 외의전 64   제목 서한 이송

수신 구 미 국 장   발신일자 1965. 6. 18.   (협조제의)

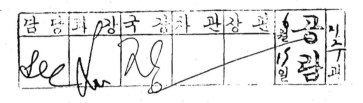

(발신명의) 의전실장 윤 호 근

(제1 의견)

1. 외의전 78 (65. 6. 7) 과 관련됩니다.

2. 한국주재 UNTAB 대표로부터 다시 별첨 서한을 접하였기

그 사본을 이송하오니 참고하시기 바랍니다.

별첨: UNTAB 으로 부터의 서한 사본. 끝

(제2 의견)

attention :

[handwritten note, illegible]

공통서식 1—23

0135 (16절지)

UNITED NATIONS ⊛ NATIONS UNIES

TECHNICAL ASSISTANCE BOARD AND SPECIAL FUND

17-1 CHANGSUNG-DONG, CHONGNO-KU
C. P. O. BOX 143
SEOUL, KOREA

Telephone
74-8503
74-8504

Cable Address:
"TECABOARD SEOUL"

REF: 3-1-1   15 June 1965

Dear Mr. Yoon,

I have to thank you for your letter of June 7, 1965 regarding use of the United States Army PX facilities. I would like to point out however that my note of June 4, 1965 did not concern only the Resident Representative of UNTAB and SF but it concerned equality of treatment for <u>all</u> United Nations personnel stationed in Korea.

With my respects,

Yours sincerely,

W. Roy Lucas
Resident Representative
and Director of Special
Fund Programmes in Korea

Mr. Yoon, Hogan
Director of Protocol
Ministry of Foreign Affairs
Seoul

0136

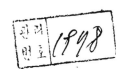

협 조 전

응 신 기 일

문기번호 외구미 722.2-   제 목 비세출자금기관 사용자의 범위

수 신: 의전실장 발 신: 구미국장 년 월 일 1965. 6. 19 제 1 의견

1. 회의접 78(1965.6.7.) 및 동 84(1965. 6. 18.)에 관련된 사항입니다.

2. 미주둔군지위협정 체결 교섭실무자회의에서 한.미 양측은 비세출자금기관(PX)의 사용자의 범위에 관하여 별첨 내용과 같이 합의를 본바 있읍니다.

3. 그 중 (b)—(e)항에 해당하는 자를 제외한 현 비세출자금기관 사용자는 협정 발효와 동시에 일단 그 사용이 금지되어야 하며 (f)항 해당자 즉 한국정부가 명시적으로 동의 함으로서 사용할 수 있는 자 또는 기관의 범위는 한.미 양국이 협의 결정케로 되었읍니다.

4. 따라서 미군 또는 미국정부권리등 (a)—(e)항 해당자 이외의 자 또는 기관의 P.X. 사용에 관하여서는 그 허가 여부가 협정에서 구체적으로 결정된바 없읍니다.

5. 그러므로 앞으로 협정 발효에 대비하여 우리 정부가 별첨 합의의사록 (f)항의 규정에 따라 P.X. 사용을 허가하여야 할 자 또는 기관이 있다면 이들을 가능한한 협정 발효 이전에 구제할 수 있도록 귀실에서 그 범위를 검토 확정하시기 바랍니다.

승인서식 1—34 (11—13330—01)   (195mm×265mm16절지)

0137

유 첨: 비세출자금기관 사용자의 범위에 관한 합의의사록. 끝

보통문서로 재분류 (1966. 12. 31)

구미국장   장 상 문

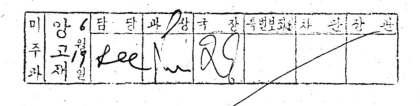

미주과	양고재 6월 19일	담 당	과 장	국 장	특별보좌	차 관	장 관
		Lee		29			

0138

AGREED MINUTE

The United States Armed Forces may grant the
use of the organizations referred to in paragraph 1 of
Article (XIII) to :
(a) other officers or personnel of the United States
Government ordinarily accorded such privileges; (b)
those other non-Korean Armed Forces in Korea under the
Unified Command which receive logistical support
from the United States Armed Forces, and their members;
(c) those non-Korean persons whose presence in the
Republic of Korea is solely for the purpose of
providing contract services financed by the United States
Government; (d) those organizations which are present
in the Republic of Korea primarily for the benefit
and service of the United States Armed forces, such
as the American Red Cross and the United Service
Organizations, and their non-Korean personnel; (e)
dependents of the foregoing; and (f) other persons
and organizations with the express consent of the
Government of the Republic of Korea.

0139

협 조 전

응신기일

분류기호 외의전 AA   제목 비세출자금기관 사용자의범위

수신 구 미 국 장   발신일자 1965. 6. 28.   (협조제의)

담 당	과 장	국 장	차 관	장 관	6월 2?일	종람	미구과
			X				

① UN CURK 및 全유엔. agencies
② 증원의 조승등을
으로 축소제하는 방향으로
향후交渉을 期해나감 jml   (발신명의) 의견신장 윤 호 군

(제1 의견)

외구미 722.2 (65.6.19) 에 대하여 아래와 같이 당신의 의견을
표시하오니 귀국에서 이문제에 관하여 미국측과 교섭견정함에 있어
참고하시기 바랍니다.

1. " 5 " 항의 범위는 미군 또는 UN 군과 직접적인 관련이
   있는 기관원에 한정하되, 의례적인 면은 고려하여 조박 외교
   공관의 공관장인 대공사 와 UNCURK   상의 대표에 대하여는
   현재 부여하고 있는 사용권은 계속인정하는것이 좋을것으로
   생각함.

2. 협정상 또는 국제 관례상 동일한 처우를하게 되어   (제2 의견)
   있는 기관간에 차별대우를 하는 결과를 초래하는 규정은 피
   해야 할 것임.

보통문서로 재분류(66. 12.31)

이z

공통서식 1—23   (16절지)

UNITED NATIONS 🌐 NATIONS UNIES

UNITED NATIONS COMMISSION FOR THE UNIFICATION AND REHABILITATION OF KOREA

Seoul, 27 January 1966

Excellency,

UNCURK has been following with close attention the negotiations between the Republic of Korea and the United States concerning the conclusion of a Status-of-Forces Agreement. Your Excellency will no doubt recall that the possible effects of the conclusion of this Agreement on the logistical support provided by the United Nations Command to UNCURK has been the subject of conversations between Your Excellency and Chairmen of the Commission and also of correspondence.

Since, according to press reports, the Agreement is to be signed in the near future, the Commission has requested me to seek from Your Excellency assurances that the conclusion of this Agreement will in no way affect the extent of logistical support which has been available without interruption to the representatives and the secretariat of UNCURK since the inception of the Commission in 1950.

The Commission believes that such assurances will provide a further manifestation of the very co-operative and understanding attitude shown by the Government of the Republic of Korea towards UNCURK and its work as the symbol of the political presence of the United Nations in Korea. As Your Excellency will recognize, it is natural and appropriate that the United Nations Command, the military component of the United Nations presence in Korea, should continue to provide logistical support to UNCURK.

Accept, Excellency, the assurances of my highest consideration.

Yuad Loesrit
Chairman

His Excellency
Mr. Lee Tong Won
Minister for Foreign Affairs
    of the Republic of Korea
Seoul

0141

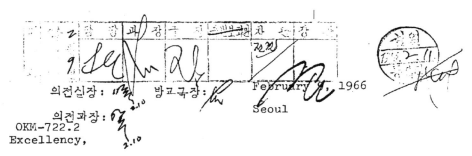

Excellency,

    I have the honour to acknowledge the receipt of
Your Excellency's note dated January 27, 1966, regarding the
logistical support provided by the United States armed forces
to UNCURK.

    Regarding the matter of logistical support provided
by the United States armed forces to the Commission in
the form of use by the Commission of certain facilities of
the United States armed forces, no detailed decision has
yet been made in the current negotiations for the Status
of Forces Agreement between the Republic of Korea
and the United States.

    However, I wish to remind Your Excellency that
whatever decisions may be made in the current negotiations,
the representatives of Member States and officials of the
Commission will, as the Foreign Minister made it clear in his note of September 9,
1964, addressed to Dr. Muammer Baykan, then the Chairman
of the Commission, enjoy such privileges and immunities,
exemptions and facilities as are granted to diplomatic envoys
of similar rank in accordance with the relevant provisions of
the Agreement between the Republic of Korea and the
United Nations.

    I avail myself of this opportunity to renew to Your
Excellency the assurances of my highest consideration.

                          Young Choo Kim
                          Acting Foreign Minister

His Excellency
    Mr. Yuad Loesrit
      Chairman of UNCURK

                          0142

OKM-722.2   Seoul, February 10, 1966

Excellency,

      I have the honour to acknowledge the receipt of Your Excellency's note dated January 27, 1966, regarding the logistical support provided by the United States armed forces to UNCURK.

      Regarding the matter of logistical support provided by the United States armed forces to the Commission in the form of use by the Commission of certain facilities of the United States armed forces, no detailed decision has yet been made in the current negotiations for the Status of Forces Agreement between the Republic of Korea and the United States.

      However, I wish to remind Your Excellency that whatever decisions may be made in the current negotiations, the representatives of member states and officials of the Commission will, as the Foreign Minister made it clear in his note of September 9, 1964, addressed to Dr. Muammer Baykan, then the Chairman of the Commission, enjoy such privileges and immunities, exemptions and facilities as are granted to diplomatic envoys of similar rank in accordance with the relevant provisions of the Agreement between the Republic of Korea and the United Nations.

      I avail myself of this opportunity to renew to Your Excellency the assurances of my highest consideration.

                       Young Choo Kim
                       Acting Foreign Minister

His Excellency
   Mr. Yuad Loesrit
     Chairman of UNCURK

0143

1966. 9. 9 일자 외무·법사 특별위 번회개최 시
제출함.

非歲出資金機關關係資料

(美八軍提供)

1966. 9. 3

合衆國軍隊의 非歲出資金機關活動은 合衆國軍隊의 本質的

이며 緊要한 部分을 이룩하고있으며. 이러한 機關은 合

衆國軍隊의 士氣昂揚, 厚生, 및 誤業關係事業을 맞고 있

음

本協定 第13條에 規定된 非歲出資金機關은 合衆国軍当

局에 依하여 公的으로 認定되고 規制되고 一般歲出資金

機関과 同一하게 緊密한 監督下에 있음.

韓国内 非歲出資金機関現況은 다음과 같다.

1. P.X.

(1) 合衆国軍隊의 韓国内、大小. P.X는 總191個所이

며 그 規模는 큰것은 現代的施設로 부터 적은것은 「트

레이러」車 또는 天幕의 一部로 되어있는것도 있으며

~/~

0144

化粧品類를 비롯하여 其他 日常必需品을 取扱하고 있음

(2) 큰 規模의 것은 다음 地域에 있음:

1. 서 울 龍山

2. 富 平

3. 烏 山

4. 大 邱

5. 釜 山

6. 第一軍司令部

7. 第二師團 本部

8. 第7師團 本部

ㄱ 劇 場

(1) 35미리 필림을 上映 할수 있는 劇場이 41個所

있으며 合衆国 陸軍 및 空軍의 *motion picture*

service 에 依하여 運営되고 있음

数百名以上을 收容할수있는 큰 規模의 것은 다음地区에

있음:

~2~

0145

1. 서울 龍山地区에 2個所

2. 富 平

3. 議 政 府

4. 烏 山

5. 大 邱

(2) 其外에도 16미리필림 上映劇場은 185個所인바
이中 56個所는 無料上映함

3. 食 堂

101個所의 將校食堂과 198個所의 士兵食堂이
있으며, 이들은 33個의 Open-mess system 에
依하여 運営되고 있음

-3-

0146

非歳出資金機関関係資料

（美八軍 提供）

1966. 9. 3

合衆國軍隊의 非歳出資金機関活動은 合衆國軍隊의 本質的이며 緊要한 部分을 이룩하고있으며, 이러한 機関은 合衆國軍隊의 士氣昂揚, 厚生, 및 誤楽関係事業을 맡고 있음

本協定 第13條에 規定된 非歳出資金機関은 合衆国軍当局에 依하여 公的으로 認定되고 規制되고 一般歳出資金機関과 同一하게 緊密한 監督下에 있음.

韓国内 非歳出資金機関現況은 다음과 같다.

1. P. X.

(1) 合衆国軍隊의 韓国内、大小, P. X 는 總191 伯所이며 그 規模는 큰것은 現代的施設로 부터 적은것은 「트레이러」車 또는 天幕의 一部로 되어있는것도 있으며

~1~

0147

한·미국 간의 상호방위조약 제4조에 의한 시설과 구역 및 한국에서의 미국군대의 지위에 관한 협정(SOFA)
전59권. 1966.7.9 서울에서 서명 : 1967.2.9 발효(조약 232호) (V.55 비세출자금기관 관계자료, 1964-66)

化粧品類를 비롯하여 其他 日常必需品들 取扱하고 있음

(2) 큰 規模의 것은 다음 地域에 있음:

    1. 서 울 龍山

    2. 富 平

    3. 烏 山

    4. 大 邱

    5. 釜 山

    6. 第一軍司令部

    7. 第二師團 本部

    8. 第七師團 本部

2. 劇 場

(1) 35미리 필림을 上映할수 있는 劇場이 41個所 있으며 合家國 陸軍 및 空軍의 motion picture Service 에 依하여 運營되고 있음

數百名以上을 收容할수있는 큰 規模의 것은 다음地区에 있음:

~2~

0148

1. 서울 龍山地区에 2個所

2. 富平

3. 議政府

4. 烏山

5. 大邱

(2) 其外에도 16미리필림 上映劇場은 165個所인바 이中 56個所는 無料上映함

3. 食堂

101個所의 將校食堂과 198個所의 士兵食堂이 있으며 이들은 33個의 Open-mess System에 依하여 運営되고 있음

-3-

INFORMATION
on
US ARMED FORCES NON-APPROPRIATED FUND ORGANIZATIONS

1. The non-appropriated fund activities of the United States armed forces are an integral and essential part of the United States armed forces worldwide and of their civilian component abroad. Although in many countries such activities and organizations are covered by appropriated funds, in the U.S. armed forces they are carried out through the use of non-appropriated funds. The difference in structure does not in any way make the non-appropriated fund (NAF) activities any less an integral part of the U.S. armed forces. Such forces are designed to promote and provide a well-rounded morale, welfare, and recreational program for the armed forces and their civilian component. The NAF organizations covered in Article XIII of the US-ROK SOFA include only those officially authorized and regulated by U.S. military authorities. Such activities are under the close and continuing supervision of US armed forces, just as are the appropriated fund activities.

2. Post Exchanges. The Far East Exchange Service of the US armed forces operates a total of 191 Post Exchanges, popularly known as PX's in Korea. These include eight major PX's located in Seoul, Ascom, Osan, Taegu, Pusan, Hq 1st Corps, Hq 2d Division and Hq 7th Division. The size of the PX's in Korea ranges widely, from the large and modern store which serves as the PX at USFK Headquarters at Yongsan to very small PX's, some located in a truck trailer or in a corner of a tent, carrying toilet articles and other daily essentials, serving units located in remote or isolated US military

0150

bases within the ROK. US military regulations require that wherever US military units are located, a PX facility be established to serve the personnel stationed there.

3. <u>Motion Pictures</u>. There is a total of 41 theaters operated by the US Army and Air Forces Motion Picture Service and showing 35 mm films – located on major US bases in Korea. The largest such theaters, which accommodate up to several hundred people, are located at Yongsan (2), Ascom, Uijongbu, Osan and Taegu. There are also 165 points, usually located on smaller US bases, at which 16 mm films are shown periodically. Many of these points are at isolated bases where only a few US troops are stationed; at 56 of these points the movies are shown free of charge because the number of troops stationed there is too few to make collection of an admission charge feasible.

4. <u>US Military Messes</u>. There are 33 open-mess systems operating on US military bases in Korea, with 101 officers open-mess branches and 198 non-commissioned officer branch messes. These facilities, open only to authorized personnel, serve as official eating places for the personnel of the US armed forces and civilian component in Korea.

5. The foregoing NAF facilities operate under the direct supervision of the US military authorities and serve a vital function in the maintenance of the US Forces in Korea. The foregoing statistics on NAF facilities include those used by all US military personnel in Korea, including MAAG personnel who are not under the SOFA. Every SOFA which United States has negotiated includes provision for these NAF organizations which are located wherever US military personnel are stationed throughout the world. It is hoped that the above information meets your requirements.

2

0151

협 조 전

분류기호 외방연 257   제 목 언커크로부터의 공한 이첩

수신 구미국장   발신일자 1966.11.17   (허조제의)

　　　　1. 언커크로부터 별첨 (1) 과 같은 공한을 접수하였는바 본건은
한미군대지위협정 시행에 금면된 사항으로 귀국 소관으로 사료되어 이를
이첩하오니 조치하여 주시기 바랍니다.

　　　시고 그 결과를 외시하

　　　　2. 동 공한에 대하여는 별첨 (2) 와 같이 일단 회보하였아오니
참고 바랍니다.

　　　　　　　　　　　　（발신명의） 방교국장 権

첨부 : 1. 언커크의장 공한 1 부   （제1의견）

　　　 2. 회한 사본 1 부 끝.

　　　　　　　　　　　　　　　　　　　　（제2의견）

0152

공통시식 1—23   （13겹지）

별첨 (1)

별첨 (2)

1966.11.10

Seoul, 1 November 1966

103495

Excellency,

The United Nations Commission for the Unification and

Rehabilitation of Korea has noted that the Agreement between

the Republic of Korea and the United States of America

Regarding Facilities and Areas and the Status of United States

Armed Forces in the Republic of Korea has now been ratified by

the Republic.

As the Commission believes that the support of your Govern-

ment is essential in facilitating the conduct of its activities

in Korea, it wishes to seek your Government's consent to the

inclusion of UNCURK among the organizations to which paragraph 1

of Article XIII of the Agreement refers. In this connexion,

your Government will no doubt give due consideration to the

unique position of UNCURK as the political component of the

United Nations presence in Korea. Furthermore, I am sure your

Government will also appreciate the special relationship, based

on various resolutions of the Security Council and the General

Assembly, which bind the Commission with the United Nations

Command as the military component of the Organization's presence

in the Republic.

The Commission has found that not only privileges and

immunities are necessary for its work in Seoul and throughout

the Republic of Korea, but that logistical support and other

../..

His Excellency
Mr. Lee Tong Won
Minister for Foreign Affairs
    of the Republic of Korea
Seoul

0153

facilities, made available to UNCURK since its inception by the
Eighth United States Army as one of the components of the United
Nations Command, have been and continue to be required for the
effective discharge of its responsibilities.

The unstinting support given by the Republic of Korea to
United Nations objectives in Korea encourages the Commission to
believe that your Government will be favourably disposed to
agree to the continued availability of the logistical support
and facilities to which UNCURK, its delegations, the international
staff of the Secretariat, and their dependents have access.

Accept, Excellency, the assurances of my highest consideration.

Pedro G. Ramirez
Chairman

0154

OBY-7098

November 16, 1966

Excellency,

I would like to acknowledge the receipt of your letter dated November 1, 1966 concerning the provision of the logistical support and other facilities to UNCURK under Paragraph 1 of Article XIII of the Agreement between the Republic of Korea and the United States of America regarding Facilities and Areas and the Status of United States Armed Forces in the Republic of Korea.

In this connection, I have the honour to advise you that the matter is under study and that when decision is made it will be informed to you without delay.

Accept, Excellency, the assurances of my highest consideration.

Young Choo KIM
Acting Minister

His Excellency
Ambassador Pedro G. Ramirez
Chairman
United Nations Commission
for the Unification and Rehabilitation
of Korea

Seoul

0155

한·미간 군대 지위협정 및 합의 의사록에 대한

합의 양해사항 발췌

제 13 조

합의 의사록

(가), (나), (다), (라) 및 (마) 항목에서 언급된것 이외의 기관 및
인원에 의한 비세출 지급 기관의 현재의 사용은 본 협정의 효력 발생시에
즉시 정지되는 것으로 양해한다. 본 의사록 (바) 항목에 따라 그러한
기관의 사용이 허용된 기관과 인원의 범위는 양국 정부의 관계 당국간의
계속적 협의에 위임한다.

0156

한·미간 군대 지위협정의 합의의사록 발췌

제 13 조

합중국 군대는 다음 각호의 자에게 제13조 제1항에 규정된 제 기관의 사용을 허용할 수 있다. (가) 통상적으로 이와같은 특권이 부여되는 합중국 정부의 기타 공무원 및 직원, (나) 합중국 군대로 부터 군수 지원을 받는 통합 사령부 산하 주한 외국 군대 및 그 구성원, (다) 대한민국 국민이 아닌 자로서, 그의 대한민국에서의 체류 목적이 합중국 정부에 의하여 재정적 지원을 받는 계약 용역의 이행만을 위한자, (라) 미 적십자사, "유.에스.오"와 같은, 주로 합중국 군대의 이익이나 용역을 위하여 대한민국에 체류하는 기관 및 대한민국 국민이 아닌 직원, (마) 전 각호에 규정된 자의 가족 및 (바) 대한민국 정부의 명시적인 동의를 얻은 기타 개인과 기관.

0157

<u>Excerpt from the Agreed Understandings to the</u>
<u>ROK-U.S. Status of Forces Agreement and Related</u>
<u>Agreed Minutes</u>

<u>ARTICLE XIII</u>

<u>AGREED MINUTE</u>

It is understood that the present use of Non-appropriated Fund organizations by organizations and persons other than those referred to in items (a), (b), (c), (d), and (e) shall immediately be suspended at the time of the entry into force of this Agreement. The extent of organizations and persons to be granted the use of such organizations under item (f) of this minute shall be left to further negotiations between the appropriate authorities of the two Governments.

0158

Excerpt from the Agreed Minutes to the ROK-U.S.
b Status of Forces Agreement

Article XIII

The United States armed forces may grant the use of the organizations referred to in paragraph 1 of Article XIII to: (a) other officers or personnel of the Government of the United States ordinarily accorded such privileges; (b) those other non-Korean armed forces in the Republic of Korea under the Unified Command which receive logistical support from the United States armed forces, and their members; (c) those non-Korean persons whose presence in the Republic of Korea is solely for the purpose of providing contract services financed by the Government of the United States; (d) those organizations which are present in the Republic of Korea primarily for the benefit and service of the United States armed forces, such as the American Red Cross and the United Service Organizations, and their non-Korean personnel; (e) dependents of the foregoing; and (f) other persons and organizations with the express consent of the Government of the Republic of Korea.

0159

협 조 전	응신기일

분류기호 외방연 265	제 목	주한 미군 지위협정 시행

수 신 구미국장   발신일자 66. 11. 23   (협조제의)
참조 미주과장

방 교 국 장

(발신명의)

1. 유엔 개발사업처 한국주재관으로 부터 별첨 공함과 같이 (제1의전)
   유엔개발사업처 직원 및 유엔전문기구에서 파견한 각종
   기술자가 주한 미군시설을 계속 이용토록 요청하는 공함을
   송부하여 왔는바 이는 주한 미군 지위협정중 특권에 관한
   사항 시행과 관련된것임으로 귀국 소관으로 사료되어 동
   공함 원본을 이첩하니 사수하시기 바랍니다.

2. 동 공함에 관하여는 당국에서 이미 접수확인공함을 (제2의전)
   유엔개발사업처 한국주재관에게 발송하였으며 귀국에서의
   동건 조치결과에 대하여도 당국에 알려주시기 바랍니다.

   첨부:1. 유엔개발사업처 공함 2-0-1/ Confidential 원본
        2. 당국의 접수확인공함 사본   끝

                                                0160

UNITED NATIONS
DEVELOPMENT PROGRAMME

PROGRAMME DES NATIONS UNIES
POUR LE DEVELOPPEMENT

UNITED NATIONS
17-1 CHANGSUNG-DONG, CHONGNO-KU
C. P. O. BOX 143
SEOUL, KOREA

Telephone: 74-8503
74-8504

Cable Address: UNDEVPRO, SEOUL

Reference:

2-0-1/Confidential

18 November 1966

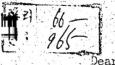

Dear Mr. Pak,

I refer to our recent discussions concerning the effect of the Status of Forces Agreement on the privileges presently extended to United Nations officials and experts by the United States 8th Army by virtue of the sponsorship of the United States Embassy.

In accordance with the provisions of the Agreement I respectfully request that the Government of Korea approve continued access to the 8th US Army facilities by the officials of the United Nations Development Programme and by the experts assigned to Korea by the Specialized Agencies of the United Nations.

This would represent a significant contribution to the Development Programme which will face increased expenses if the privileges are removed. Furthermore the difficulties would extend into the more sensitive areas of recruitment and retention of the programme experts.

I have been asked by my Headquarters, to stress that, in any event, it is expected the Government will observe equality of treatment of all United Nations Agencies in Korea in this matter.

With my respects,

Yours sincerely,

W. Roy Lucas
Resident Representative

Mr. Pak, Kun
Director
Bureau of International Relations
Ministry of Foreign Affairs
Seoul

6 11.18
1213

0161

OBY –   November 21st, 1966

Dear Mr. Lucas,

    I wish to acknowledge the receipt of your letter 2-0-1/Confidential, dated 18 November 1966, requesting approval of the Korean Government for the continued access to the 8th US Army facilities by the officials of the United Nations Development Programme and by the experts assigned to Korea by the Specialized Agencies of the United Nations.

    In this connection, I have the honour to inform you that your request is under consideration and that when decision is made it will be advised to you without delay.

    With best personal regards, I remain.

                    Kun Pak
                    Director, Bureau of
                    International Relations

W. Roy Lucas
Resident Representative,
United Nations Development Programme,
C.P.O. Box 143, Seoul, Korea

0162

분류기호 외방연 282 제 목 UNMCK 요청에 대한 조치 의뢰

수신 구 미 국 장 　　　　 발신일자 　 66.12.1 　　 (협조재의)

(발신명의) 방 교 국 장

(제1의 건)

　　1. 유엔군묘지(UNMCK) 관리인으로부터 유엔 사무총장을 대신하여 별첨과 같은 공한을 보내왔는바, 귀국소관사항으로 사료되어 이를 이첩하오니 필요한 조치를 취하여 주시기 바랍니다.

　　2. 당국으로서는 한국에 주재해 있는 유엔 구 기관의 특수한 지위, 유엔과 우리나라와의 특별한 관계와 종전의 관행 및 특권과

(제2의 건)

면제에 관련된 현실적인 문제점 등을 고려하여 본건에 대한 신중한 검토가 필요한것으로 사료되오니 참고 바랍니다.

첨부 : UNMCK 관리인 공한 원본 끝.

0163

공통서식 1—23 　　　　　　　　　　　　　 (18겹지)

별첨 (3)

Seoul, 28 November 1966

Excellency,

I have the honour, on behalf of the Secretary-General, to refer to the recently ratified Agreement between the United States of America and the Republic of Korea Regarding Facilities and Areas and the Status of United States Armed Forces in the Republic of Korea.

In this connexion, permit me to bring to Your Excellency's attention certain considerations regarding the effects which some provisions of the Agreement may have on the future operation of the United Nations Memorial Cemetery in Korea.

Your Excellency will recall that the Agreement between the United Nations and the Republic of Korea for the establishment and maintenance of a United Nations Memorial Cemetery in Korea was signed on 6 November 1959. Ever since March 1960, when the United Nations commenced the administration and maintenance of the Cemetery, the operation of the Cemetery has been totally dependent upon the logistic support provided by the United States Forces serving in Korea under the United Nations Command and also on the sustained support and co-operation of the Government of the Republic of Korea, the authorities of the municipal government as well as the ROK Army Command at Pusan.

As I trust that the Government of the Republic of Korea would wish to continue to assist the United Nations in the efficient discharge of its responsibilities in the administration of the Cemetery, I have been directed by the Secretary-General to request the consent of Your Excellency's Government to the inclusion of UNMCK, the Custodian, his international staff and their dependents among the organizations and persons which may be granted continued access to the "non-appropriated fund organizations" enumerated in Article XIII of the Agreement between the Republic of Korea and the United States of America.

This consent will be considered as a further manifestation of the spirit which motivated the Government of the Republic of Korea to offer generously to the United Nations the ground of the Cemetery at Pusan for the establishment of a memorial to those who gave their lives in defence of the ideals of the Organization.

Accept, Excellency, the assurances of my highest consideration.

Ali Nekunam
Custodian

His Excellency
Mr. Kim Young Choo
Acting Minister for Foreign Affairs
   of the Republic of Korea
Seoul

0164

OKM 7170.   Seoul, December 2, 1966

Dear Mr. Nekunam:

   Your note of November 28, 1966, addressed to the Acting
Minister of Foreign Affairs, concerning certain effects of some
provisions of the R.O.K. - U.S. Status of Forces Agreement upon
the future operation of the United Nations Memorial Cemetery
in Korea, has been referred to me, *and*

   In this connection, I ~~wish~~ to inform you that the
                         am pleased   *as soon as*
matter is under study, ~~and~~ you will be duly informed ~~when~~ any
          by the relevant authorities of the gov't.
decision ~~has been taken~~ on the subject.
one this will be made.
   With best regards, I am,

                              Yours sincerely,

                              Ha Jong Yoon,
                              Director, Bureau of
                              European and American Affairs

Mr. Ali Nekunam,
Custodian,
United Nations Memorial
   Cemetery in Korea,
Seoul.

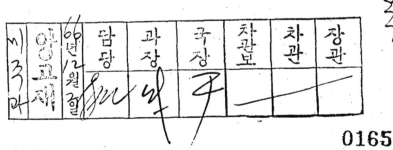

0165

Seoul, December 5, 1966

Dear Mr. Nekunam:

Your note of November 28, 1966, addressed to the Acting Minister of Foreign Affairs, concerning certain effects of some provisions of the R.O.K. - U.S. Status of Forces Agreement upon the future operation of the United Nations Memorial Cemetery in Korea, has been referred to me, and I am pleased to inform you that the matter is receiving due attention and that relevant study is being made by the authorities concerned of the Government.

You will be duly informed as soon as any decision is made on the subject.

With best regards, I am,

Yours sincerely,

Ha Jong Yoon,
Director, Bureau of
European and American Affairs

Mr. Ali Nekunam,
Custodian,
United Nations Memorial
  Cemetery in Korea,
Seoul.

0166

MEMO

196 . . . .

제목: 한.미 군대지위협정 발효에
따르는 미군 비세출자금
기관 이용제한 문제

본건은, 국장 지시에 의하여
영문가로 보완. *[서명]*

~~외무부의 전신~~

165

0167

외 무 부

1966 년 *12* 월 *14* 일

本件에 關하여는 UNCURK側
으로부터 누차 非公式으로 UNCURK
에 對하여도 特惠措置를 政府가
取하여 줄것을 要請한바 있으며,
(邦交局長에게 口頭로) 또 UN本
部에서도 나라시만 事務次長이
駐口韓大使에게 이미 關하여 通
心은 希한바 있음(UNW-1098)에
비추어 또 UNCURKK의 特殊住
區에 비추어 特別考慮함이 可한것
으로 思料됨.

방 교 장.

0168

외　무　부

196 . . .

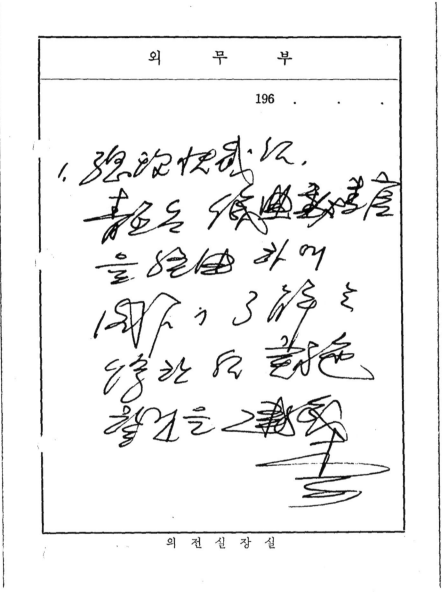

의 전 실 장 실

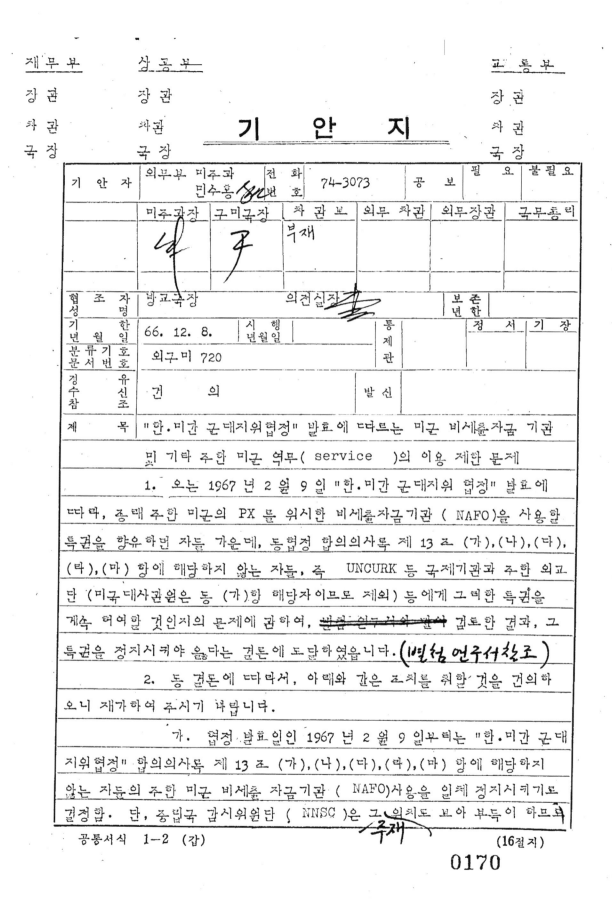

재 무 부	상 공 부				교 통 부
장 관	장 관				장 관
차 관	차 관				차 관
국 장	국 장				국 장

기 안 지

기 안 자	외무부 미주과 민수홍 /뗸	전 화 번 호	74-3073	공 보	필 요	불 필 요

	미주과장	구미국장	차관보	외무 차관	외무장관	국무총리
			부재			

협 조 자 성 명	방교국장		의전실장		보 존 년 한	
기 안 년 월 일 한	66. 12. 8.	시 행 년월일		통 제 관	정 서	기 장
분 류 기 호 문 서 번 호	외구미 720					
경 수 참 유 신 조	건 의		발 신			

제 목 "한·미간 군대지위협정" 발효에 따르는 미군 비세출자금 기관

및 기타 주한 미군 역무(service)의 이용 제한 문제

1. 오는 1967 년 2 월 9 일 "한·미간 군대지위 협정" 발효에

따라, 종래 주한 미군의 PX 를 위시한 비세출자금기관 (NAFO)을 사용할

특권을 향유하던 자들 가운데, 동협정 합의의사록 제 13 조 (가),(나),(다),

(라),(마) 항에 해당하지 않는 자들, 즉 UNCURK 등 국제기관과 주한 외교

단 (미국 대사관원은 동 (가)항 해당자이므로 제외) 등에게 그러한 특권을

계속 허여할 것인지의 문제에 관하여, ~~본부 연구과와 함께~~ 검토한 결과, 그

특권을 정지시켜야 옳다는 결론에 도달하였습니다. (별첨 연구서 참조)

2. 동 결론에 따라서, 아래와 같은 조치를 취할 것을 건의하

오니 재가하여 주시기 바랍니다.

가. 협정 발효일인 1967 년 2 월 9 일부터는 "한·미간 군대

지위협정" 합의의사록 제 13 조 (가),(나),(다),(라),(마) 항에 해당하지

않는 자들의 주한 미군 비세출 자금기관 (NAFO)사용을 일체 정지시키기로

결정함. 단, 중립국 감시위원단 (NNSC)은 그 위치도 보아 부득이 하므로

예외적으로 동기관을 계속 사용하도록 허가함.

　　　　　나. 교통부 산하의 특정외래품 판매쇼 (Foreigners'
Commissary)를 최단시일내에 확대시켜, 위의 가.항 해당자들의 편의~~유~~
~~수파와 의차확보~~를 도모하는 조치를 취하기로 ~~건의~~함.

　　　　　다. 특정외래품 판매쇼가 이들 외국인들의 수요를 충족시킬
수 있다고 외무부와 교통부가 인정할 때까지는 잠정적 조치로서 위의 가.항
해당자들의 미군 Commissary 사용을 허가하기로 ~~건의~~함.

　　　　　라. 위의 결정 사항을 별첨 구둣로 ~~같은 공한으로~~ 미국측에
통고함.

　　　　　3. 한편, UNCURK 와 UNMCK 등이 종래 이용하던 미군의
기타 각종 역무는 별첨 연구서의 첨부물 내역과 같은 바, 이러한 각종 사항
중에서 우리나라 법규에 저촉되는 것은 1967 년 2 월 9 일을 기하여 일체
허락하지 않는다는 기본 원칙 한에, 그에 대한 구체적 내용은
한.미 합동위원회에서 협의하기로 건의합니다.

첨부: ~~1. 미국대사관 앞 구술서 안.~~
　　　1. 별첨 연구서. 끝.

Draft

OKM-

MEMORANDUM

Reference is made to item (f) of Agreed Minutes regarding Article XIII of the R.O.K.-U.S. Status of Forces Agreement, concerning the extent of organizations and persons to be granted the use of the non-appropriated fund organizations and commissaries of the United States armed forces in Korea, and the Ministry of Foreign Affairs wishes to inform the Embassy of the United States of America of the following position of the Government of the Republic of Korea regarding the matter:

1. The Government deems it proper to suspend the present use of the non-appropriated fund organizations and commissaries by any organizations and persons other than those referred to in items (a) through (e) of the Agreed Minutes of the said Article effective February 9, 1967, when the Status of Forces Agreement comes into force, except for the Swedish and Swiss components of the Neutral Nations Supervisory Commission, whose continued use of such commissaries and non-appropriated fund organizations is considered necessary.

2. However, it is an intent of the Government of the Republic of Korea to minimize any possible inconveniences

0172

that might be caused to members of the diplomatic corps,
UNCURK, UNMCK, UNDP, UNICEF, WHO, and the Scandinavian
Mission to the National Medical Center. For this reason,
it is the opinion of the Korean Government that continued
use by the above-mentioned persons of the commissaries of
the United States armed forces in Korea be permitted temporarily until such time as certain Korean commissary facilities
are provided to satisfactorily serve for a supply of their
daily provisions.

Seoul, December 12, 1966.

0173

협 조 전

응신기일

분류기호 의정383 제목 주한외교관 및 국제연합기관원에 의한 미군 비세출자금기관 사용

수신 구미국장 발신일자 1966.12.15 (협조제의)

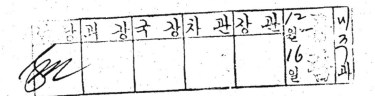

(발신명의) 의 견 십 장

(제1 의견)

　행정협정 발효에 따른 주한외교관 및 국제연합기관원에 의한 미국 비세출자금기관 사용 여부문제에 관한 당부 의견을 별첨과 여히 송부하오니 동문제에 관한 정책결정에 반영하여 주시기 바랍니다.

첨부: 1. 행정연구서 1통
　　　2. 미군 비세출자금기관의 사진자료 2걸

(제2 의견)

0174

Commisary
사 건

0176 0100

외 무 부 문 서 보 존 실

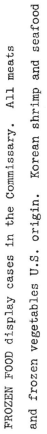

FROZEN FOOD display cases in the Commissary. All meats and frozen vegetables U.S. origin. Korean shrimp and seafood also available.

0177

DISPLAY OF KOREAN BOOTS in the Sporting Goods section

of the Post Exchange.

0178

HUNTING BOOTS

READY-TO-WEAR CLOTHING SECTION of the Post Exchange. All
US merchandise except for some Korean ready-to-wear.

0179

LUGGAGE SECTION of the Post Exchange. All merchandise is US

except for a small amount of Korean briefcases.

0180

RECORD AND STEREO SECTION of the Post Exchange. Over 90% of the radios and television sets are of US manufacture and a small quantity of Japanese and Korean radios are also stocked. 0181

SOFT DRINK SECTION of the Post Exchange. All products are US except for Korean beer.

FRESH PRODUCE AREA of the Commissary. All fresh vegetables
are Korean-procured except for citrus fruits.

0133

BREAD, PASTRY, and cracker section of the Commissary, with additional frozen food storage on the right.

0184

CHECK-OUT COUNTERS at the Commissary, similar to those found in US supermarkets.

CHECK-OUT COUNTERS at the Commissary, similar to those found in US supermarkets.

0186

기록물종류	문서-일반공문서철	등록번호	26049 9627	등록일자	2006-07-27
분류번호	741.12	국가코드	US	주제	
문서철명	한.미국 간의 상호방위조약 제4조에 의한 시설과 구역 및 한국에서의 미국군대의 지위에 관한 협정 (SOFA) 전59권. 1966.7.9 서울에서 서명 : 1967.2.9 발효 (조약 232호) ★원본				
생산과	미주과/조약과	생산년도	1952 - 1967	보존기간	영구
담당과(그룹)	조약	조약		서가번호	--
참조분류					
권차명	V.56 형사재판관할권 관계자료				

내용목차	★ 일지 :
	1953.8.7　　　　　이승만 대통령-Dulles 미국 국무장관 공동성명
	- 상호방위조약 발효 후 군대지위협정 교섭 약속
	1954.12.2　　　　정부, 주한 UN군의 관세업무협정 체결 제의
	1955.1월, 5월　　미국, 제의 거절
	1955.4.28　　　　정부, 군대지위협정 제의 (한국측 초안 제시)
	1957.9.10　　　　Hurter 미국 국무차관 방한 시 각서 수교 (한국측 제의 수락 요구)
	1957.11.13, 26　정부, 개별 협정의 단계적 체결 제의
	1958.9.18　　　　Dawling 주한미국대사, 형사재판관할권 협정 제외 조건으로 행정협정 체결 의사 전달
	1960.3.10　　　　정부, 토지, 시설협정의 우선적 체결 강력 요구
	1961.4.10　　　　장면 국무총리-McConaughy 주한미국대사 공동성명으로 교섭 개시 합의
	1961.4.15, 4.25　제1, 2차 한.미국 교섭회의 (서울)
	1962.3.12　　　　정부, 교섭 재개 촉구 공한 송부
	1962.5.14　　　　Burger 주한미국대사, 최규하 장관 면담 시 형사재판관할권 문제 제기 않는 조건으로 교섭 재개 통고
	1962.9.6　　　　 한.미국 간 공동성명 발표 (9월 중 교섭 재개 합의)
	1962.9.20~　　　제1-81차 실무 교섭회의 (서울)
	1965.6.7
	1966.7.8　　　　 제82차 실무 교섭회의 (서울)
	1966.7.9　　　　 서명
	1967.2.9　　　　 발효 (조약 232호)

마/이/크/로/필/름/사/항				
촬영연도	★롤 번호	화일 번호	후레임 번호	보관함 번호
2006-11-24	I-06-0073	01	1-278	

0001

刑事裁判 管轄條項

韓·美, 兩側提案 差異点.

1964. 2. 20.

3. 管轄權 內容.

	한 국 안	미 국 안
(가) 行使機關	(1) 한국 --- 대한민국 当局、 (2) 미국 --- 미국 軍当局.	(1) 한국 --- 대한민국 民事当局、 (2) 미국 --- 미국 当局、
		韓國 軍法會議에서 裁判 받지 아니 한다.
(나) 適用人員	(1) 軍隊構成員 (2) 軍屬	(1) 軍隊構成員. (2) 軍屬 (3) 家族
(다) 適用範圍	(美國의 一次裁判管轄權 行使에 있어서) 公務執行中 그公務와 직접 關聯된 作爲 또는 不作爲의 범죄	(美國의 一次裁判管轄權 行使에 있어서) 公務 執行中의 作爲 또는 不作爲의 범죄
	公務執行 與否의	公務執行 與否의

－1－

0002

한 국 안	미 국 안
最終決定은 韓國側이 한다.	最終決定은 美國側이 한다.
	韓國軍人이 犯한 범죄라면 一般法院 보다도 軍法會議에서 裁判받게되는, 그러한 범죄를 美國軍隊 構成員이 犯하였을 境遇 그 범죄는 美國側이 一次的 裁判管轄权을 가진다.
	協定 發効 以前의 범죄는 大田協定에 依하여 管轄한다.
	戒嚴地域内의 범죄는 美國이 專屬管轄权을 가진다.
	韓國 以外의 地域에서 犯한 범죄에 對하여는 韓國의 裁判管轄權이 미치지 못한다.

(다) 適用範囲.

(라) 適用地域

0003

— 2 —

	한 국 안	미 국 안
(마) 適用 時期		戒嚴令下에서의 犯罪는 該當地域內에서의 美國 側이 專屬裁判權을 가진다
		相互防衛條約 第二條, 規定下의 交戰狀態가 發生 하면 刑事裁判管轄條 項의 効力이 即時 停止되고 美國側이 專屬的 管轄權을 가진다.
(바) 管轄權 포 기		韓國이 專屬管轄權을 가지는 境遇에도 행정처벌 또는 징계 처분이 効果的일 경우, 美國側의 관할권포기요청 에 대하여 韓國側은 호의적 考慮를 한다.
		韓國이 一次的 管轄權을 가지는 경우에도 이를 포기 한다.

—3—

0004

	한 국 안	미 국 안
(바) 管轄權 포기		美國側은 如斯한 포기에 該当하는 事件을 個別的으로 韓國側에 通告한다. 韓國側은 管轄權行使를 하는것이 特히 重要하다고 認定하는 경우에는 前記 通告로부터 15日 以内에 合同委員會에서 同事件의 管轄權포기 撤回를 為하여 合意하도록 試図하여야 한다.
		以上의 規定을 條件으로, 韓國側의 管轄權拋棄는 놓件 이고 最終的 이며 韓國 政府나 國民을 莫論하고 刑事節次를 取할수 없다. 韓美범죄를 迅速히 처리하기 위하여, 通告로서 처리 할수 있는

—4—

0005

	한 국 안	미 구 안
(바) 재판의 폭기		約程을 兩 當軍國 間에 締結한다.

2. 管轄 節次

	한 국 안	미 구 안
(가) 피 의 자 의 체 포 및 구 속	韓國側은 美國軍人. 軍屬. 家族의 체포를 美軍當局에 通告한다.	韓國側은 美國軍人.軍屬. 家族의 체포를 即時 美軍 當局에 通告한다
	美國當局은, 專屬管轄權을 行使하는 경우를 除外하고, 軍人, 軍屬. 家族의 逮捕를 지체 없이 韓國側에 通告한다.	(管轄權 拋棄 關聯 條項 參照.)
	韓國이 管轄權을	韓國이 管轄權을

—5—

	한 국 안	미 국 안
(가) 被의者의 逮捕 및 拘束	行使하게될 피의자가 美國手中에 있는 경우에는 美國은 이를 拘禁하되, 韓國의 拘束令狀을 提示하면 지체없이 韓國当局에 引渡한다.	韓國이 當轄權을 行使하게 될 피의자의 拘禁은, 그가 美國手中에 있는 경우에는, 모든 裁判節次가 끝나고 또한 韓國当局의 引渡 要求가 있을때까지 美國側이 이를 계속 맡는다.
		그러한 피의자가 韓國側手中에 있는 경우에는 即時美國側에 引渡하고, 모든 裁判節次가 끝나고 또한 韓國側이 引渡를 要求할때까지 美國側이 계속 이를 맡는다. 美國当局은 이러한 피의자를 韓國当局이 調査하고 또한 韓國法逆에 나가도록한다. 美國側이 韓國側에 対하여 피의자 구금에 関한

—6—

	한 국 안	미 국 안
(가) 편의 제공 및 지원		원조를 요청하면, 韓國 側은 이에 對하여 好意 的 考慮를 한다
(나) 服役		美國側이 韓國側에 對하여 이 한국재판 결과로 服役하는 者 의 拘禁을 要請하는 경우 에는, 韓國側은 이에 對 하여 호의적 고려를 한다. 服役者를 美國側에 引渡 하는 경우에는 美國側은 刑期가 르終了할때까지 또는 한국당국에 依하여 석방이 許容될때 까지 적당한 施設內에 拘禁할 의무를 가진다
(다) 총칙 협조		(美國안은 合意의사록에서 증인, 라고인출 控訴事實內容의 通知, 證人의 特权 免除, △的 등

0008

	한 국 안	미 국 안
(다) 訴訟節次의 協調		提案內容의 처리등 여러 問題에 關하여 韓國側 많은 義務를 賦課하고 있음)
(라) 二重처벌의 禁止		(美國側은, 刑罰이 免除 減刑 또는 停止 되는 경우에도 그 刑罰에 對하여 다시 처벌 하지 못하게하고 있음)
(마) 訴訟節次上의 待遇	辯護人	그 당시 (for the time being)의 사정에 따라 - - - -
	通譯 通譯을 提供받을 權利	통역을 갖일 權利
		通譯을 갖일 權利는 逮捕 또는 抑留순간 부터 가진다
	재판관 몇 재판정	試補期間을 마친 判事로서만 構成되는 公平한 法廷에서 公開裁判을 받을 權利

0009

한·미국 간의 상호방위조약 제4조에 의한 시설과 구역 및 한국에서의 미국군대의 지위에 관한 협정(SOFA)
전59권. 1966.7.9 서울에서 서명 : 1967.2.9 발효(조약 232호) (V.56 형사재판관할권 관계자료)

한 국 안	미 국 안
<u>裁判官 및 裁判소</u>	실당한 理由없이 逮捕,抑留, 못하며, 그 理由를 지체없이 청취할 權利를 갖이며, 타당한 理由없으면 직시석방한다 逮捕,抑留卽時로 告發 內容을 그가 解得할수 있는 言語로 알려야한다. 裁判開始 以前 適当한 時期에 自己負罪記據 內容을 알려야 하며, 辯護人으로하여금 裁判 以前에 記人 陳述書 사본을 볼수 있게 한다.
<u>記人</u>	被告人은 記人의 一切審問過程에 參席하고 記人을 심문할수 있는 充分한 機会를 준다
<u>辯護人</u>	辯護를 받을 權利는 逮捕및 抑留 순간부터 存在 하며

(다) 訴訟節次上의 待遇

0010

	한 국 안	미 국 안
(마) 訴訟節次上의待遇	<u>변호인</u>	모든 過程에서 변호인이 同席하고 被告人과 辯護人이 秘密로 相談할수 있게 하여야 한다
	<u>美國政府 代表에 關하여</u>	逮捕 또는 抑留순간부터 美國 政府代表와 連絡한 權利가 있으며, 同代表의 參席없이 行한 피의자의 陳述은 證據로 삼을수 없다. 同代表는 모든 訴訟過程에 參席할 權利가 있다.
	<u>人權옹호</u>	美國 軍人·軍屬·家族은 韓國市民에 賦與된 모든 節次上 또는 실체상의 權利를 賦與받는다. 如斯한 權利가 거부되었거나 거부될 가망성이 있는 경우에는 兩國政府 代表는 合同委員會에서 그 시정 조치를 위하여 協議한다

0011

	한 국 안	미 국 안
	其他의 待遇條件	(합의의사록 RE. Paragraph의 참조)
(따) 訴訟節次上의 待遇	不法證據	不法 또는 不適当한 호法에 依한 자백, 시인, 기타진술 또는 實証은 한국재판에서 利用할수 없다.
	檢事의 上訴制限	被告人에 不利한 上訴의 制限.
	行刑施設	美國 当局은 韓國 行刑施設의 視察权을 가진다. 行刑施設, 其他 收容施設은 合同委員会에서 合意한 最低水準을 充足하여야 한다. 美國 当局은 拘留 또는 抑留中인 者와 언제던지 접촉하고, 침식 기타

0012

	한국안	미국안
(라) 訴訟節次上의 促進	1 行刑施設	편의를 돌보아 줄수 있다.
	2 訴訟狀態 ┐의조치	韓國側은 未決 또는 既決囚에 對한 모든 可能한 保護措置를 取하고, 美國側의 引渡要求를 好意的으로 考慮하여야 한다. 이를 위한 必要節次는 合同委員會에서 合意한다.

0013

| 협 조 전 | 응 신 기 일 |

문서번호 외구미 722.2— 　　제 목 주둔군지위협정 체결 교섭
　　　　　　　　　　　　　　　실무자회의 회의록 송부.

수 신: 방교국장　발 신: 구미국장　년 월 일 1964.10.6.　제 1 의 견
　　　참조: 조약과장

　　　주둔군지위협정 체결 교섭 실무자회의에서 토의되고 있는

헝사재판관할권에 관한 Joint Summary Record (중요 조항 별) ✓

1 부를 송부하오니 보관 참고하시기 바랍니다.

　　　유 첨: 헝사재판관할권에 관한 Joint Summary Record
　　　　　　　(중요 조항 별) 1 부.　　　끝.

　　　본문: 　첨부건에서 분리되면 보통문서로 재분류

　　　첨부물: 　보통문서로 재분류 (1966. 12. 31.

　　　구 미 국 장　　　장 상 문

The authorities of the United States to have the
right to exercise jurisdiction

At the 45th Session (March 6, 1964)

A further difference between the two drafts, Mr. Habib
continued, is that in many critical paragraphs the Korean
text omits the word "dependent" and limits the coverage
of this article to members of the armed forces and the
civilian component. The United States Government is certainly
as much concerned about the treatment of dependents as about
the treatment of members of the armed forces and civilian
employees. The U.S. negotiators must insist, therefore,
that dependents be covered in the SOFA with the ROK Government in the same way that they are covered in the agreements
with Japan and all the NATO governments. If the Korean
negotiators were concerned about the effect of the U.S.
Supreme Court decisions in 1960 regarding military jurisdiction over civilians, Mr. Habib stated, the U.S. negotiators
would like to point out that: (a) the U.S. armed forces have
as much jurisdiction over dependents as they do over the
civilian component, which has been included in the Korean
draft; and (b) all of the status of forces agreements
concluded since the 1960 decisions have included the word
"dependent", just as the earlier ones did.

0015

Mr. Chang noted that the Korean draft uses the term "military authorities of the United States" whereas the U.S. draft uses the term "authorities of the United States". The Korean negotiators hoped that this did not imply that the U.S. negotiators were thinking in terms of some U.S. authority other than U.S. military authorities having jurisdiction in the Republic of Korea.

0016

<u>At the 46th Session</u> (March 13, 1964)

With regard to dependents, Mr. Habib stated that the Korean negotiators apparently did not agree with the coverage given by the U.S. draft. He pointed out that the number of dependents who would be covered by the SOFA would be relatively small, since most of the military dependents in Korea were MAAG dependents who would not be covered by the SOFA. The Korean negotiators should consider the fact that dependents are covered by this article in every other status of forces agreement.

Mr. Chang asked whether the U.S. negotiators had any further comments to make regarding the Korean position. Mr. Habib replied that the Korean negotiators had expressed some concern over the fact that the U.S. draft used the term "authorities of the United States" rather than "military authorities of the United States." He said this was a matter of internal concern for the United States and should not worry the Koreans. The language had been made broad enough to provide for any possible exercise of jurisdiction by U.S. authorities.

0017

<u>At the 47th Session</u> (March 20, 1964)

With regard to dependents, Mr. Chang continued, the status of the dependents is substantially different from that of the members of the U.S. armed forces and civilian component. Dependents of members of the U.S. armed forces in Korea are not in the same position as members of the forces and the civilian component. Moreover, they are not subject to the same strict discipline as are members of the armed forces. However, as the Korean negotiators had indicated at the last meeting, they are not trying to be inflexible in their approach to this problem.

With regard to the term "authorities of the United States", Mr. Chang continued, the U.S. negotiators had stated that the language had been made broad enough to provide for any possible exercise of jurisdiction by U.S. authorities. He said the Korean negotiators would like to emphasize that the subject and matters of discussion throughout this SOFA negotiation is the military status of the U.S. armed forces but not any other U.S. authority in Korea. It is utterly inconceivable that any United States authority other than the U.S. military authorities would have jurisdiction in Korea. Moreover, the Korean

0018

negotiators could not find any similar provision in any
other SOFA. In this respect, they would appreciate an
explanation of any possible difficulty envisaged by the
U.S. negotiators in case the word "military" is inserted.

Mr. Habib stated that Mr. Chang had made two statements indicating willingness on the part of the Korean
negotiators to consider the U.S. point of view. The first
of these was Mr. Chang's statement that the enumeration of
trial safeguards was consistent with ROK law and that if the
U.S. negotiators wished to include such an enumeration in
this article, the Korean negotiators would not object in
principle. The second was Mr. Chang's statement that the
Korean negotiators were not inflexible on the subject of
dependents. Mr. Habib said the U.S. negotiators would defer
discussion on these points until the Korean position had
been somewhat refined.

The negotiators then began paragraph by paragraph
discussion and in paragraph 1(a) noted that the Korean
draft contained the word "military" in front of the
word "authorities" while the U.S. draft contained the
phrase "and their dependents" and referred to "all"
criminal and disciplinary jurisdiction.

0019

Mr. Habib stated that if the Korean negotiators
were unwilling to include the phrase "and their dependents"
in this subparagraph, their position was not very flexible.
He pointed out that if dependents were to be subject to
U.S. jurisdiction, they would have to be mentioned in
this subparagraph.

Mr. Chang replied that inclusion or exclusion of
the word "all" was not an important matter and could be
discussed later. On the other hand, the question of
whether to refer to "authorities" or "military authorities"
was a very important question which was not just simply
a matter of wording but a question which affects the
judicial rights of the Korean people as a whole. With
regard to dependents, the Korean negotiators believed that
measures could be worked out to include them in this
article without specifically referring to them in this
subparagraph. He pointed out that the U.S. negotiators
had not made any definite explanation as to how far the
U.S. military courts have jurisdiction over dependents.
The Korean negotiators wished to know what the U.S.
authorities would do regarding those persons over whom
the armed forces would have no jurisdiction.

Mr. Habib replied that the U.S. armed forces would
have disciplinary jurisdiction over such persons. It was

0020

also possible that in future, jurisdiction will be provided
that does not exist at present. In wartime, the armed
forces would have jurisdiction over dependents under the
provisions of the "hostilities" paragraph in the U.S. draft.
In this connection, Mr. Habib urged the Korean negotiators to
study carefully the provisions of paragraph 2(b), which
provides that the Republic of Korea will have exclusive
jurisdiction over offenses not punishable by U.S. law.

0021

At the 52nd Session (May 20, 1964)

Now I would like to explain our new proposals item by item. First, in paragraph 1(a) of our draft, we offer to replace the phrase "the members of the United States armed forces and the civilian components" with a new phrase reading "all persons subject to the military law of the United States."

Our new proposal may not sound to you like a very new idea. However, by proposing this phrase, we are prepared to recognize the jurisdiction of U.S. military authorities in Korea over the dependents to the extent they are subject to U.S. military law. Whether the dependents are covered by the uniform code of military justice or not is an internal matter on your side.

With regard to "authorities of the United States" to exercise criminal jurisdiction in Korea, we have designated the U.S. military authorities as sole authorities to exercise criminal jurisdiction since it is inconceivable for us that authorities other than U.S. military authorities would exercise jurisdiction within the Republic of Korea.

The chief U.S. negotiator stated at the 46th session that this is a matter of internal concern for the U.S. and that the language had been made broad enough to provide for any possible exercise of jurisdiction by U.S. authority.

0022

However, we are of the opinion that it is not the internal concern solely for the U.S. We believe that the exercise of Criminal Jurisdiction in Korea by the authorities of the United States, whether they be military authorities or other than military authorities, has to be mutually agreed upon. We have serious concern over the statement which implies the possibility of U.S. authorities in Korea other than military authorities exercising judicial power in Korea.

Mr. Habib asked whether the Korean negotiators' position regarding U.S. jurisdiction over dependents was limited to the provisions of Paragraph 1. Mr. Chang replied that it was not limited to Paragraph 1, but would apply to the relevant paragraphs. However, the rights and privileges of dependents to be covered by the rest of the article should be dealt with through further negotiation.

0023

<u>At the 58th Session</u> (July 16, 1964)

Mr. Habib recalled that the Korean negotiators had proposed the substitution in Paragraph 1(a) of the Korean draft of the phrase "all persons subject to the military law of the United States" for the phrase "the members of the United States armed forces and the civilian components". They had also expressed concern over the possibility that the language in the U.S. draft would permit the exercise in Korea of judicial power by some U.S. authority other than military authorities. The U.S. negotiators wished to give a categorical assurance that the U.S. Government has no intention to establish civil courts which could exercise jurisdiction in the Republic of Korea. There is no intention that U.S. other than military authorities will exercise jurisdiction in Korea over U.S. personnel. At the same time, however, the U.S. negotiators would like to call attention to the possibility that legislation may be passed eventually in the United States which would provide that accused U.S. civilians abroad could be returned to the United States for trial. Paragraph 1(a) of the U.S. draft had been drafted specifically so as not to preclude this possibility. The U.S. negotiators, therefore, believed the U.S. draft preferable to the proposed change in the Korean draft, since

0024

it would not preclude the applicability of any legislation
which might be passed to bridge the present "jurisdiction
gap" over U.S. civilians abroad.

<u>At the 59th Session (July 28, 1964)</u>

Mr. Chang then made the following statement:

"a. <u>All persons subject to the military law of the
U.S., Para 1(a)</u>

"With respect to our proposal to substitute the
phrase 'all persons subject to the military law of the
United States' for the phrase 'the members of the U.S.
armed forces and the civilian components,' the U.S. side
gave an assurance that the U.S. Government has no intention
to establish civil courts which could exercise jurisdiction
in the Republic of Korea. At the same time, the U.S.
negotiators indicated their preference for the language in
their draft to the Korean proposal, on the grounds that
legislation may be passed eventually in the U.S. which
would provide that any accused U.S. civilian abroad could
be taken to the U.S. for trial.

"We have no objection to the principle that the SOFA
language should be flexible enough to accommodate all
eventualities foreseen in the near future. However, it is
inconceivable that such an uncertain eventuality as the
legislation referred to by the U.S. negotiators should affect
in any way our Status of Forces negotiations. Furthermore,
decisions of the Supreme Court of the United States on the

0026

matter have been subject to reversal since 1956. Therefore, we can think not only of the possibility over which the U.S. negotiators are concerned but also of the possibility that the U.S. Supreme Court may eventually reverse its decision of 1960 so that civilian offenders may be tried by U.S. Court Martial overseas.

"Moreover, in our view, the proposed idea of taking the accused civilians back to the U.S. for trial is neither consonant with the established principle of judicial proceedings nor acceptable to any sovereign nation hosting foreign troops. We believe the contemporary principle and practice of trial in any given country demand that the trial should be held at the place where the offense is committed or at least at a place reasonably distant from the site of the crime. We also believe that if an accused who committed an offense in the territory of one sovereign country is brought to another sovereign country for trial there would arise a serious question as to possible infringement of sovereignty."

Regarding Paragraph 1(a), Mr. Habib noted that the Korean negotiators had expressed the wish to retain the phrase "all persons subject to the military law of the United States," despite the assurance given by the U.S.

0027

negotiators that no U.S. courts would be established in Korea and despite the desire of the U.S. negotiators to retain flexibility in case legislation should be passed in the future which would establish jurisdiction over U.S. civilians abroad. The objections of the Korean negotiators were apparently based on: (a) a feeling that the passage of such legislation was inconceivable, and (b) the possibility of a reversal of the 1960 Supreme Court decision. In stating these objections, the Korean negotiators were attempting to exercise the right of review of U.S. legislation, which was certainly not relevant to the question at hand. The Korean negotiators were seeking to differentiate between military personnel and civilians in the application of U.S. law. If U.S. law is to apply, it should apply equally to military personnel and civilians, who are in Korea for the accomplishment of the same mission under the provisions of the Mutual Security Treaty. The U.S. negotiators were concerned that the application of rights under the SOFA should not be discriminatory between the military personnel and the civilians who were in Korea under identical conditions and for the same purpose. Mr. Habib asked what the attitude of the Korean negotiators would be if the Supreme Court decision of 1960 had not been made.

0028

<u>At the 60th Session</u> (August 7, 1964)

With regard to Paragraph 1(a), Mr. Habib continued, the Korean negotiators had objected to the concept of jurisdiction contained in the U.S. draft, which would allow for the exercise of jurisdiction by the U.S. authorities at some future time outside the Republic of Korea. The Korean negotiators had stated at the 59th meeting that any future return of accused civilians to the United States for trial would be inconsistent with judicial principles and not acceptable to any sovereign nation hosting foreign troops. They also had stated that if a person accused of committing a crime in one sovereign country was taken to another sovereign country for trial "there would arise a serious question as to possible infringement of sovereignty".

Mr. Habib stated that the U.S. negotiators did not agree with this interpretation of the proposed provision. He pointed out that it is a recognized principle of international law that a sovereign state retains jurisdiction over its nationals whether they are within the territorial jurisdiction of the asserting state or within that of a foreign state. This jurisdiction is based upon the personal supremacy of a sovereign state over its own nationals rather than on any

0029

question of territorial sovereignty. The rights and duties of a national are solely determined by the law of his sovereign state and he is subjected to such penal jurisdiction for acts committed abroad as is provided for in that law.

Jurisdiction based upon the supremacy of a state over its nationals, Mr. Habib continued, is not in derogation of the sovereignty of the foreign state in which the offense is committed. Unless there are contrary treaty provisions, the state claiming jurisdiction based on nationality is under the obligation not to infringe upon the territorial supremacy of a foreign state by performing acts of sovereignty in the foreign state. This does not detract from the state's right under international law to punish its nationals when they are again within its territorial jurisdiction for acts committed abroad.

Mr. Habib pointed out that the Republic of Korea has exercised this right through implementation of Korean law. The Korean negotiators had said that this would be contrary to international law and judicial principles. The U.S. negotiators, however, wished to point out that the laws of the Republic of Korea recognize this principle and make specific provisions for this very situation. Article 3, Criminal Code, Korean Law 293, reads as follows:

0030

"Crimes Committed by Koreans Abroad

"This Code shall apply to all Korean nationals outside the territory of the Republic of Korea."

In fact, Mr. Habib continued, Korean law carries the principle of jurisdiction over crimes committed abroad much further than is applicable to the issue under discussion. Article 5 of the Korean Criminal Code provides that the Code shall apply to aliens who commit certain specified crimes outside the territory of the Republic of Korea. Article 6 reads as follows:

"Crimes Committed Abroad Against the Republic of Korea and Korean Nationals

"This Code shall apply to aliens who commit, outside the territory of Korea, against the Republic of Korea or her nationals, crimes other than those specified in the preceding article, except where they do not constitute crimes at the place of commission or where their prosecution or execution of the punishment imposed has been remitted."

Mr. Habib stated that the United States had no counterpart to Article 3 of the Korean Criminal Code whether or not this will be accomplished in future legislation is a matter wholly reserved to the United States Government in the exercise of its sovereign right of supremacy over its own nationals. If such legislation is passed, it would not derogate from the unquestioned sovereignty of the Republic of Korea. It is difficult to understand, he continued, why

0031

the ROK negotiators are concerned over a principle recognized by international law and specifically provided for in their own Criminal Code.

Mr. Habib said the U.S. negotiators had clearly stated the purpose of the language in the U.S. draft, which was to provide for the possibility of future legislation in the United States. The Korean negotiators had objected on the grounds that there was no basis in judicial practice for such a provision and that it would derogate against the sovereignty of the Republic of Korea. The U.S. negotiators had clearly demonstrated that there was no lack of precedents in judicial practice and that the provision would not derogate against the sovereignty of the Republic of Korea.

Mr. Habib added that the U.S. negotiators believe the Korean negotiators might be basing their objection also on the fact that this provision does not appear in this form in other status of forces agreements. He reiterated the frequently expressed view of the U.S. negotiators that this agreement was being negotiated on the basis of accumulated experience and not on the basis of language in other agreements. There was nothing in this provision which was inconsistent with the spirit of other status of forces agreements, nor with judicial precedents, including those contained in Korean law.

Mr. Habib asked whether the Korean negotiators wished to comment.

0032

Mr. Chang replied that the U.S. negotiators had quoted articles of the Korean Criminal Code to justify their position that an accused could be taken from one country to another for trial without causing any infringement upon the territorial jurisdiction of the former. The spirit underlying them was that the Government of the Republic of Korea would exercise jurisdiction over the accused when the accused come within reach of ROK sovereignty or under an extradition agreement. In other words, the Korean articles do not call for unilateral and involuntary waiver of territorial jurisdiction, while the U.S. draft in question and the explanation of the U.S. negotiators clearly demand unconditional waiver, voluntary or involuntary, of territorial jurisdiction on the part of the Republic of Korea. The Korean negotiators did not believe that the U.S. Government would automatically waiver jurisdiction over a Korean offender in the United States. In the absence of an extradition agreement between the two countries, which is the case at present, if the ROK Government tried to extradite a Korean civilian or soldier accused of an offense in the United States for trial in the Republic of Korea, the U.S. Government not only could, but would probably object.

0033

In case the U.S. Government feels, for one reason or another, that the territorial jurisdiction can not be waived, the accused Korean can not be brought to Korea for trial. In brief, waiver of territorial jurisdiction is traced to the consent of the territorial sovereign.

Mr. Habib replied that the negotiators were not arguing on the specifics of Korean law. Nor were they discussing the subject of extradition. They were discussing the principle of the right of each government to exercise its sovereignty, a principle which the Korean negotiators had questioned at the last meeting. The U.S. negotiators were not questioning the way in which the Korean authorities applied ROK law. With regard to the attitude of the U.S. Government, Mr. Habib reminded the Korean negotiators of the recent case of a member of the ROK Navy who had got into trouble in Guam. Although the changes against him had been of a very serious nature, including manslaughter, the U.S. Government, acting in response to the request of the ROK Government, had agreed to permit him to be returned to the Republic of Korea for trial.

Mr. Habib reiterated that the provision in question would result in no derogation of sovereignty and was based on judicial precedents. The Korean negotiators had raised the question of comparability with other status of forces

0034

agreements. In this case, the U.S. negotiators were not arguing in favor of their language on the basis of the existence of a different set of conditions in Korea than in other countries where U.S. armed forces are stationed. They wished to point out that at the time when the status of forces agreements with Japan and with the NATO governments were negotiated, the Supreme Court decision of 1960 had not yet been handed down. At the time when the agreement with Japan was negotiated, the U.S. negotiators had believed that U.S. military courts had jurisdiction over certain U.S. civilians. Therefore, in this respect the two agreements were not comparable.

Reverting to Paragraph 1(a), Mr. Chang stated that when an accused is taken from the host country to another country for trial, the host country voluntarily waives its jurisdiction. If such a case arose in the Republic of Korea and the ROK authorities were not prepared to waive ROK jurisdiction, the accused could not be taken to another country for trial. In effect, the language of the U.S. draft called for a voluntary waiver of jurisdiction over dependents by the ROK Government.

Mr. Chang asked whether the United States, following the 1960 Supreme Court decision, had received assurances from other governments with whom it has negotiated status of forces agreements that civilians may be taken to the

0035

United States for trial. Mr. Habib replied that, to his
knowledge, the question had not arisen.

0036

The authorities of the ROK to exercise jurisdiction

<u>At the 45th Session</u> (March 6, 1964)

Mr. Chang stated that the Korean negotiators had noticed that the U.S. draft used the term "civil authorities of the Republic of Korea" rather than "authorities of the Republic of Korea." This appeared to imply that members of the U.S. armed forces would be subject to Korean civilian courts but not to Korean military courts. However, under Korean law, even civilians are subject to court-martial for specific offenses under special circumstances. Nevertheless, the Korean Supreme Court has final appellate jurisdiction over courts-martial, thereby guaranteeing to every defendant his basic human rights to the maximum extent.

0037

<u>At the 47th Session</u> (March 20, 1964)

With regard to the phrase "authorities of the Republic of Korea", Mr. Chang said the Korean negotiators do not want to limit Korean authority to the civil side. As he had mentioned at the previous meeting, a member of the American forces, their civilian component, or one of their dependents may have to be subject to trial by the Korean military tribunals in case where ordinary Korean civilians would be triable by the Korean military courts. The Korean Constitution, in Article 106, states that in cases of espionage on military affairs, offenses against sentinels and sentry-posts, distribution of harmful food to armed forces, and offenses against prisoners of war, civilians and soldiers alike would be subject to the military tribunal in accordance with provisions of law. If the Korean negotiators accepted the U.S. version of "civil authorities of the Republic of Korea", the Korean authorities would have to initiate criminal proceedings against such offenses only in a civil court. It is the understanding of the Korean negotiators that espionage or violation of any law relating to official secrets of the state may be tried by the civil court. However, they believe that offenses involving espionage on military affairs should be dealt with by the military court rather than the civil court for security reasons.

0038

In paragraph 1(b), Mr. Habib identified the key difference as being the use of "civil authorities" in the U.S. draft, compared with "authorities" in the Korean draft. Also, the U.S. draft states that the Korean authorities "shall have the right to exercise jurisdiction" whereas the Korean draft says they "shall have jurisdiction". This is not a substantial point, Mr. Habib said, but the language of the U.S. draft is similar to the language of paragraph 1(a) in both drafts.

0039

At the 52nd Session (May 20, 1964)

　　As for the authorities of the Republic of Korea
exercising criminal jurisdiction, we understand your intention
of limiting our authirities to the civil side is motivated
from apprehension that the U.S. military personnel might be
tried by Korean court-martial. We are prepared to assure
you that we would not exercise jurisdiction over U.S.
military personnel by military tribunal under any circumstances.
Accordingly we propose to record this assurance in the joint
minutes and we believe you would accept our version. We
are sure that our new proposal will certainly meet your
requirements.

0040

<u>At the 58th Session</u> (July 16, 1964)

Mr. Habib recalled that at the 52nd meeting, the Korean negotiators had stated that the ROK Government would not exercise jurisdiction over U.S. military personnel by military tribunal under any circumstances. They had also given the same assurance with regard to the civilian component. The U.S. negotiators welcomed these assurances. They wished to point out again that the language of Paragraph 1(b) of the U.S. draft plainly sets forth the ROK Government's intention, since it states that "the civil authorities of the Republic of Korea shall have the right to exercise ...". The U.S. draft of this subparagraph contained the phrase "the right to exercise", which was not contained in the Korean draft. On restudying the subparagraph, the U.S. negotiators had found the Korean phraseology to be clear and acceptable and agreed to the deletion of the phrase "the right to exercise". The only remaining difference in language in the two drafts of the subparagraph, therefore, was the inclusion of the word "civil" in the U.S. draft. Since the Korean negotiators had already given the assurances just referred to, they should be able to agree to the inclusion of this word.

0041

At the 59th Session (July 28, 1964)

"b. The civil Authorities of the Republic of Korea,
    Para. 1(b)

"Regarding the provision of Paragraph 1(b), the United
States negotiators stated that the language of paragraph 1(b)
of the U.S. draft, 'the civil authorities of the Republic of
Korea', sets forth the Korean Government's intention as
expressed in assurances given by the Korean negotiators
that the Korean Government will not exercise jurisdiction
over U.S. military personnel by military tribunal under any
circumstances.

"The assurance was intended to meet the requirement
of the U.S. negotiators, who have expressed their concern
over the possibility of subjecting their military personnel
to Korean military tribunal.

"Inasmuch as such a significant assurance was given
to your side, we have naturally expected that you would no
longer insist on retaining the word 'civil'. Since this
word 'civil' cannot be found in other SOFAs we wonder what
were your understandings or arrangements with other countries
in agreeing to the provision without the word 'civil'.

"If the Korean negotiators would accept such
unprecedented wording as appeared in the U.S. draft, this

0042

would undoubtedly cause very delicate problems in the Korean
Government as well as with the Korean people. Neither the
sentiment of the Korean people nor the atmosphere of the
National Assembly would tolerate acceptance of such a version.

Regarding Paragraph 1(b), Mr. Habib stated that the
position of the U.S. negotiators that jurisdiction over
the U.S. armed forces by the host government should be limited
to the civil authorities of the government was a firm U.S.
position in every country in which a SOFA is in force.
The U.S. negotiators wanted to have it stated explicitly
in the SOFA with the ROK. If the Korean negotiators were
willing to give the assurances that they had given in this
respect, why were they unwilling to spell the assurances out
in the Agreement? The absence of the phrase "civil authorities"
from other agreements is no reason why it should not be
included in this Agreement. The experience of the past
two years had clearly shown that the ROK Government does
not hesitate to resort to military courts to try civil crimes.
The Korean negotiators had argued that it would be difficult
to explain this provision to the public and to the National
Assembly. Why could the National Assembly not be told
simply that the U.S. authorities were unwilling to pass
jurisdiction from U.S. military courts to Korean military

0043

courts. The U.S. negotiators believed that such an explanation would be palatable and acceptable to the National
Assembly. They believed the Korean objections to this
provision to be shallow and urged the Korean negotiators to
reconsider.

0044

At the 60th Session (August 7, 1964)

Mr. Habib stated that similar reasoning lay behind the language of Paragraph 1(b) of the U.S. draft. The U.S. negotiators of the status of forces agreements with Japan and the NATO governments had not conceived of the possibility that military authorities of the host country could exercise jurisdiction. Inasmuch as that possibility does exist in the Republic of Korea, the U.S. negotiators, in drafting this more modern agreement, wish to make the language of the provision quite clear by having it read "the civil authorities of the Republic of Korea". This is not an unreasonable provision and should be fairly easy to explain. It is fully consistent with the statements of the Korean negotiators for the negotiating record that the Korean authorities have no intention of subjecting U.S. personnel covered by this SOFA to military courts. The objection of the Korean negotiators to this provision appeared to be solely the fact that such language does not appear in the SOFA with Japan. The U.S. negotiators were of the opinion that this was not a valid objection.

With regard to Paragraph 1(b), Mr. Chang stated that the Korean negotiators had given an unequivocal assurance for the negotiating record that under no circumstances would members of the U.S. armed forces be subject to trial by Korean military authorities, in the hope that the U.S. negotiators would agree to the deletion of the word "civil". Mr. Habib replied that the simplest way of handling this question was to leave the word "civil" in the text of the paragraph.

Mr. Chang stated that the Korean negotiators believed both sides were trying to negotiate an agreement that would be acceptable to their respective citizens and legislatures. They were trying to find acceptable wording regarding this question. The Korean negotiators believed that the effect would be the same, whether the assurance appeared in the text of the Agreement or in the Agreed Joint Summary. Inasmuch as the effect was same, the U.S. negotiators should and could be responsive to the concern of their counterparts. Utter disregard by the U.S. side of the Korean concern was not a constructive way of conducting negotiation. The Korean negotiators could not understand the U.S. insistance on the inclusion of the word "civil" in the text.

In an attempt to clarify the Korean position, Mr. Habib asked whether the Korean negotiators were proposing to include their assurance in the Agreed Joint Summary or as an Agreed Munite. Mr. Chang replied that they were neither

0046

making any suggestion nor proposal. They merely wished to clarify the U.S. position whether the U.S.negotiators would accept the assurance as an Agreed Minute and delete the word "civil" from the text.

0047

Duty Certificate

At the 45th Session (March 6, 1964)

Having thus discussed the six points raised by the
Korean negotiators in Mr. Chang's statement of February 28,
Mr. Habib said he would like to discuss several points
not mentioned in that statement. A major point of difference
between the two drafts is the manner in which they deal
with the "performance of duty certificate". While the
U.S. draft makes it clear that the issuance of this
certificate by U.S. military authorities is conclusive,
the Korean draft provides that the final determination
of the validity of such a certificate would be made not by
the U.S. authorities, nor even by a Korean court, but
instead would be made administratively by a local prosecutor.
The U.S. position expresses world-wide practice in status
of forces agreements since their beginning in 1952. There
is no precedent anywhere for the Korean proposal. In the
case of NATO, the negotiating record makes it clear that
it was the understanding of the negotiators that the question
of the performance of duty could be determined only by the
authorities of the visiting forces. This has been the
universal practice in NATO ever since. In only one case
did a NATO government question a duty certificate. In the

0048

Martin case in France, the Court of Cassation, the highest
court in France, decided for all time that such a certificate
was final and could not be questioned by the French Government. In many agreements, the finality of the duty certificate
is spelled out; in those cases where it is not spelled
out, it has been accepted in practice. This is entirely
reasonable, as no one other than a military commander is
competent to determine whether one of his soldiers is or
is not performing an assigned duty.

　　With regard to the question of duty certificates,
Mr. Chang said the Korean negotiators had defined specific
procedures in the Korean draft in order to prevent this
matter from becoming a controversial issue in the future
in actual application. They had tried to avoid ambiguity
by defining the exact meaning of "duty offenses."

At the 46th Session (March 13, 1964)

　　With regard to the official duty certificate, Mr. Habib
recalled that the Korean negotiators had indicated that
their reason for providing the procedures contained in
paragraph 3(a) (ii) of their draft and for including a
definition of official duty in the Agreed Minutes of their
draft was to avoid disputes over the interpretation of

0049

"official duty". Far from avoiding disputes, the Korean provisions would foster disputes. In keeping with worldwide precedents, the U.S. negotiators believe that duty is best defined by those who assign the duty. In actual fact, the definition suggested by the Korean negotiators was illogical and contrary to reality.

As an example, Mr. Habib asked the Korean negotiators to consider the case of artillery firing practice on a firing range. Korean nationals wander onto the range while the firing is in progress and are hit. Under the Korean definition, firing of the shells which hit the Koreans would not be considered in line of duty, since wounding civilians is not a "normal function" of artillery practice firing. This definition is palpably unacceptable to the U.S. negotiators. Mr. Habib reminded the Korean negotiators that this article deals with criminal jurisdiction, not civil liability, which is provided for elsewhere in the Agreement. If the Korean negotiators were concerned that U.S. officers might abuse their trust in executing duty certificates, the U.S. negotiators could assure the Korean negotiators that the execution of the duty certificates would be done in a responsible manner by responsible officers. This is the procedure followed elsewhere; there is no reason to establish an entirely new precedent which

0050

is inconsistent with normal worldwide practice. The U.S. negotiators, therefore, could not agree to the Korean draft.

At the 47th Session (March 20, 1964)

Regarding the official duty certificate, the Korean negotiators do not challenge the contention of the U.S. negotiators that the local commander may well determine whether one of his soldiers is or is not on duty. However, determination of whether an offense arising out of an act or omission committed on duty has a genuine link with the performance of official duty should not be made by a field commander but by a judicial officer who has the sole authority to take up criminal cases under Korean laws. The example given by the U.S. negotiators of artillery firing practice on a firing range is irrelevant to the criminal case under discussion and not to the point. The Korean negotiators would like to give an example, said Mr. Chang, which would justify their concern on this point. Suppose a soldier was ordered to proceed from Seoul to Suwon on official business. He had to park his car on the street somewhere along the Yongdongpo main street and unfortunately became involved in a quarrel with a Korean and committed assault and battery or serious injury.

0051

Even though this example sounds like a hypothetical case, we cannot rule out the possibility of such unfortunate cases occurring. What the Korean negotiators contend in such a case is that a local commander may well certify that the offense was committed during the hours of the soldier's duty, but he is not empowered to determine whether the offense arose out of an act or omission directly related to the official order he issued.

Further, Mr. Chang said, the U.S. draft has not attempted to formulate any concise explanation of when an offense does arise out of an act or omission done in the performance of official duty. This is why the Korean negotiators had prepared in their draft the exact meaning of "official duty". If the U.S. negotiators don't like some of the wording in the Korean draft, the Korean negotiators would propose to modify it in line with a circular of the United States Army, Far East, which was published in January, 1956. The Korean negotiators believe that the U.S. authorities could have no objection to accepting the Korean proposal, because such definition of "official duty" is their own interpretation.

In other respects, Mr. Habib continued, there appeared
to be no recognition on the part of the Korean negotiators
of other problems existing with regard to this article or
of the explanations given by the U.S. negotiators. In
particular, the Korean negotiators' discussion of the duty
certificate was difficult to accept. He pointed out that
there was a profound difference between the example given
by the U.S. negotiators and that given by the Korean
negotiators. In the Korean negotiators' example, the offense
was clearly not an on-duty offense. But in the example given
by the U.S. negotiators, an on-duty offense would be
construed as an off-duty offense, according to the definition
of off-duty offenses which the Korean negotiators wished to
include in the Agreement. Mr. Habib again pointed out that
in no status of forces agreement is there any such definition,
the reason being that only the commander who assigns the
duty is able to determine whether or not an offense was
committed in the line of that duty. In some status of
forces agreements, there is provision for a review system.
Where such a system has been used, the finding has always
been that only the commander is competent to determine what
constitutes duty.

With regard to the duty certificate question, the
U.S. negotiators should not have any difficulty in accepting

0054

0053

the definition published in the January, 1956 circular of the U.S. Army, Far East, either as part of the text or as an understanding in the negotiating record.

In subparagraph (a) (ii) of the Korean draft appeared the definition of on-duty offenses which the Korean negotiators had just indicated need not necessarily be included in the text of the Agreement.

Mr. Chang stated that if agreement could be reached by the negotiators on the definition contained in the U.S. Army Far East circular which he had mentioned, it need not be included in the text. Mr. Habib replied that the U.S. negotiators would not agree on a definition of duty. There is no such definition in any status of forces agreement. By definition, duty is what the commander calls duty. This is a universally accepted principle.

Mr. Chang replied that if the U.S. negotiators would accept the second and third sentences of subparagraph (a) (ii) of the Korean draft, the Korean negotiators would be willing to delete the first sentence, which constituted the definition of duty. Mr. Habib replied that this proposal was unacceptable to the U.S. negotiators. He said the U.S. negotiators were prepared to discuss how the commanding officer could responsibly fulfill his function of defining duty but they were unable to agree to any proposal which

0054

would vest that function in some person not connected with the duty.

Mr. Chang stated that the Korean negotiators were not insisting that agreement on the definition of duty contained in the U.S. Army Far East circular be included in the text of the article or even in an Agreed Minute. If the negotiators could just reach agreement on that definition, there would be no problem in solving this question.

At this point, the negotiators broke off substantive discussion to spend the last few minutes of the meeting in bidding farewell to General Fuller and to Mr. Kang, each of whom was attending his last negotiating session prior to departure on another assignment.

At the 49th Session (April 10, 1964)

Turning to the Criminal Jurisdiction Article, Mr. Habib recalled that at the last previous meeting devoted to this article, discussion had not been completed on paragraph 3. He suggested, therefore, that discussion be resumed with subparagraph (a) (ii), which dealt with the question of duty offenses. During the previous discussion, the Korean negotiators had stated that they would not insist that the definition of duty, as contained in the circular published

0055

by the U.S. Army, Far East in January, 1956, be included in
the text of the Agreement or in the Agreed Minutes. The
Korean chief negotiator had stated that if agreement could
be reached on that definition, there would be no problem in
solving this matter. The U.S. negotiators had considered
the Korean suggestion that the definition might be included
in the negotiating record. They believed that this might
offer a sound and satisfactory way of handling the problem.
Therefore, if the Korean negotiators would accept the
Agreed Minute #2 in the U.S. draft re paragraph 3(a), the
U.S. negotiators agreed that the following definition could
be placed in the negotiating record as the basis on which
duty certificates would be issued:

"The term 'official duty' as used in Article ____
and the Agreed Minutes is not meant to include all
acts by members of the Armed Forces and the civilian
component during periods when they are on duty,
but is meant to apply only to acts which are required
to be done as functions of those duties the individuals
are performing. Thus, a substantial departure from
the acts a person is required to perform in a particular
duty usually will indicate an act outside of his
'official duty'".

Mr. Habib called the attention of the Korean negotiators
to the fact that the above definition was based on the
full text of the definition which had appeared in the Army
circular which they had cited, and not on the partial
text suggested by the Korean negotiators.

0056

Mr. Chang stated that the Korean negotiators would examine the U.S. proposal and give their views at a later meeting. He suggested that the negotiators resume their paragraph by paragraph consideration of this article.

At the 50th Session (April 23, 1964)

Regarding the second Agreed Minute re Paragraph 3(a), Mr. Habib reminded the Korean negotiators that the U.S. negotiators had made a proposal at the last meeting to agree to insert the definition of official duty into the negotiating record, provided the Korean negotiators would accept the second Agreed Minute re Paragraph 3(a) in the U.S. draft. He asked for the comments of the Korean negotiators regarding this proposal.

Mr. Chang replied that the Korean negotiators believed that the definition of official duty should be considered to be a separate matter from that of the issuance of a duty certificate. They did not agree, therefore, to the proposal of the U.S. negotiators. However, they had no objection to inclusion in the summery record of the definition of official duty tabled by the U.S. negotiators at the previous meeting without referring to the issuance of a duty certificate. They would present a counter-proposal at the next meeting.

0057

<u>At the 52nd Session</u> (May 20, 1964)

The Korean negotiators would like to delete from the provision of paragraph 3(a) (ii) of the Korean draft the following language "provided that such act or omission is directly related to the duty. The question as to whether offenses were committed in the performance of official duty shall be decided by a competent district public prosecutor of the Republic of Korea. In case the offender's commanding officer finds otherwise, he may appeal from the prosecutor's decision to the Ministry of Justice within ten days from the receipt of the decision of the prosecutor, and the decision of the Minister of Justice shall be final." We propose the following alternative draft as Agreed Minute re Paragraph 3(a) (ii). If the U.S. negotiators accept the proposed alternative draft, the Korean negotiators would give favorable consideration to the U.S. proposal made at the previous meeting to record in the Joint Summary the definition of official duty modified after the FEAF version of 1956:

"<u>Re Paragraph 3(a) (ii)</u>

"Where a member of the United States armed forces or civilian component is charged with an offense, a certificate issued by a staff judge advocate on behalf of his commanding officer stating that the alleged offense, if committed by him, arose out of an act or omission done in the performance

0058

of official duty, shall be sufficient evidence of the fact
for the purpose of determining primary jurisdiction, unless
the contrary is proved.

"If the chief prosecutor of the Republic of Korea
considers that there is proof contrary to the certificate
of official duty, he will refer the matter to the Joint
Committee for decision.

"The above statements shall not be interpreted to
prejudice in any way Article 308 of the Korean Code of
Criminal Procedure."

The Korean negotiators believe the alternative draft
would meet the desires expressed by the United States
negotiators with respect to the issuance of a duty certificate
for determining primary jurisdiction over offenses arising
out of an act done in the performance of official duty.

However, the Korean negotiators, taking into account
the highly legal affairs involved, deem it proper that a
Staff Judge Advocate should exercise the right to make such
determination on behalf of the commanding officer at
divisional level.

With respect to the validity of a duty certificate,
the Korean draft provides that a certificate shall be
sufficient evidence of the fact for the purpose of determining

0059

primary jurisdiction, unless the contrary is proved, whereas the U.S. draft provides that it shall be conclusive. The Korean negotiators believe that the Korean authorities should be accorded the opportunity to express their views as to the validity of a certificate in the event they find evidence contrary to the certificate.

The Korean draft provides the Joint Committee as the reviewing system of disputes to work out a mutually acceptable solution.

Further, the Korean negotiators reserve to the court the power to make determination of fact by referring to Article 308 of the Korean Code of Criminal Procedure.

At the 58th Session (July 16, 1964)

Turning to the subject of the Duty Certificate, Mr. Habib recalled that at the 47th meeting, the Korean negotiators had proposed that the definition of official duty based on that contained in the U.S. Army, Far East, circular of January 1956 be read into the Agreed Joint Summary. At the 49th meeting, the U.S. negotiators had agreed to this proposal, provided the Korean negotiators would agree to Agreed Minute #2 Re Paragraph 3(a) of the U.S. draft. Instead of agreeing

0060

to this package proposal of the U.S. negotiators, the Korean negotiators at the 52nd meeting had proposed an alternative Agreed Minute Re Paragraph 3(a) (ii). Before commenting on this Korean counter-proposal, the U.S. negotiators wished to seek clarification of the Korean position and, at the same time, wished to make the U.S. position regarding duty certificate quite clear.

Mr. Habib stated that in the view of the U.S. negotiators, the duty certificate would be definitive unless it is modified by the U.S. authorities, either as a result of a request by the ROK authorities for modification or otherwise. There was no intention to foreclose requests by the Korean authorities for reconsideration of duty certificates in specific cases where there is a justifiable basis for questioning the correctness of the certificate. What is important, in the view of the U.S. negotiators, is that the certificate will be conclusive unless modification is agreed upon. This is not made clear in the Korean draft. A second matter of concern to the U.S. negotiators is that the accused should not be deprived of his entitlement to a prompt and speedy trial as a result of protracted reconsideration of the duty certificate. If agreement to modification were not reached within a specified time, the U.S. authorities would expect the duty certificate to be conclusive for that case, although discussions could continue concerning the propriety of issuing a duty certificate under similar circumstances in a future case.

0061

The U.S. negotiators had been instructed to inform the Korean negotiators, Mr. Habib continued, that the U.S. Government was concerned lest modification of the U.S. position on duty certificates was being sought by the Korean negotiators as a means of acquiring jurisdiction in cases involving action taken by sentries to protect U.S. property. In the absence of special circumstances, such cases would be certified as official duty. The U.S. authorities would be willing to reconsider the duty certificate in such a case, if requested to do so by the Korean authorities. However, the duty certificate would be definitive unless it were modified as a result of the reconsideration. Mr. Habib made it clear that the U.S. negotiators were not responding to the revised draft of the Agreed Minute tabled by the Korean negotiators and, before doing so, wished to clarify the views of the Korean negotiators on the points he had mentioned.

Mr. Chang replied that whereas the U.S. draft provides that the duty certificate shall be "conclusive" (Agreed Minute #2 Re Paragraph 3(a)), the Korean draft uses the word "sufficient" (revised Agreed Minute Re Paragraph 3(a) (ii)). The Korean draft provides for specific procedures to be followed if the Korean authorities raise an objection

0062

to a duty certificate, while the U.S. draft does not outline any procedure. The Korean negotiators, therefore, preferred the Korean draft.

Mr. Habib stated that the U.S. negotiators wished to make it clear that a Korean appeal regarding a duty certificate would not alter the conclusive nature of the certificate unless the U.S. authorities agreed to modify the certificate after reconsideration. He asked what procedure the Korean negotiators had in mind.

Mr. Chang reviewed the position stated by the U.S. negotiators. They held that once the duty certificate were issued, it would remain valid unless modified by the U.S. authorities after considering objections raised by the Korean authorities. According to the U.S. position, there were two possibilities: the duty certificate would either be conclusive or it would be modified by the U.S. authorities. Mr. Chang stated that this was contrary to the position set forth in the revised draft tabled by the Korean negotiators. They had in mind that if the Korean authorities objected to a duty certificate, agreement would then be reached by the Joint Committee, not unilaterally by the U.S. authorities. The Korean negotiators also believed that the Joint Committee must be allowed sufficient time to reach a decision. There

0063

might be cases in which the validity of the duty certificates would be ambiguous; therefore it would take some time for both sides to reach agreement. For these reasons, the Korean negotiators could not agree to the two points made by the U.S. negotiators.

In reply to Mr. Habib's request for clarification of the concept of "sufficient time", Mr. Chang stated that "appropriate time" might be a better phrase. The Korean negotiators believed that agreement could be reached on a certain number of days as a time limit for Joint Committee consideration of duty certificate cases.

Referring to the Korean revised draft, Mr. Habib asked who would determine that "the contrary is proved" or that a decision had been reached. Mr. Chang replied that the Korean draft provided that the Korean authorities could base an objection to a duty certificate on the belief of the chief prosecutor that there was proof contrary to the certificate. Mr. Chang added that the third paragraph of the Korean revised draft of the Agreed Minute re Paragraph 3(a) (ii) provided for referral of the case to the Korean courts if the Joint Committee were unable to reach agreement regarding modification of a duty certificate to which the Korean authorities had objected.

0064

At the 59th Session (July 28, 1964)

"c. Official Duty Certificate, Agreed Minutes Re
Para 3(a) (ii)

"Regarding the official duty certificate, the U.S.
side stated at the last session the following two points:

(1) The certificate will be conclusive unless
modification is agreed upon;

(2) The accused should not be deprived of his entitlement to a prompt and speedy trial as a result of
protracted reconsideration of the duty certificate.

"The Korean negotiators should like to concentrate
on the first point alone at this meeting. The Korean
negotiators have studied the U.S. statement, and we have
found that the statement indicates an improvement over the
U.S. Agreed Minute re Paragraph 3(a).

"The provision of the U.S. Agreed Minute re Paragraph
3(a) reads as follows: 'A certificate issued by or on behalf
of his commanding officer etc..... shall be conclusive for
the purpose of determining primary jurisdiction.' However,
the U.S. negotiators at the last session stated that unless
modification is agreed upon either through request of the
Korean authorities or otherwise, the certificate will be
conclusive. The indication of possible modification at the
request of the Korean authorities is an improvement from
our point of view.

0065

"In our view, any possible controversy over the duty certificate, though we do not expect to encounter many of them, should be solved by mutual consultation and to mutual satisfaction. Therefore, if a controversy arises over the certificate, the matter should be handed over to the Joint Committee for reconsideration. Whatever way we may take to solve this problem of duty certificate, we must find a mechanism under which mutual consultation and agreement are provided for resolution of controversy over the validity of the official duty certificate.

With regard to the question of the duty certificate, Mr. Habib reminded the Korean negotiators that the U.S. negotiators had not responded specifically to the proposed revision of the Agreed Minute Re Paragraph 3(a) (ii) of the Korean draft. Now that the U.S. negotiators had received further explanation of what the Korean negotiators had in mind, they would respond in detail to this proposed revision at the next meeting.

At the 60th Session (August 7, 1964)

Mr. Habib stated that the U.S. negotiators wished to clarify further the U.S. position with regard to the duty certificate and to bring to the attention of the Korean

0066

negotiators certain precedents and other factors of which they might not be aware. The U.S. negotiators had stated their view that the duty certificate is conclusive. The Korean negotiators had taken the position that if the Korean authorities objected to a duty certificate, they should be able to refer the matter to the Joint Committee. If the Joint Committee could not reach agreement, the matter would then be referred to the Korean courts, under the terms of the third paragraph of the revised Agreed Minute Re Paragraph 3(a) (ii) of the Korean draft. The Korean negotiators had expressed the hope that the U.S. military authorities would be prepared to entertain requests for modification of duty certificates. The U.S. negotiators, Mr. Habib continued, did not wish to mislead the Korean negotiators regarding the firmness of the U.S. belief in the conclusive nature of the duty certificate. This belief was based on a lengthy body of experience. The U.S. negotiators wished to call the attention of the Korean negotiators to the following information.

In Belgium, Mr. Habib stated, duty certificates are prepared by the unit commanding officer and submitted to the Army Attache at the U.S. Embassy in Brussels. The Army Attache either submits the duty certificate to the local

0067

authorities or advises them informally regarding the duty status of the accused. The Belgian authorities have never questioned U.S. determinations regarding duty status of an accused.

In Denmark, Mr. Habib continued, no formal procedures have been established for the determination of official duty status and no official duty cases have arisen to date. If such a case should occur, the determination would be made by the U.S. Representative on the Joint Committee, who would advise appropriate Danish authorities.

In France, the U.S. Staff Judge Advocate notifies the French prosecutor of official duty cases. The French Ministry of Justice issued a circular in 1956, which recognized the primary responsibility of the United States, as sending state, to determine the duty status of the accused. The French Court of Cassation in the case of James Martin (a partie civile prosecution brought by an injured claimant) decided that only the sending state may make the determination of the performance of official duty referred to in Article VII of the NATO Status of Forces Agreement and that the sending state's duty certificate is conclusive as a matter of law.

0068

In Germany, Mr. Habib continued, criminal jurisdiction over U.S. personnel is exercised by the sending state only. However, the Agreement to Supplement the NATO Status of Forces Agreement in Germany provides as follows:

> "1. Whenever, in the course of criminal proceedings against a member of a force or of a civilian component, it becomes necessary to determine whether an offence has risen out of any act or omission done in the performance of official duty, such determination shall be made in accordance with the law of the sending State concerned. The highest appropriate authority of such sending State may submit to the German Court or authority dealing with the case a certificate thereon.

> "2. The German court or authority shall make its decision in conformity with the certificate. In exceptional cases, however, such certificate may, at the request of the German court or authority, be made the subject of review through discussions between the Federal Government and the diplomatic mission in the Federal Republic of the sending State."

Mr. Habib went on to point out that in Greece official duty certificates are issued by the Staff Judge Advocate and, if approved by the U.S. Representative on the Joint Committee, are submitted through diplomatic channels to the Ministry of Foreign Affairs. Greek authorities have never questioned official duty status determinations made by U.S. authorities.

In Italy, Mr. Habib continued, the determination of official duty status is made by a service Legal Officer or by the command Staff Judge Advocate on the basis of information provided by the unit commander. The determination is then submitted to the appropriate Italian official

0069

with a statement that the command will exercise its primary right of jurisdiction over the accused. It is well established in Italy that official duty certificates submitted by U.S. authorities are accepted without question by Italian authorities, including those issued with regard to acts or omissions which occur during travel incident to temporary duty or permanent change of station or while traveling between residence and place of duty in privately-owned vehicles.

In Luxembourg, official duty determinations are made by the U.S. Representative on the Joint Committee on the basis of information provided by the immediate commander of the individual concerned and are transmitted by him to the Chief Public Prosecutor of the appropriate arrondissement. Authorities of Luxembourg in all cases have accepted United States official duty determinations.

Mr. Habib stated that he could go on, relating the precedents established in the Netherlands, Norway, Portugal the United Kingdom, and the United States. Without taking the time to do that, he could state that again and again, in the countries cited, duty certificates are not questioned but are accepted as conclusive. In view of the many precedents he had cited and others which he had not cited, the U.S. negotiators did not believe that their requirement

0070

that the duty certificate be considered conclusive was an extraordinary requirement. He suggested that further discussion on this question be deferred until the U.S. negotiators responded specifically to the revised Agreed Minute Re Paragraph 3(a) (ii) proposed by the Korean negotiators.

0071

<u>Waiver of primary right to exercise Jurisdiction</u>

<u>At the 44th Session</u> (February 28, 1964.)

Furthermore, your draft request the Korean authorities to waive in cases where there are concurrent rights, except under special circumstances in the specific case, in recognition of the primary responsibility of the U.S. military authorities for maintaining good order and discipline among the members of the United States armed forces, civilian component and their dependents.

0072

<u>At the 45th Session</u> (March 6, 1964)

Mr. Habib then referred to the second point regarding which Mr. Chang had expressed concern: the U.S. proposal for waiver of cases where there are concurrent rights of jurisdiction. Mr. Habib pointed out that this is a standard provision in most of the U.S. status of forces agreements. He cited particularly the Netherlands and Greek bilateral agreements with the United States in the NATO area; and West Indies agreement in the western hemisphere; the new German agreement, which applies to the situation which is the closest approach to the combat conditions existing in Korea; and the 12 years of practice under the Japanese agreement in the Pacific area. He then provided to the Korean negotiators a copy of <u>Department of Defense Statistics on the Exercise of Criminal Jurisdiction by Foreign Tribunals over United States Personnel, 1 December 1961 - 30 November 1962</u>, an annual publication which shows the percentages of waiver in all countries where U.S. forces are stationed. This book shows that during the latest year for which published reports are available, of all cases in which the host government had the primary right to exercise jurisdiction about 60% were waived to the United States. In Japan over 90% of such cases were waived to the United States. Mr. Habib remarked that these figures have been fairly constant over the entire 12-year experience of the U.S.

0073

armed forces with status of forces agreements. There
appears to be nothing objectionable to the host governments
in waiving jurisdiction granted to them under these agreements.

Mr. Chang noted also that the U.S. draft provides for
a general waiver of the primary right to exercise jurisdiction. He said such a provision is not consonant with the
principle of mutual recognition by each government of the
primary right of jurisdiction of the other which was
specifically set forth in both texts. With regard to
precedents in other status of forces agreements regarding
waiver, Mr. Chang indicated that the Korean authorities
were prepared to waive in as many cases as in the precedents
referred to by the U.S. negotiators, but believed that this
Agreement should contain the same language and expressions
as other status of forces agreements.

0074

<u>At the 47th Session</u> (March 20, 1964)

With respect to waiver of concurrent jurisdiction, Mr. Chang continued, the Korean negotiators are well aware that the rate of waiver in other countries had proved to be very high. As he had mentioned before, the Korean authorities are prepared to waive in as many cases as in the precedents referred to by the U.S. negotiators. However, the Korean negotiators are unable to understand why the provision in this agreement should be differently worded than similar provisions in other agreements. The U.S. negotiators had said further that the provision as stated in the U.S. draft is a standard provision in most Status of Forces Agreements, but so far as the Korean negotiators know, there is no such provision in any of the existing Status of Forces Agreement, particularly the last paragraph of the U.S. draft, barring the host country and its nationals from instituting criminal proceedings in case the Joint Committee fails to come to an agreement on the question of waiver.

Mr. Habib pointed out that the U.S. negotiators had not claimed that the provision in the U.S. draft providing for waiver of concurrent jurisdiction was a standard provision in all status of forces agreements. What he had said previously was that the reference to waiver in the text

0075

of both the U.S. and Korean drafts of this article was
standard language. The Agreed Minutes, of course, were
another matter. The language in the U.S. draft of the
Agreed Minutes was not the standard language.

In paragraph 3(a), Mr. Habib noted the same differences
in language regarding the use of the term "military authorities"
and the phrase "and their dependents" in the Korean and
U.S. drafts, respectively. Subparagraph (a) (i) in both
drafts was identical.

0076

<u>At the 50th Session</u> (April 23, 1964)

Mr. Habib stated that another basis difference in the two drafts lay in the Agreed Minute re Paragraph 3 proposed by the U.S. negotiators. He stated that the exercise of the waiver of jurisdiction has developed to a high degree in the countries where the United States has status of forces agreements. In Japan, for instance, over 90% of the cases are waived by the Japanese Government. The U.S. negotiators believe that the Korean authorities do not intend to try all cases and do intend to exercise the right of waiver. The U.S. Agreed Minute would provide that the ROK Government could seek a recall of waiver in those cases in which it wished to exercise jurisdiction. The presumption in the Korean draft is that in cases of particular importance to the ROK Government, it will not waive its jurisdiction. In the U.S. draft, the presumption is that in such cases, the ROK Government will recall its waiver. The ROK Government is interested in establishing its right to exercise jurisdiction; this would be spelled out in the text of the Article. The U.S. negotiators are interested in obtaining a maximum degree of waiver in order to maintain discipline and order among the U.S. armed forces.

Mr. Chang replied that the ROK authorities, as he had already indicated, were willing to waive in as many

0077

cases as other governments. The status of forces agreements
with Japan and the NATO countries do not contain this provision; yet they waive jurisdiction in a high percentage of
cases. There is no reason why the Korean authorities should
not do the same. Furthermore, the Korean negotiators did
not like this particular provision because it would not
permit them to exercise the right of recall of waiver
without going through the Joint Committee. The Korean
negotiators would present a counter-proposal at the next
meeting.

0078

At the 52nd Session (May 20, 1964)

With respect to the Agreed Minute re paragraph 3(c) of our draft concerning the problem of waiver of primary right to exercise jurisdiction, we offer to add the following paragraph as the first paragraph "the authorities of the Republic of Korea will, upon the notification of individual cases falling under the waiver provided in Article _____ paragraph 3(c) from the military authorities of the United States, waive its primary right to exercise jurisdiction under Article _____ except where they determine that it is of particular importance that jurisdiction be exercised by the authorities of the Republic of Korea."

Further, we propose to add the words "In addition to the foregoing provisions" before the second paragraph which has been placed as the first paragraph in our original draft. We are also prepared to consider the U.S. paragraph which reads "To facilitate the expeditious disposal of offenses of minor importance, arrangements may be made between United States authorities and the competent authorities of the Republic of Korea to dispense with notification".

As you may notice in our proposal, we are greatly binding ourselves by this paragraph, because under this clause we have to waive most of the cases by simple notifica-

0079

tion from the U.S. side. Under this clause, our ground for retaining primary right despite the waiver request is extremely limited due to the key phrase "particular importance". We would like to recall that at the previous meeting your side stated that the U.S. intention is to obtain maximum waiver. We believe that our new proposal would effectively meet your requirements.

As to the procedure for mutual waiver, we would prefer to settle the detailed arrangements through the Joint Committee. However, in accordance with the principle set forth above, we could conceive the following detailed procedures for future reference: "When the Korean authorities hold the view that by reason of special circumstances in a specific case, major interests of the Korean administration of justice make imperative the exercise of the Korean jurisdiction, they will notify the military authorities of the United States of that opinion within a reasonable period. In case an understanding cannot be reached in discussion between the both sides, the U.S. military authorities will seek agreement of the Joint Committee within fifteen days from the date of receipt of such notification. If the U.S. authorities do not reply within fifteen days, the request for waiver will be deemed to have recalled."

0080

We have mentioned the above procedures as an example. We
would propose that the final procedures would be negotiated
at the Joint Committee.

0081

<u>At the 58th Session</u> (July 16, 1964)

The Korean negotiators had also requested deletion from the U.S. draft of Agreed Minute #1 Re Paragraph 3(a), which would give the U.S. authorities primary right to exercise jurisdiction over court martial offenses. Having carefully studied the Korean request, the U.S. negotiators were prepared to make a significant counter-proposal in an effort to reach full agreement on the waiver question. The U.S. negotiators would agree to the deletion of the two Agreed Minutes just mentioned if the Korean negotiators would accept the Agreed Minute Re Paragraph 3 of the U.S. draft. This would be a substantial concession by the U.S. negotiators.

0082

<u>At the 59th Session</u> (July 28, 1964)

"d. <u>The Concept of the Combat Zone and the Waiver</u>
<u>of the Primary Jurisdiction</u>

"At the previous session, the United States negotiators proposed that if the Korean negotiators would accept the Agreed Minute Re Paragraph 3 of the United States draft with respect to the waiver of primary jurisdiction, the U.S. side would delete the clause on the combat zone of Agreed Minute #1, Re Paragraph 1(b) and Agreed Minute #1, Re Paragraph 3(a). At the same time, the U.S. negotiators added that this proposal was a substantial concession by the U.S. side.

"The Korean negotiators appreciate the significant suggestion made by the U.S. side. We take the suggestion as an indication on the U.S. part to accommodate our concern over the proposed concept of the combat zone. Although the suggestion was conditioned upon the acceptance by the Korean side of the provision of the Agreed Minute Re Paragraph 3 of the U.S. draft, we welcome the qualified responsiveness of the U.S. side.

"However, to our regret, we cannot view the U.S. proposal as a significant concession, as the U.S. negotiators have claimed. Even if the U.S. negotiators withdraw the concept of the combat zone, the U.S. negotiators, by retaining

0083

the provisions of the Agreed Minute Re Paragraph 3 of the
U.S. draft, would accomplish their ultimate purpose of
obtaining total waiver from the Korean authorities. A
quick review of the U.S. draft of the waiver clause would
show clearly that the contents of the clause amount to
what we call 'total waiver'.

"According to the provisions of U.S. draft:

(a) The Korean authorities have to waive automatically
their primary jurisdiction upon the receipt of notice
instead of the request for waiver from the U.S. side.

(b) The Korean authorities are also required to seek
agreement of the Joint Committee in case they desire to
recall the waiver for any particular case.

"You have to note that the recall of waiver which
has automatically been made by the Korean side is not
granted by the U.S. side on the same automatic basis.
In other words, while the Korean waiver is automatic, U.S.
grant of recall is conditioned upon approval by the Joint
Committee.

(c) Furthermore, the U.S. draft provides that the
waiver thus granted by the Korean authorities shall be
unconditional and final for all purposes and shall bar both
the authorities and the nationals of the Republic of Korea
from instituting criminal procedures. It is extremely

0084

unfair that the United States side, by the mere fact of
waiver granted by the Korean authorities, intends not only
to bar Korean nationals from initiating appropriate remedial
actions, but also to prevent the authorities of the Korean
Government from instituting criminal procedures even in a
case where the U.S. has not tried the waivered case.
In this regard, we are unable to find any international
precedents similar to the U.S. draft in any other SOFA.

"We are willing to assure you that we are prepared
to waive the primary jurisdiction as generously as any
NATO party does under the very simple provision in NATO
SOFA. However, as a matter of principle, we believe that
the Korean authorities, as the authorities of the receiving
state, should have the right to determine whether or not to
waive primary jurisdiction.

"This right can not be replaced by the automatic
waiver clause which the U.S. side seeks. We should like
to reiterate our position that whatever the final agreement
we may reach on this subject, the agreement has to retain
the language and mechanism that would provide for the
principle of self-determination by the Korean authorities
on waiver of primary jurisdiction.

With regard to the waiver provision, Mr. Habib said
the Korean negotiators appeared to be concerned over the

0085

question of automaticity. The concern of the U.S. negotiators was to obtain the maximum possible degree of waiver. The implication of the remarks made by the Korean Chief Negotiators was that the Korean authorities did not desire to try all cases that may arise and that only in special circumstances would they wish to try a case. The U.S. draft does not preclude this and provides the means whereby the Korean authorities could seek recall of their waiver.

0086

At the 60th Session (August 7, 1964)

Turning to the waiver provisions, Mr. Habib recalled that the Korean negotiators had rejected the idea of an automatic waiver on the grounds that no precedent existed for such a provision. In the view of the U.S. negotiators, there was general agreement on the desirability of some sort of waiver provision. The U.S. negotiators had proposed a general waiver by the ROK Government, with the power to recall that waiver in special circumstances; the ROK negotiators had proposed that the U.S. authorities be given the power to request a waiver in special circumstances. Mr. Habib asked whether the Korean negotiators could elaborate on, or restate, their position in the light of the discussions which had taken place since these positions had first been stated.

Mr. Chang replied that the provisions regarding waiver were more important than those regarding the duty certificate because the waiver provisions would play a heavier role in determining which side would exercise jurisdiction than the other provisions would. This was a very sensitive subject. The Korean negotiators could not accept the automaticity of waiver provided for in the U.S. draft. They wished to reserve to the Korean authorities the right to determine whether or not to waive when requested to do so by the

0087

U.S. authorities. The Korean position was based not on
a lack of precedents but on principle. The principle is
that the waiver is granted by the authorities who hold
the jurisdiction and could not be exercised by the authorities
lacking the jurisdiction. The automatic waiver provisions
proposed by the U.S. negotiators are diametrically opposite
to this principle. Under the system of automatic waiver,
the U.S. authorities, who lack the original jurisdiction,
are to exercise waiver, while the Korean authorities are
to ask for recall of waiver. The Korean negotiators had
already stated, and wished to state again, that the Korean
authorities would waive in as many cases as possible but
they must retain the discretion whether or not to waive.
The Korean negotiators therefore could not think of a
SOFA with a waiver clause providing for an automatic waiver.

0088

<u>Custody of an Accused</u>

<u>At the 44th Session</u> (February 28, 1964)

Your draft also requests that the U.S. military
authorities should have primary right in the custody
of an accused member of the United States armed forces
or civilian component or of a dependent even if he is
in the hands of the Republic of Korea. It further provides
that the Korean authorities should give sympathetic
consideration to the request of the U.S. authorities asking
for turn-over of offenders who are serving a sentence of
confinement imposed by a Korean court. The acceptance of
this request would mean almost total waiver of our remaining
token right.

0089

<u>At the 45th Session</u> (March 6, 1964)

Mr. Habib noted that the Korean negotiators had also raised the question of pre-trial custody. The U.S. negotiators had proposed that such custody be retained by the U.S. armed forces. They had made this proposal partly because an examination of the ROK pre-trial detention facilities had indicated that they are not satisfactory places for an American soldier, civilian employee, or dependent to be confined while awaiting trial and partly because of the many cases reported in Korean newspapers in which persons awaiting trial in Korean courts have been subjected to torture and compulsion to incriminate themselves. The U.S. armed forces do not intend to subject their personnel to such pre-trial treatment. The U.S. armed forces will undertake to guarantee that accused persons will be held in Korea if they are to be tried in Korean courts and will not be allowed to escape ROK jurisdiction. With such an undertaking on the part of the U.S. armed forces, there should be no need for the Korean negotiators to insist upon pre-trial custody in ROK facilities. Mr. Habib pointed out that the U.S. proposal would provide economic benefits to the ROK Government since it would avoid making it necessary for the ROK authorities to make any special provisions for detention of U.S. personnel awaiting trial. He also

0090

noted that the U.S. armed forces in Germany retain full
pretrial custody in all cases.

Mr. Habib recalled that Mr. Chang had also questioned
the U.S. proposal that the ROK Government give sympathetic
consideration to a request from the U.S. authorities that
an offender serve his post-trial sentence in a U.S. prison
rather than in a Korean prison. He pointed out that this
proposal had been made first not by the U.S. negotiators
but by Foreign Ministry officials during a conference with
Embassy officers in 1961. This proposal also would be
economically beneficial to the ROK Government.

0091

<u>At the 46th Session</u> (March 13, 1964)

Regarding pre-trial custody, Mr. Habib asked why the Korean authorities desired it when the U.S. armed forces were prepared to obligate themselves to produce defendants on request and to prevent them from escaping Korean jurisdiction. He pointed out that in actual practice, the Japanese authorities have shown no desire for pretrial custody.

Regarding post-trial custody, Mr. Habib reiterated that the U.S. authorities had previously received from the ROK Government a suggestion that the U.S. authorities might take post-trial custody of defendants convicted under ROK jurisdiction. The U.S. negotiators had thought that they were responding to this suggestion. The U.S. draft would not obligate the Korean authorities in any way but would merely call on them to entertain a request for post-trial custody. Unless this provision were included in the Agreement, the U.S. authorities would not have the right to take post-trial custody, even if the Korean authorities wanted them to do so.

0092

<u>At the 47th Session</u> (March 20, 1964)

Mr. Habib reminded the Korean negotiators that the question of pre-trial custody was also a matter of concern to the U.S. negotiators. Noting that Mr. Chang had not discussed this question in his just-concluded remarks, Mr. Habib asked for a statement of the Korean position regarding pre-trial custody. Mr. Chang replied that pre-trial custody was closely connected with the question of post-trial custody. The Korean negotiators wished to withhold comment on both subjects until a later meeting.

<u>At the 49th Session</u> (April 10, 1964)

In paragraph 5(a), Mr. Habib pointed out that the
U.S. draft uses the language "have custody" while the Korean
draft uses "exercise jurisdiction". This difference arises
out of the differing provisions in the two drafts with regard
to custody. When the question of language relating to custody
is settled, agreement on the language of paragraph 5(a)
will be almost automatic.

Mr. Habib noted that paragraph 5(b) of the Korean
draft omitted the word "promptly". The U.S. negotiators
believed that it was important that there should be
prompt notification of arrest. Mr. Chang stated that the
Korean negotiators believed this to be a reciprocal
matter and that if the U.S. military authorities promptly
notified the ROK authorities, as provided for in paragraph
5(c) of the Korean draft, the ROK authorities would
reciprocate.

Mr. Habib replied that paragraph 5(c) of the Korean
draft had no counterpart in the U.S. draft. Nor did it
have any precedents in the NATO Agreement or the Agreement
with Japan, the reason being that it imposes on the U.S.
military forces an onerous requirement which serves no
fundamental purpose. The absence of such a provision has

0094

created no problems in the countries mentioned but its inclusion in this Agreement would undoubtedly create problems. Why did the Korean negotiators wish to include it? Mr. Chang replied that he would give the Korean views on this question at a subsequent meeting.

Mr. Habib pointed out that the U.S. draft of paragraph 5(c) used the phrase "a dependent" instead of the phrase "their dependents" which appeared in the Korean draft. The U.S. negotiators considered "a dependent" to be standard usage and preferable. Mr. Chang said the Korean negotiators accepted usage of the phrase " a dependent".

With regard to paragraph 5(c) of the U.S. draft and its counterpart, 5(d) of the Korean draft, Mr. Habib stated that in these provisions the question of custody arises. Whereas, the U.S. language provides procedure for retention of custody by the U.S. authorities, the Korean language is a considerable revision of the similar paragraphs in the NATO and Japanese Agreements and provides for a handing over to Korean custody upon the issuance of a warrant. Mr. Habib added that the U.S. negotiators do not believe that retention of custody by the U.S. authorities will interfere with the course of justice. On the contrary, they believe that such a provision has much to commend it. This is a matter of major, substantial interest to the U.S. Government. The U.S. authorities have reservations about existing Korean

0095

facilities for both pre-trial and post-trial custody.
He noted that the proposal for post-trial custody, contained
in the last sentence of the U.S. draft of paragraph 5(c),
was a response to indications given by earlier Korean
negotiators that they would prefer that post-trial custody
not be a Korean responsibility and that they would welcome
a provision such as this one. The U.S. negotiators believed
that neither pre-trial nor post-trial custody by the U.S.
authorities would interfere with the judicial proceedings.
Furthermore, they saw many advantages to the proposal.

Mr. Chang asked whether the phrase in the U.S. draft
"pending completion of all judicial proceedings" was intended
to include all the proceedings of the trial or trials up
to final sentencing. If that were the cases, the phrase
"until custody is requested by the authorities of the
Republic of Korea" would have no meaning at all. Mr. Habib
replied that the phrase meant until all appellate proceedings have
been completed.

0096

<u>At the 50th Session</u> (April 23)

Mr. Habib stated that the Agreed Minute re Paragraph 5(b) in the Korean draft was related to the question of pre-trial custody. From the point of view of the U.S. negotiators, this Agreed Minute was not necessary. However, when a decision was finally reached on pre-trial custody, the fate of this Agreed Minute would be determined.

0097

<u>At the 52nd Session</u> (May 20, 1964)

With respect to the provisions of paragraph 5(d) of the Korean draft regarding the pre-trial custody of the accused, we wish to propose the following revision and an additional paragraph 5(e):

"<u>Paragraph 5(d)</u> An accused member of the United States Armed Forces or civilian component over whom the Republic of Korea is to exercise jurisdiction will, if he is in the hands of the United States, be under the custody of the United States during all judicial proceedings and until custody is requested by the authorities of the Republic of Korea.

"The military authorities of the United States may transfer custody to the Korean authorities at any time and shall give sympathetic consideration to any request for the transfer of custody which may be made by the Korean authorities in specific cases."

"<u>Paragraph 5(e)</u> In respect of offenses solely against the security of the Republic of Korea provided in Paragraph 2(c), custody shall remain with the authorities of the Republic of Korea."

In order to meet the desires of the U.S. negotiators to the maximum extent, we propose to provide some additional

0098

provisions to facilitate expeditious investigation and trial on the part of the authorities of the Republic of Korea.

With respect to the provisions regarding the custody in the hands of the Republic of Korea, we are assuring you that custody will be turned over to the hands of the United States unless there is any specific reason and if there arises any question as to the existence of adequate cause and necessity to retain such accused, it will be determined at the Joint Committee.

With respect to pre-trial custody of the security offenses, we would like to emphasize that the custody of such offender should rest with the authorities of the Republic of Korea since an offender of the security offenses against the Republic of Korea could disclose security information to others, while he is in the hands of the authorities other than Korea. Accordingly the Korean negotiators find no reason why the military authorities of the United States should take custody of such an offender.

0099

<u>At the 58th Session</u> (July 16, 1964)

Regarding the subject of pre-trial custody, Mr. Habib recalled that at the 52nd meeting, the Korean negotiators had tabled a revised draft of Paragraph 5(d) and a new Paragraph 5(e). The U.S. negotiators believed the revised version of Paragraph 5(d) to be an improvement over the original language but they still considered Paragraph 5(c) of the U.S. draft to be preferable. Transfer of an accused to Korean custody is adequately covered by the last sentence of the latter paragraph. The U.S. negotiators had studied the proposed new Paragraph 5(e), regarding Korean custody of offenders against the security of the Republic of Korea. The U.S. armed forces in Korea are there to help protect and preserve the security of the ROK and will continue to do everything possible to carry out that mission. Therefore, the U.S. negotiators were prepared to agree to inclusion of the new ROK paragraph 5(e), e.i. to Korean custody in security cases if the Korean negotiators would agree to the following two understandings:

a. There must be mutual U.S.-ROK agreement as to the circumstances in which such custody is appropriate;

b. Korean confinement facilities must be a adequate by U.S. standards.

0100

<u>At the 59th Session</u> (July 28, 1964)

"e. <u>Pre-trial Custody, Paragraph 5(d) and 5(e)</u>

"Regarding the subject of pre-trial custody, the U.S. chief negotiator stated that the revised draft of Paragraph 5(d) is an improvement over the original language but they still believed Paragraph 5(c) of the U.S. draft to be preferable. At the same time he stated that the U.S. side was prepared to agree to the revised Paragraph 5(e) of the Korean draft regarding custody in security offenses.

"With respect to pre-trial custody in the hands of the U.S., the revised Korean version of Paragraph 5(d) is almost identical with the language of the U.S. draft and fully reflects the views of the U.S. side. However, the Korean negotiators believe that they should reserve the language which would guarantee the U.S. side's sympathetic consideration to any request for the transfer of custody which may be made by the Korean authorities in specific cases.

"With respect to Korean custody in security offenses, the Korean negotiators appreciate the acceptance by the U.S. side of the revised proposal made by the Korean side. However, we have noted that the acceptance by the U.S. side is conditioned upon the acceptance by the Korean negotiators of the two understandings:

0101

(a) The first proposed understanding is not acceptable to the Korean negotiators, since we believe that in security offenses, the Korean authorities should be the only and final authorities to determine whether or not such custody is appropriate. This does not necessarily mean that we would not consult with U.S. authorities as to the necessity of such custody. But, as a matter of principle, we believe agreement with U.S. side is not necessary in a security case.

(b) Regarding the second question, the Korean negotiators are prepared to accept the proposed understanding.

With regard to pre-trial custody, Mr. Habib noted that the Korean negotiators had made no concessions to meet what the U.S. negotiators consider to be a serious problem. With respect to this subject, also, the U.S. negotiators based their position on experience. The U.S. draft was clear. It provided that defendants in the custody of the U.S. authorities would be produced promptly at the request of the Korean authorities. The U.S. negotiators did not understand the Korean desire to retain custody, except in the case of security cases, with regard to which the U.S. negotiators had made a concession. The U.S. negotiators had also pointed out that the final sentence of Paragraph 5(c) of the U.S. draft was related to this question and

0102

would permit the Korean authorities to take custody when requested to do so. In view of the assurances on presentation of the accused already given by the U.S. negotiators, the Korean authorities could exercise jurisdiction just as effectively if the U.S. military authorities retain custody.

0103

<u>At the 60th Session</u> (August 7, 1964)

Turning to the question of pre-trial custody, Mr. Habib recalled the remaining difference of opinion pertains to the question of custody in security cases. The U.S. negotiators had indicated their willingness to agree to Paragraph 5(e) of the Korean draft, provided the Korean negotiators would agree to the inclusion in the Agreed Joint Summary of the following two understandings:

a. There must be mutual U.S.-ROK agreement as to the circumstances in which such custody is appropriate; and

b. Korean confinement facilities must be adequate by U.S. standards.

The Korean negotiators had accepted the second of these two understandings but had rejected the first on the grounds that the Korean authorities should be the only and final authorities to determine whether or not such custody is appropriate. Earlier, the Korean negotiators had stated that the Korean authorities required custody of individuals charged with security offenses in order to prevent further threats to the security of the Republic of Korea or to prevent destruction of evidence. It was inconceivable, Mr. Habib stated, that the United States Government would be a party to threats to the security of the Republic of Korea. The U.S. armed forces were not present in the

0104

Republic of Korea to pose a threat to its security. The
U.S. authorities desired to participate in the determination
of the circumstances under which Korean custody of the
accused would be appropriate. This position did not
reject the right of the Korean authorities to hold custody.
As a matter of practical implementation, mutual discussion
would be called for in a security case. Let both sides
consider this question further.

Mr. Chang replied that in the light of the special
and close relationship existing between the two countries,
the Korean negotiators were not unprepared to reconsider
this matter. They viewed it as a matter of principle,
however. The Korean authorities were prepared to consult
with U.S. military authorities concerning a security case
and to recognize the U.S. right to participate in the
determination of circumstances leading to custody by the
Korean authorities but the final decision concerning custody
must be made by the Korean authorities, not the U.S.
authorities. Agreement between them was not necessary.

Mr. Habib replied that the U.S. negotiators believed
that agreement was necessary - agreement as to the circumstances
in which custody would be appropriate. In order to preclude
the temptation to the Korean authorities to make a unilateral

0105

decision, there should be consultation. The U.S. negotiators were proposing these two understandings for inclusion in the Agreed Joint Summary in view of the importance of the Joint Summary as a document providing specific guidelines for those who will be charged with implementing the Agreement. Mr. Chang replied that the Korean negotiators fully shared the views of the U.S. negotiators concerning the importance of the Agreed Joint Summary and its function as a guide for implementation of the Agreement.

0106

At the 66th Session (November 24, 1964)

Taking up first the use in Paragraph 1(b) of the U.S. draft of the phrase "civil authorities of the Republic of Korea", Mr. Chang made the following statement:

"a. With respect to the phrase 'civil authorities of the Republic of Korea' in the U.S. draft, the U.S. negotiators had previously stated that the position that jurisdiction over the U.S. armed forces by the host government should be limited to the civil authorities of the government was a firm U.S. position in every country in which a SOFA is in force. The U.S. negotiators wanted to have it stated explicitly in the SOFA with the ROK Government. At the 60th session, the U.S. negotiators had again reiterated that the U.S. negotiators of the Agreements with Japan and the NATO governments had not conceived of the possibility that military authorities of the host country could exercise jurisdiction. Inasmuch as that possibility does exist in the Republic of Korea, the U.S. negotiators wished to make the language of the provision quite clear by having it read 'the civil authorities of the Republic of Korea'.

"b. To accommodate the oft-repeated U.S. concern above, and to meet the Korean requirement, the Korean negotiators had given to the U.S. negotiators an unqualified assurance for the negotiating record that under no circumstances would members of the U.S. armed forces and civilian

0107

components be subject to trial by Korean military authorities, in the hope that the U.S. negotiators would agree to the deletion of the world 'civil' from the draft.

"c. The Korean negotiators had further wished at the 60th session to clarify the U.S. position by asking whether the U.S. position was to accept the assurance as an agreed minute and delete the word 'civil' from the text. Although the U.S. side declined to respond to the question on the ground that the question was a hypothetical one, we wish to reiterate our position that the assurance made for the Joint Summary Record should be sufficient to settle the problem. In other words, we cannot accept the word 'civil', either in the text or in an agreed minute, but are prepared to negotiate to meet the U.S. requirement through assurances in a form other than text or agreed minute. We wonder what still keeps the U.S. negotiators from accepting the Korean assurances which squarely meet the U.S. requirement. If the U.S. negotiators have in mind any other reasons for insisting on the word 'civil in the text, we have so far no way of knowing them.

"d. The Korean negotiators ask the U.S. negotiators to take into consideration the position of the Korean negotiators and accept it."

0108

<u>At the 66th Session</u> (November 24, 1964)

Turning to the question of waiver of jurisdiction, Mr. Chang made the following statement:

"a. The Korean negotiators wish to review their position on the draft regarding the waiver of primary right to exercise jurisdiction, thereby reminding the U.S. negotiators of outstanding issues and difficulties which confront us in connection with the waiver problem.

"b. According to the U.S. draft, even though we consider it absolutely necessary to try an accused in specific cases, we would be obliged to hand him over to the U.S. authorities and then undergo afterwards necessary procedures to recall the waived case by seeking agreement at the Joint Committee. Furthermore, the U.S. draft does not guarantee any assurance which enables us to obtain successful recall in specific cases.

"c. In the past, the U.S. negotiators had emphasized that it was the intention of the U.S. negotiators to obtain maximum waiver from the Korean authorities. To meet the U.S. concern, the Korean negotiators had reiterated that we would waive as many cases as other countries do under their SOFA's. Nevertheless, we firmly maintain that our position is to retain the principle so that we could waive primary right to

0103

the U.S. authorities except when we determine that it
is of particular importance to try an accused in the Korean
court.

"d. Time and again, we are ready to assure the U.S.
negotiators that the Korean authorities will waive as
generously as other SOFA countries do; however, we wish
to retain discretion on our part as to whether or not to
waive. In this connection, we believe that we are asking
the U.S. negotiators not any new or unique provisions
but only universal ones which have been generally accepted
by other "SOFA's so that we could reserve as a hosting
country primary right to exercise jurisdiction not in
general but in specific cases under special circumstances.

"e. We ask once again that the U.S. negotiators
reconsider our difficulties toward this problem and accept
the Korean views."

0110

형사 재판 관할권에 관한 미국측안 중 합의의사록의

번역문 (가역)

외 무 부

조 약 과

0111

합 의 의 사 록

본조의 규정은 미군이외에 한국에 주둔하고 있는 유엔군에 대한 재판관할권의 행사에 관한 현행의 협정, 약정 또는 관행에는 영향을 미치지 아니한다.

제 1 항 (2) 에 관하여

1. 합중국당국은 전투지역이 있다면 그 지역에 있는 합중국군대의 구성원, 군속 및 가족에 대하여 전속적 관할권을 행사할 권리를 갖는다. 전투지역의 한계는 합동위원회가 이를 정하며 이는 비무장지역으로부터 합중국 군단(전투단) 및 이 지역에 배치되어 있는 한국군의 군 규모만한 부대의 후방경계선에 이르기까지의 지역을 포함한다.

2. 대한민국이 계엄령을 선포한 경우에 있어서는 계엄령하에 있는 대한민국의 지역에 있어서는 본조의 규정은 그 적용이 즉시 정지되며 합중국 당국은 계엄령이 해제될때까지 합중국 군대의 구성원, 군속 및 가족에 대하여 전속적 관할권을 행사할 권리를 가진다.

3. 합중국 군대의 구성원, 군속 및 가족에 대한 대한민국 당국의 재판관할권은 대한민국 영역외에서 범한 어떠한 범죄에도 미치지 아니한다.

제 2 항에 관하여

대한민국은 합중국 당국이 적의한 경우에 합중국 군대의 구성원, 군속 및 가족에 과하게 되는 행정적 및 징계적인 재제의 유효성을 인정하여 합동위원회에서 제 2 항에 의한 재판관할권을 행사할 권리의 포기를 요청하는 경우에는 이에 대하여 호의적인 고려를 하여야 한다.

제 2 항 (3) 에 관하여

각기정부는 이 세항에 규정된 안전에 관한 모든 범죄의 상세한 내용과 이러한 범죄에 관한 법령상의 규정을 통고하여야 한다.

(1)

제 3 항에 관하여

    대한민국은 합중국 군대의 구성원. 군속 및 가족간의 질서와
규율을 유지함이 합중국 당국의 주된 책임임을 시인하여 대한민국
당국의 제 3 항에 의한 재판관할권을 행사할 권리를 포기한다.
합중국 당국은 상기 권리 포기에 해당하는 개별적 사건을 대한민국
관계당국에 통고한다. 특정사건에 있어서 특정의 사정을 이유로
대한민국이 이러한 경우에 재판관할권을 행사함이 특히 중요하다고
인정할 경우에는 상기 통지를 받은 날로부터 15 일 이내에 그들은 이
특정사건에 대한 권리의 포기를 철회하기 위하여 합동위원회의 협의를
구하여야 한다. 전기 규정에 따라 대한민국이 허용한 권리 포기는
어떠한 경우에 있어서나 무조건이며 최종적이고 또한 이에 따라서 대한
민국 당국이나 국민은 형사소송을 제기할수 없다. 경미한 범죄의
신속한 처리를 촉진하기 위하여 합중국 당국과 대한민국 관계당국은
상기 통고를 철회할 약정을 체결할수 있다.

제 3 항 (1) 에 관하여

  1. 합중국 당국은 만일 대한민국의 군대가 범죄를 범한다면 민간
법원에 의하지 않고 군법회의에 의하여 재판될 범죄에 관련된 합중국
군대의 구성원에 대하여 재판관할권을 행사할 제 1 차적인 권리를
갖는다.

  2. 합중국 군대의 구성원 또는 군속이 어떠한 범죄의 혐의를 받을
경우에는 그가 범죄를 범하였다면 혐의 받는 범죄가 공적직무의 수행중
행하여 진 작위 또는 부작위에 기인하였다고 기재한 범죄 혐의자의
지휘관이 또는 그를 대신하여 발행한 증명서는 제 1 차적인 재판관할권을
결정하기 위한 충정자료가 된다.

제 3 항에 관하여

  1. 합중국 당국과 대한민국 당국은 대한민국내에서 관계당국이 행하는

형사 소송상 필요한 증인을 출두토록 하기 위하여 상호 협조한다. 한국에 주둔하고 있는 합중국 군대의 구성원이 증인이나 피고인으로서 대한민국 법정에 출두 소환을 받을때에는 합중국 당국은 군사상의 비상사태로 인하여 달리 요청되지 않는 한 이러한 출두가 대한민국 법률상 강제적인 것을 조건으로 그를 출두토록 하여야 한다. 군사상의 비상사태로 인하여 그가 출두할수 없을 때에는 합중국 당국은 출두불능의 예정기간을 기재한 증명서를 제출한다. 증인이나 피고인으로서 합중국 군대의 구성원, 군속 및 가족에 대하여 발부되는 영장은 영어로 작성하여 직접 송달 되어야 한다. 영장의 발부 송달은 군사시설이나 지역내에 있는 자에 대하여 한국 송달인에 의하여 집행될 경우에 합중국 당국은 한국 송달인이 그와 같은 송달을 집행토록 필요한 제반 가능한 조치를 취하여야 한다. 이에 부가하여 합중국 군대의 구성원, 군속 및 가족을 포함하는 모든 대한민국 형사소송 절차에 있어서 대한민국 당국은 지체없이 형사상의 모든 영장 (구속영장, 소환장, 공소장 및 호출장을 포함한다)의 사본을 합중국 당국이 지정한 영장 영수인에게 송달하여야 한다. 합중국 당국이 대한민국의 국민이나 거주인을 증인이나 전문가로서 필요할 때에는 대한민국의 법원 또는 기타 당국은 대한민국의 법률이 정하는 바에 따라 이러한 자로 하여금 출두토록 한다. 이러한 경우에 있어서 합중국 당국은 대한민국 검찰총장 또는 대한민국 당국이 지정하는 기타 기관을 통하여 행한다. 증인에 대한 비용 및 보수는 _____조에 의하여 설치된 합동위원회가 이를 정한다.

2. 증인의 특권과 면제는 그가 출두하는 법원, 공판정 또는 기타 당국에 관한 법률의 정하는 바에 따른다. 이러한 경우에 있어서도 증인은 자기의 부죄의 우려가 있는 증언을 할 필요가 없다.

3. 형사 소송의 진행중에 대한민국이나 합중국 당국의 앞에서 그 어떠한 국가의 공적 기밀의 발로 또는 그 어떤 국가의 안전을 침해할 우려성이

(3)

0114

있는 정보의 발로가 소송절차의 정당한 필요할 경우에는 관계당국은
관계국가의 관계당국의 이러한 발로를 하여도 좋다는 서면상의 허가를
구하여야 한다.

제 9 항 (1) 에 관하여

대한민국에 의한 지체없는 신속한 재판을 받을 권리는 시보기간을
이수한 법관으로서 전격으로 구성되는 공정한 법정에 의한 공개재판을
포함한다. 합중국 군대의 구성원, 군속 및 가족은 대한민국의 군법
회의에 의한 재판을 받지 않는다.

제 9 항 (2) 에 관하여

합중국 군대의 구성원, 군속 및 가족은 상당한 사유가 없이는
대한민국 당국에 의하여 체포 또는 구금되지 아니하며 그러한 사유가
자신이나 변호인이 참석한 공개법정에서 밝혀져야 하는 직접적인 심문을
받을 권리가 있다. 상당한 사유가 밝혀지지 않을 때에는 지체없이
석방을 명하여야 한다. 체포되거나 구금되었을 때에는 즉시 그가
이해하는 언어로서 그에 대한 혐의 사실을 통고받을 권리를 가진다.
그는 그에게 불리하게 이용될 증거의 재판에 앞서 상당한 기간을 통보
받아야 하며 당해 피의자의 변호인은 청구에 따라서 사건의 재판을 담당
할 대한민국 법원에 송부된 서류에 포함되어 있고 대한민국 당국이 채증한
증인의 진술을 조사하고 또 독취할 기회가 재판에 앞서 부여되어야 한다.

제 9 항 (3) 및 (4)

대한민국 당국에 의하여 기소된 합중국 군대의 구성원, 군속 및
가족은 그에게 유리하거나 불리한 모든 증인의 증언, 제반 심리, 재판권의
변론, 심판자체, 기타 소송을 통하여 출석할 권리를 가지며 증인을 심문
하기에 충분한 기회가 허용된다.

제 9 항 (5) 에 관하여

변호인의 구조를 받을 권리는 체포 또는 구금되는 때로부터 존재
하며 피의자가 출석하는 모든 사건 조사, 심리, 재판권의 변론, 심판자체

0115

(4)

및 기타 소송절차에 변로인을 선임할 권리와 그 변호인과 비밀히
상의할 권리를 포함한다.

제 9 항 (6) 에 관하여

유능한 통역인의 구조를 받을 권리는 체포 또는 구금되는 때로
부터 존재한다.

제 9 항 (7) 에 관하여

합중국 정부의 대표자와 접견 교통할 권리는 체포 또는 구금되는
때로부터 존재하며 동 대표자가 결석중에 피고인이 한 진술은 피고인에
대한 유죄의 증거로서 채증되지 아니한다. 동 대표자는 피의자가 출석
하는 모든 사건 조사, 심리, 재판전의 변론, 심판 자체 및 기타 소송
절차에 참여할 권리를 갖는다.

제 9 항에 관하여

대한민국 당국이 재판하는 합중국 군대의 구성원, 군속 및 가족은
대한민국의 법률상 대한민국 국민에게 보장한 제반 절차상 및 실체상의
권리가 보장된다. 대한민국 법률상 대한민국 국민에게 보장하고 있는
모든 절차상 또는 실체상의 권리가 당해 피의자에게 거부되었거나
거부될 우려가 있을 경우에는 양 정부의 대표자는 그러한 권리의 거부를
방지하거나 시정하기 위하여 합동위원회에서 협의한다.

본조 본항 (1) 에서 (7) 까지에 열기된 권리에 부가하여 대한민국
당국에 의하여 기소된 합중국 군대의 구성원, 군속 및 가족은

(1) 그의 재판에 관하여 영어로 된 축어적 보고를 받을 권리

(2) 유죄판결 또는 형의 선고에 대한 상소권, 이에 부가하여 유죄판결
이나 형의 선고시에 대한민국 법원으로부터 상소권이 있다는 것과 상소권
행사기간을 고지받을 권리

(3) 합중국 또는 대한민국의 유치장에서의 판결선고전의 구류기간을 구류
형에 산입받을 권리

(5)

0116

(4) 행위시 대한민국 법률에 의하여 범죄를 구성하지 아니하는 작위 또는 부작위로 인하여 범죄 유죄를 소추받지 아니하는 권리

(5) 혐의받는 범죄가 범하여졌을 때 또는 원판결로서 원심법원이 유죄판결을 하였을 때에 적용되는 형보다도 중한 형을 받지 아니하는 권리

(6) 범죄의 범행후 피고에게 불리하게 변경된 증거 법칙이나 증명 요건에 기하여 범죄의 유죄로 소추받지 아니하는 권리

(7) 의사에 반하여 증언을 강제당하지 아니하거나 답티 자기 부죄를 강제당하지 아니하는 권리

(8) 참혹하거나 과중한 처벌을 받지 아니하는 권리

(9) 입법행위나 행정행위에 의하여 형의 소추를 받거나 처벌을 받지 아니하는 권리

(10) 동일 범죄에 대하여 이중으로 형의 소추를 받거나 처벌을 받지 아니하는 권리

(11) 심판에 출두하거나 자기의 변호에 있어서 육체적으로나 정신적으로 부적당한 때에는 심판에 출두하도록 요청되지 아니하는 권리

(12) 군인이나 민간인으로서 적절한 정장을 타고 수갑을 채우지 않는다는 것을 포함하여 합중국 군대의 위엄과 합당하는 조건임을 제외하고는 심판을 받지 아니하는 권리

위법하거나 부당한 방법에 의하여 수집된 자백, 자인(승인), 기타 진술이거나 진실한 증거는 대한민국 법원이 본조에 의하여 형의 소추를 하는 데 있어서 채증하지 아니한다.

본조에 의하여 대한민국 당국이 기소하는 어떠한 경우에 있어서나 기소측에서 유죄가 아니거나 무죄 석방되었음을 이유로 상소하지 못하며 또한 법률 적용의 착오를 이유로 제외하고는 피의자가 상소하지 아니하는 것을 것을 이유로 상소하지 못한다.

합중국 당국은 합중국 군대의 구성원, 군속 및 가족이 수감되거나

수급되어질 대한민국의 구류시설을 조사할 권리를 가진다.

전투발생시에는 대한민국은 재판이전이거나 대한민국 법원이 선고한 형의 복역중이거나를 불문하고 대한민국 구류시설에 수급되고 있는 합중국 군대의 구성원, 군속 및 가족을 보호할 모든 가능한 수단을 취하여야 한다.

대한민국은 이러한자를 석방하여 책임있는 합중국 당국의 비호하에 두자는 요구에 대하여 호의적인 고려를 한다.

시행에 필요한 규정은 합동위원회를 통하여 양정부가 협의한다. 합중국 군대의 구성원, 군속 및 가족에 대한 사형선고, 구류, 금고 또는 징역의 기간 또는 유치의 집행을 위하여 이용되는 시설은 합동위원회에서 협의한바에 따라서 최소한도의 수준을 충족시켜야 한다. 합중국 당국은 청구에 따라 언제든지 합중국 군대의 구성원, 군속 및 가족과 접견 교통할 권리를 가진다.

합중국 당국은 대한민국 구류시설에 구류되고 있는 피구류자와의 접견시에 당해 피구류자를 위하여 의류, 음식, 침대, 의학적 및 치아의 치료와 같은 보조적인 의료품 및 양식을 공급할수 있다.

제 10 항 (1) 피 제 10 항 (2) 에 관하여

합중국 당국은 원칙적으로 합중국 군대의 사용중인 시설과 지역내에서 누구든지 체포할수 있다. 대한민국 당국은 합중국당국이 사용하고 시설과 지역내에 있는 사람이나 재산의 일체 또는 소재 여하를 불문하고 합중국의 재산에 대하여 수사, 압수 또는 수색할 권리를 원칙적으로 행사하지 아니한다. 다만 합중국 당국이 대한민국 당국으로하여금 이러한 사람이나 재산에 대하여 이러한 수사, 압수 또는 수색하는 것에 동의할때에는 그러하지 아니한다. 대한민국 당국이 합중국이 사용하고 있는 시설과 지역안에 있는 사람이나 재산 또는 대한민국 내에 있는 합중국 재산에 대하여 수사, 압수 또는 수색을 하고저 할때에는

(7)

0118

합중국 당국의 청구에 따라 수사, 압수 또는 수색을 행한다.

합중국 정부가 그 기관이 소유하거나 사용하는 재산을 제외하고 상기 재산에 관한 판정의 경우에는 합중국은 판정에 따른 처리를 위하여 대한민국 당국에 그 재산을 법률이 정하는 바에 따라 인도한다.

합중국 당국은 시설 또는 지역의 주변에서 시설이나 지역의 안전에 대한 범죄를 범하고 있거나 기도한자를 누구든지 체포 또는 구금할수 있다.

합중국 군대의 구성원, 군속 및 가족이 아닌자의 경우에는 즉시 대한민국 당국에 인도하여야 한다.

162

(8)

한·미국 간의 상호방위조약 제4조에 의한 시설과 구역 및 한국에서의 미국군대의 지위에 관한 협정(SOFA) 전59권. 1966.7.9 서울에서 서명 : 1967.2.9 발효(조약 232호) (V.56 형사재판관할권 관계자료) 311

Re paragraph 2(c)

Both Governments shall inform each other of the details of all the security offenses mentioned in this subparagraph and the provisions governing such offenses in the existing laws of their respective countries.

Re paragraph 3(c)

Mutual procedures relating to waivers of the primary right to exercise jurisidction shall be determined by the Joint Committee.

Trials of cases in which the authorities of the Republic of Korea waived the primary right to exercise jurisdiction, and trials of cases involving offenses described in paragraph 3(a) (ii) committed against the State or nationals of the Republic of Korea shall be held promptly in the Republic of Korea within a reasonable distance from the places where the offenses are alleged to have taken place unless other arrangements are mutually agreed upon. Representatives of the authorities of the Republic of Korea may be present at such trials.

Re paragraph 4

Dual nationals, the Republic of Korea and United States, who are the members of the United States armed forces and the civilian component and are brought to the Republic of Korea shall not be considered as nationals of the Republic of Korea, but shall be considered as United States nationals for the purposes of this paragraph.

Re paragraph 5(d)

In case the authorities of the Republic of Korea have arrested an offender who is a member of the United States armed forces, the civilian component or a dependent with respect to a case over which the Republic of Korea has the primary right to exercise jurisdiction, the authorities of the Republic of Korea will, unless they deem that there is adequate cause and necessity to retain such offender, release him to the custody

- 1 -

0120

of the United States military authorities provided that he shall, on request, be made available to the authorities of the Republic of Korea, if such be the condition of his release. The United States authorities shall, on request, transfer his custody to the authorities of the Republic of Korea at the time he is indicted by the latter.

Re paragraph 9

1. The rights enumerated in items (a) through (e) of this paragraph are guaranteed to all persons on trial in the Korean courts by the provisions of the Republic of Korea Constitution. In addition to these rights, a member of the United States armed forces, the civilian component or a dependent who is prosecuted under the jurisdiction of the Republic of Korea shall have such other rights as are guaranteed under the laws of the Republic of Korea to all persons on trial in the Korean courts. Such additional rights include the following which are guaranteed under the Republic of Korea Constitution:

(a) He shall not be arrested or detained without being at once informed of the charge against him or without the immediate privilege of counsel, nor shall he be detained without adequate cause, and upon demand of any persons such cause must be immediately shown in open court in his presence and the presence of his counsel;

(b) He shall enjoy the right to a public trial by an impartial tribunal;

(c) He shall not be compelled to testify against himself;

(d) He shall be permitted full opportunity to examine all witnesses;

(e) No cruel punishments shall be imposed upon him.

2. The United States authorities shall have the right upon request to have access at any time to members of the United States armed forces the civilian component, or their dependents who are confined or detained under the authorities of the Republic of Korea.

- 2 -

한·미국 간의 상호방위조약 제4조에 의한 시설과 구역 및 한국에서의 미국군대의 지위에 관한 협정(SOFA) 전59권. 1966.7.9 서울에서 서명 : 1967.2.9 발효(조약 232호) (V.56 형사재판관할권 관계자료) 313

Re paragraphs 10(a) and 10(b)

1. The United States military authorities will normally make
all arrests within facilities and areas in use by and guarded under
the authority of the United States armed forces. This shall not
preclude the authorities of the Republic of Korea from making arrests
within facilities and areas in cases where the competent authorities
of the United States armed forces have given consent, or in cases of
pursuit of a flagrant offender who has committed a serious crime.

Where persons whose arrest is desired by the authorities of the
Republic of Korea and who are not subject to the jurisdiction of the
United States armed forces are within facilities and areas in use by
the United States armed forces, the United States military authorities
will undertake, upon request, to arrest such persons. All persons arres
by the United States military authorities, who are not subject to the
jurisdiction of the United States armed forces, shall immediately be
turned over to the authorities of the Republic of Korea.

The United States military authorities may, under due process of
law, arrest in the vicinity of a facility or area any persons in the
commission or attempted commission of an offense against the security
of that facility or area. Any such person not subject to the jurisdiction of the United States armed forces shall immediately be turned over
to the authorities of the Republic of Korea.

2. The authorities of the Republic of Korea will normally not
exercise the right of search, seizure, or inspection with respect to
any persons or property within facilities and areas in use by and guar
under the authorities of the United States armed forces or with
respect to property of the United States armed forces wherever situat
except in cases where the competent authorities of the United States
armed forces consent to such search, seizure, or inspection by the
authorities of the Republic of Korea of such persons or property.

- 3 -

0122

Where search, seizure, or inspection with respect to persons or property within facilities and areas in use by the United States armed forces or with respect to property of the United States armed forces in the Republic of Korea is desired by the authorities of the Republic of Korea, the United States military authorities will undertake, upon request, to make such search, seizure, or inspection. In the event of a judgement concerning such property, except property owned or utilized by the United States Government or its instrumentalities, the United States will turn over such property to the authorities of the Republic of Korea for disposition in accordance with the judgement.

- 4 -

0123

Witnesses

Germany

Article 37 (Apperances before Courts or authorities)

1. a) Where a member of a force or of a civilian component is summoned to appear before a German court or authority, the military authorities, unless military exigancy requires otherwise, shall secure his attendance provided that such attendance is compulsory under German law. The liaison agency shall be requested to ensure execution of such summons.

b) The provisons of sub-paragraph (a) of this paragraph shall apply mutatis mutandis to dependants insofar as the military authorities are able to secure their attendance; otherwise dependents will be summoned in accordance with German law.

2. Where persons whose attendance cannot be secured by the military authorities are required witnesses or experts by a court or a military authority of a sending State, the German courts and authorities shall, in accordance with German laa secure the attendance of such persons before the court or military authority of that State.

Article 39 (Witnesses and Experts)

Privileges and immunities of witnesses and experts shall be those accorded by the law of the court or authority before which they appear. The court or authority shall, however, give appropriate consideration to the privileges and immunities which witnesses and experts, if they are mambers of a force or of a civilian component or dependents, would have before a court of the sending State or, if they do not belong to these categories of persons, would have before a German court.

Ethiopia (U.S. - Ethiopia) 1953

Article XVII, paragraph 4.

In such cases the appropriate authorities of the Imperial authorities

0124

Imperial Ethoiapian Government shall, upon request, assist in the collection
of evidence and in the carrying out of all necessary investigations.
Necessary arrangements will be made by the appropriate authorities of
Ethoipia to secure the presence of Ethoipian nationals and other persons
in Ethiopia (except members of the United States forces) as witnesses for official
investigations and for military tribunals, and, in appropriate cases, to
seize and hand over evidence, exhibits and objects connected with the
offense. The United States authorities shall, in like United States
forces and assist the Ethiopian authorities in the case of an offense to
be tried in the Ethiopian courts.

Iceland (U/S. - Iceland) 1951
Article 2, paragraph 7 (b).

    (b) If the case is one within the jurisdiction of the United States,
the authorities of Iceland will themselves carry out the necessary
arrangements to secure the presence of and obtain evidence from Icelandic
nationals and other persons in Iceland, except from members of the
United States forces and their dependents, outside the agreed areas.
In case where it is necessary under the laws of the United States for the
authorities of the United States to obtain themselves information from
Icelandic nationals, the Icelandic suthorities will make all possible
arrangements to secure the attendance of such nationals for interrogation in
the presence of Icelandic authorities at places designated by them.
    The military authorities will, in a similar manner, carry out the
collection of evidence from members of the United States forces and their
dependents in the case of an offense within the jurisdiction of the
Icelandic authorities.

Libya (U.S. - Libya) 1954.
Article XX, paragraph 4.

    The United States and Libyan authorities will assist each other in the
carrying out of all necessary investigation into offenses, and in the

0125

collection and production of evidence, including the attendance of
witnesses at the trial and the seizure and, in proper cases, the handing
over of objects connected with an offense. The handing over of such
objects may, however, be made subject to their return within the time
specified by the authority delivering them.

Paragraph 7

Witnesses who are alleged to have committed perjury or contempt of
court in proceedings before the United States service tribunals or
authorities and who are not subject to the law administered by those
tribunals and authorities will be turned over to the Libyan authorities.
Provision will be made by the laws of Libya for the trial and punishment of such
offenders.

Spain

Article 9 (a), (b)

(a) The authorities of the United States and Spain will assist
each other in the collection of evidence, conducting investigation and
securing the presence of witnesses for investigations and trials. The
Mixed Commission on Jurisdiction and representatives of the Joint United
States Military Group, Spain, shall confer frequently for the purpose of
developing and maintaining a satisfactory method of operation

(b) Spanish nationals and other persons in territory under
Spanish jurisdiction, (except members of the United States Forces) who
are required to appear as witnesses before United States Military Courts will
be paid fees and allowances at rates to be determined by the Chief, Joint
United States Military Group in coordination with pertinent Spanish
authorities.

West Indies

Article 9 paragraph 6 (a)

To the extent authorised by law, the authorities of the Territory and
of the United States shall assist each other in the carrying out of all

necessary investigations into offences, in providing for the attendance of witnesses and in the collection and production of evidence, including the seizure and in proper cases, the handling over of objects connected with an offence.

한·미국 간의 상호방위조약 제4조에 의한 시설과 구역 및 한국에서의 미국군대의 지위에 관한 협정(SOFA) 전59권. 1966.7.9 서울에서 서명 : 1967.2.9 발효(조약 232호) (V.56 형사재판관할권 관계자료) 319

necessary investigations into offences, in providing for the attendance of witnesses and in the collection and production of evidence, including the seizure and in proper cases, the handling over of objects connected with an offence.

EXIGENCE, or EXIGENCY.

Demand, want, need, imperativeness; emergency, something arising suddenly out of the current of events; any event or occasional combination of circumstances, calling for immediate action or remedy; a pressing necessity; a sudden and unexpected happening or an unforeseen occurrence or condition. United States v. Atlantic Coast Line Co., D.C.N.C., 224 F. 160, 1962; Los Angeles County v. Payne, 8 Cal.2d 563, 66 P.2d 658, 663. Something arising suddenly out of circumstances calling for immediate action or remedy, or where something helpful needs to be done at once, yet not so pressing as an emergency. State ex rel. Odenwald v. District Court of Tenth Judicial Dist. in and for Fergus County, 98 Mont. 1, 38 P.2d 269, 271.

0128

Japan, Administrative Agreement (Signed 1952 and expired 1960)

Art. XXIV

In the event of hostilities, or imminently threatened hostilities, in the Japan area, the Governments of the United States and Japan shall immediately consult together with a view to taking necessary joint measures for the defense of that area and to carrying out the purposes of Article I of the security Treaty.

Japan (1960)

Art. 17

11. In the event of hostilities to which the provisions of Article V of the Treaty of Mutual Cooperation and Security apply, either the Government of the United States or the Government of Japan shall have the right, by givening sixty days notice to the other, to suspend the application of any of the provisions of this Article. If this right is exercised, the Governments of the United States and Japan shall immediately consult with a view to agreeing on suitable provisions to replace the provisions suspended.

NATO (1953)

Art. XV

1. Subject to paragraph 2 of this Article, this Agreement shall remain in force in the event of hostilities to which the North Atlantic Treaty applies, except that the provisions for settling claims in paragraph 2 and 5 of Article VIII shall not apply to war damage, and that the provisions of the Agreement, and, in particular of Article III and VII, shall immediately be reviewed by the Contracting

0129

Parties concerned, who may agree to such modifications as they may consider desirable regarding the application of the Agreement between them.

2. In the event of such hostilities, each of the Contracting Parties shall have the right, by going 60 days' notice to the other Contracting Parties, to suspend the application of any of the provisions of this Agreement so far as it is concerned. If this is exercised, the Contracting Parties shall immediately consult with a view to agreeing on suitable provisions to replace the provisions suspended.

German (1959)

Art. 80

The provisions of Article XV of the NATO Status of Forces Agreement shall apply to the present Agreement, it being understood that references in that Article to other provisions of the NATO Status of Forces Agreement shall be deemed to be references to those provisions as supplemented by the present Agreement.

Philippines (1947)

Art. 13

6. Notwithstanding the foregoing provisions, it is mutually agreed that in time of war the United States shall have the right to exercise exclusive jurisdiction over any offenses which may be committed by members of the armed forces of the United States in the Philippines.

0130

Philippines (1947)

Art. XIV
Arrest And Service Of Process

1. No arrest shall be made and no process, civil or
criminal, shall be served within any base except with the
permission of the commanding officer of such base; but
should the commanding officer refuse to grant such
permission he shall (except in cases of arrest where the
United States has jurisdiction under Article XIII) forthwith
take the necessary steps to arrest the person charged and
surrender him to the appropriate authorities of the
Philippines or to serve such process, as the case may be,
and to provide the attendance of the server of such
process before the appropriate court in the Philippines
or procure such server to make the necessary affidavit
or declaration to prove such service as the case may require.

Dominican Republic (1957)

Art. XII

1) (b) Except during a period of hostilities in which
either Government is engaged, the Government of the United
States of America and the Government of the Dominican Rep.
shall have concurrent jurisdiction over offenses committed
outside the areas referred to in Article 11 by persons
described in subparagraph (a) against a Dominican national
or nationals of a third country. In each such case, the two
Governments through the Mixed Military Commission provided
for under Article XI shall decide which Government shall
exercise jurisdiction and shall give consideration to whether
the offense arose out of any act or omission done in the
performance of official duties. During a period of hostilities
in which either Government is engaged, the principle stated
in subparagraph (a) shall apply.

0131

미군가족에 대한 군사재판 관할건

가. 1. Kinsella, v. Krueger Case (1956. 6. 11.)

(주일미군 소속 육군대령인 남편을 부인인
Mrs. Dorothy Krueger Smith 이 교살한

사건이 군재에 회부된데 대한 상고)
미대심원은 다음과 같은 이유를 들어 접수국과의
군대지위협정 하에 가족이 미군법재판에 복하는
것은 위헌이 아니라고 판결하였다.
(1) 미국의 국방상 군대를 해외에 파견함에 따라
    가족이나 민간인이 동반하게 될 필요성은
    미국회나 정부가 다같이 인정하는 바이며
(2) 민간인도 파견군을 중심으로 하여 하나의
    군대사회를 형성하게 되면 관할군사령관은
    그 군대사회의 규율을 확립하기 위하여 군대
    구성원 뿐만 아니라 가족에 대하여서도
    일률적으로 제재권을 행사할 필요가 생기게
    된다.
(3) 국회가 헌법에 따라 필요한 경우에 legislative Court
    를 설치할수 있는 권한이 있는 이상 가족이
    영사재판 지도, 속령재판지도 또는 군사재판제도
    중 어느 제도에 복할 것이냐를 결정하는 것은
    그 권한에 속하는 사항들이며
(4) 또한 접수국의 협정에서 그 국가의 재판권의
    일부를 이양하는 것은 파견군당국이 공정
    신속한 재판을 실시할 것을 신뢰하고 있기
    때문이며 또 재판제도가 각양각상인 접수국의
    재판권에 복하는 것 보다는 비록 배심제도가
    결여되었다 할지라도 미의지위 인권 상세하게
    보장되고 있는 미국군사재판에 복하는 것이
    피의자를 위하여서도 유리할 것이다.

0132

2. Reid V. Corert Case (1956.6.11.)

(주영국미군 소속 군인의 부인인 Mrs. Clarice Covert 이

남편을 살해한 범죄로 미군법재판에 회부되어 무기징역을

언도 받고 상고)

외국에서 군사재판을 받은 가족이 본국으로 호송

되었을 경우에는 그 재판의 효력의 연장으로 봄으로

합헌적이라고 판결하였다.

3. 1957년도에 상기 각 판결은 다음과 같은 이유로

위헌적이라고 하여 번복되었다.

(1) 평화시에 있어서 극형에 관련된 가족의 재판은

그 회복될수 없는 최종적이고도 절대적인 점에

감하여 미헌법에서 보장된 배심제도에 의한 재판

을 받아야 하며 군사재판에 복하는 것은 위헌이다.

4. Kinsella v. Singleton Case (1960.1.8)

(주독미군 인의 처인 Mrs. Joanna S. Dial 이 동거자녀를

상해하고 군사재판에 복한데 대하여 그 모친인 Mrs.

Singleton이 불복 상고한 사건)

미대심원은 다음과 같은 이유를 들어 평화시에는 범죄의

경중을 막론하고 가족이 군법재판에 복하는 것은 위헌

이라고 판결하였다.

(1) 미군형법은 신분에 의하여 그 관할권을 결정하였으며

죄의 경중에 따라 관할권을 결정한 바는 없다.

(2) 따라서 민간인의 극형에 해당하는 사건이 헌법에

보장된 배심제도가 없는 군사재판에 복하는 것이

위헌이라면 경죄에 대하여서는 배심제도가 결여된

재판에 복하여도 가하다는 것은 모순된 것이다.

다. 결론 : 상기 각 대심원 판결에 따라 해외미군에 동반

하는 가족이 군법재판에 복하는 것은 평화시에 관한한

위헌이라고 판결되었음에 따라 우리측이 가족을 미군

당국의 재판권 행사 대상에 추가할것을 수락하면

0133

(1) 국회가 그 건안 내에서 영사재판제도에 유사한
    Legislative Court 를 설치하여 가족에 관한
    범죄를 관할케 할 가능성이 있으며
(2) 적어도 중죄에 관한한 본국으로 이송하여 재판할
    가능성이 농후함으로 미초안 제1항의 미국당국의
    관할권 행사기관에 관련하여 미군당국으로 규정할
    것을 지속 주장하여야 할것으로 본다.

0134

WEST INDIES

Aericle 9

3.   (c) If the authorities having the primary right
decide not to exercise jurisdiction, they shall
notify the other authorities as soon as
practicable. The United States authorities shall
give sympathetic consideration to a request from
the authorities of the Territory for a waiver of
their primary right in cases where the authorities
of the Territory consider such waiver to be of
particular importance. The authorities of the
Territory will waive, upon request, their primary
right to exercise jurisdiction under this Article,
except where they in their discretion determine
and notify the United States authorities that it
is of particular importance that such jurisdiction
be not waived.

0135

<u>Offenses arising in performance of</u>
<u>Official Duty</u>

<u>Circular, U.S. Army Forces, Far East (Jan. 1956)</u>

The term "official duty" as used in Article XVII, Official Minutes, and the Agreed Views is not meant to include all acts by members of the armed forces and civilian component during periods while they are on duty, but is meant to apply only to acts which are required to be done as a function of those duties which the individuals are performing. Thus, a substantial departure from the acts a person is required to perform in a particular duty usually will indicate an act outside of his "official duty."

<u>Iceland (May 8, 1951)</u>

<u>Art. 2, Par. 4(a) 2.</u>

Offenses arising out of any act done in the performance of official duty.

<u>Philippine (March 26, 1947)</u>

<u>Art. XIII, par. 4</u>

Whenever for special reasons the Philippines may desire not to exercise the jurisdiction reserved to it in paragraph 2 of this article, the fiscal (prosecuting attorney) of the city or province where the offense has been committed shall so notify the officer holding the offender in custody within ten (10) days after his arrest, and in such a case the United States shall be free to exercise jurisdiction. If any offense falling under paragraph 2 of this Article is committed by any member of the armed forces of the United States:

(a) while engaged in the actual performance of a specific military duty, or

0136

(b) during a period of national emergency declared
by either Government and the fiscal (prosecuting attorney)
so finds from the evidence, he shall immediately notify
the officer holding the offender in custody that the United
States is free to exercise jurisdiction. In the event
the fiscal (prosecuting attorney) finds that the offense
was not committed in the actual performance of a specific
military duty, the offender's commanding officer shall
have the right to appeal from such finding to the Secretary
of Justice within ten days from the receipt of the decision
of the fiscal and the decision of the Secretary of Justice
shall be final.

Japan (June 23, 1960

Art. XVII, par. 3(a) (ii) (Agreement)

Offenses arising out of any act or omission done in
the performance of official duty.

Art. XVII, Re Par. 3(a) (ii) (Agreed Minute)

Where a member of the United States armed forces or the
civilian component is charged with an offense, a certificate
issued by or on behalf of his commanding Officer stating
that the alleged offense, if committed by him, arose out of
an act or omission done in the performance of official duty,
shall, in any judicial proceedings, be sufficient evidence
of the fact unless the contrary is proved.

The above statement shall not be interpreted to prejudice
in any way Article 318 of the Japanese Code of Criminal
Procedure.

한·미국 간의 상호방위조약 제4조에 의한 시설과 구역 및 한국에서의 미국군대의 지위에 관한 협정(SOFA)
전59권. 1966.7.9 서울에서 서명 : 1967.2.9 발효(조약 232호) (V.56 형사재판관할권 관계자료) 329

Agreed View No.43

If the Chief Prosecutor of Japan considers that there is proof contrary to the certificate of official duty, the matter is referred to the Joint Committee for decision.

Visiting Forces Act (1952)

In the United KINGDOM, THE Visiting Forces Act of 1952 provides that a certificate issued by the appropriate military authority stating that, if the alleged offense was committed by the accused, it arose out of and in the course of the accused's duty as a member of the force or civilian component, shall "be sufficient evidence of that fact unless the contrary is proved."

Turkey (June 23, 1954)

1) By legislation enacted on 16 July 1956, the language of the Agreement is to be applied to any "offense arising out of any act or omission done in the performance of official duty or done in connection with the performance of official duty." The addition was made in order to permit agreement on this point between the Turkish and American authorities.

2) On July 16, 1956, a law was enacted providing that "the basis regarding the establishment of the status of duty would be determined between the government of the Turkish Republic and the government of the sending State.

3) U.S.-Turkey, Aide-memoire (July 28, 1956)

An official certificate bearing the signature of the person holding the highest ranking office of the United States military forces in Turkey, stating that an act was done in connection with or in the performance of official duty, will be accepted by Turkish judicial authorities.

0138

Federal Republic of Germany (March 3, 1959)

Art. 18

1. Whenever, in the course of criminal proceedings against a member of a force or of a civilian component, it becomes necessary to determine whether an offence has arisen out of any act or omission done in the performance of official duty, such determination shall be made in accordance with the law of the sending State concerned. The highest appropriate authority of such sending State may submit to the German court or authority dealing with the case a certificate thereon.

2. The German court or authority shall make its dicision in conformity with the certificate. In exceptional cases, however, such certificate may, at the request of the German court or authority, be made the subject of review through discussions between the Federal Government and the diplomatic mission in the Federal Republic of the sending State.

France (Circular of the Ministry of Justice)

French authorities must accept a determination of this question by American military authorities only when that determination is made by a staff judge advocate or other legal officer. A decision by a local commander is not acceptable.

Dominican Republic, (March 19, 1957)

Art. XII, 1) (a),(b)

1) (a) Except as provided in subparagraph (b), the Government of the United States of America shall have the

right to exercise exclusive criminal jurisdiction over any offense committed in the Dominican Republic by (1) members of the United States Armed Forces and (2) other persons subject to United States military law except Dominican nationals or nationals of a third country.

(b) Except during a period of hostilities in which either Government is engaged, the Government of the United States of America and the Government of the Dominican Republic shall have concurrent jurisdiction over offenses committed outside the areas referred to in Article II by persons described in subparagraph (a) against a Dominican national or nationals of a third country. In each such case, the two Governments through the Mixed Military Commission provided for under Article XI shall decide which Government shall exercise jurisdiction and shall give consideration to whether the offense arose out of any act or omission done in the performance of official duties. During a period of hostilities in which either Government is engaged, the principle stated in subparagraph (a) shall apply.

Art. XI

A Mixed Military Commission composed of the Secretary of State of the Armed Forces of the Dominican Republic and Senior officials of the United States Armed Forces appointed by the Government of the United States of America, shall decide all question with regard to the operations under this agreement.

0140

West Indies SOFA (Feb. 19, 1961)

Art. IX, Par. (3) (n) (ii)

(ii) offenses arising out of any act or omission
done in the performance of official duty.

Art. IX, Par. (11)

A certificate of the appropriate United States
commanding officer that an offense arose out of an act or
omission done in the performance of official duty shall
be conclusive, but the commanding officer shall give
consideration to any representation made by the Government
of the Territory.

Agreement between U.S. and Bolivia for the Establishment
of a United States Army Mission to Bolivia, (June 30, 1956)

Art. 14

Mission members shall be immune from the civil jurisdiction of the courts of the Republic of Bolivia for acts
or omissions arising out of the performance of their
official duties. Determined as to whether an act or omission
arose out of the performance of official duties shall be
made jointly by the Chief of Mission and the Minister of
National Defense.

Ethiopia SOFA (May 22, 1953)

Art. XVII, Par. 3

Members of the United States forces shall be immune
from the criminal jurisdiction of Ethiopian courts, and,
in matters arising from the performance of their official
duties, from the civil jurisdiction of Ethiopian courts,
provided that, in particular cases, the United States
authorities may waive such immunity. In all other cases,
Ethiopian courts shall have jurisdiction.

0141

Philippines (1947)

Art. XIII.Par. 5

5. In all cases over which the Philippines exercise jurisdiction the custody of the accused, pending trail and final judgment, shall be entrusted without delay to the commanding officer of the nearest base, who shall acknowledge in writing that such accused has been delivered to him for custody pending trail in a competent court of the Philippines and that he will be held ready to appear and will be produced before said court when required by it. The commanding officer shall be furnished by the fiscal (prosecuting attorney) with a copy of the information against the accused upon the filing of the original in the competent court.

Libya (1954)

Art. XX, Par. 3

(3) The United States and Libyan authorities will assist each other in the arrest and handing over to the appropriate authority of members of the United States forces for trial in accordance with the above provisions, and the Libyan authorities will immediately notify the United States authorities if they arrest any member of the United States forces. The Libyan authorities will, if the United States authorities request the release on remand of an arrested member of the United States forces, release him from their custody on the United States authorities' undertaking to present him to the Libyan courts for investigatory proceedings and trial when required.

0142

NATO (1953)

Art. VII. Par. 5(c)

(c) The custody of an accused member of a force or civilian component over whom the receiving State is to exercise jurisdiction shall, if he is in the hands of the sending State, remain with that State until he is charged by the receiving State.

Japan (1960)

Same as NATO Provision.

Australia (1963)

Art. 8. Par. 5(c)

(c) The custody of an accused member of the United States forces or of the civilian component or of a dependant over whom Australia is to exercise jurisdiction shall, if he is in the hands of the United States authorities, remain with the United States to the extent authorised by United States law until he is charged by Australia.

Iceland (1951)

Art. 2. Par. 6(c)

(c) The custody of an accused over whom Iceland is to exercise jurisdiction shall, if he is in the hands of the authorities of the United States, remain in the hands of such authorities until he is charged by Iceland.

Ethiopia (1953)

Art. XVII. Par. 5, 6

5. Ethiopian authorities may arrest members of the United States forces outside the Installations for the commission or attempted commission of an offense, but,

0143

in the event of such an arrest, the member or members shall
be immediately turned over to the United States authorities.
Except for Ethiopian nationals and other persons normally
resident in Ethiopia, any person fleeing from the jurisdiction of the United States forces and found in any place
outside the Installations may, on request, be arrested by
the Ethiopian authorities and turned over to the United
States authorities.

6. The United States authorities shall deliver to the
Ethiopian authorities for trial and punishment all Ethiopian
nationals and other persons normally resident in Ethiopia
who have been charged by the Ethiopian or the United States
authorities with having committed offenses within the
limits of the Installations.

Germany (1959)

Art. 20, 21

ARTICLE 20

1. The military authorities of a sending State may,
without a warrant of arrest, take into temporary custody
any person not subject to their jurisdiction.

    (a) if such person is caught or pursued in flagrante
        delicto and either

        (i) the identity of the person cannot be
            established immediately, or

        (ii) there is reason to believe that the person
            may flee from justice; or

    (b) if so requested by a German authority; or

    (c) if such person is a member of the force or of
        the civilian component of another sending
        State, or a dependent of any such member,
        upon request by an authority of that State.

0144

2. If there is danger in delay and a German public prosecutor or German police officer cannot be called in time, the military authorities of a sending State may, without a warrant of arrest, take into temporary custody a person not subject to their jurisdiction if there are strong reasons to suspect (dringender Verdacht) that such person has committed or is making a punishable attempt to commit an offence within, or directed against, an installation of that State, or an offence punishable under Article 7 of the Fourth Law Amending the Criminal Law dated 11 June 1957 (Bundesgesetzblatt Teil I, page 597) in conjunction with Sections 99, 100, 100c, 100d, 100e, 100f, 109g and 363, of the German Criminal Code, or under such legislation as may replace these provisions in future. This provision shall apply only if the person in question is a fugitive from justice or in hiding or if there are good reason to fear that he is seeking to evade criminal proceedings consequent upon the commission of such offence or punishable attempt.

3. In cases falling within paragraph 1 or 2 of this Article the military authorities may, to such extent as may be necessary, disarm the person so taken into temporary custody, and may search him and seize any items in his possession which may serve as evidence for the purpose of the investigation of the suspected or alleged offence.

4. The military authorities shall, without delay, deliver any person taken into temporary custody in accordance with this Article, together with any weapons or other items so seized, to the nearest German public prosecutor or police officer or judge or to the military authorities.

0145

of the sending State to whose force or civilian component
the person belongs either as a member or as a dependent
of such member.

5. The provisions of this Article shall not affect
the constitutional immunities of the parliaments of the
Federation and the Laender.

Article 22

1. (a) Where jurisdiction is exercised by the authorities of a sending State, custody of members of the force,
of the civilian component, or dependents shall rest with
the authorities of that State.

(b) Where jurisdiction is exercised by the German
authorities, custody of members of a force, of a civilian
component, or dependents shall rest with the authorities
of the sending State in accordance with paragraphs 2 and
3 of this article.

2. (a) Where the arrest has been made by the German
authorities, the arrested person shall be handed over to
the authorities of the sending State concerned if such
authorities so request.

(b) Where the arrest has been made by the authorities
of a sending State, or where the arrested person has
been handed over to them under subparagraph (a) of this
paragraph, they

(i) may transfer custody to the German authorities
at any time;

(ii) shall give sympathetic consideration to
any request for the transfer of custody
which may be made by the German authorities
in specific cases.

0146

(c) In respect of offences solely against the security of the Federal Republic, custody shall rest with the German authorities in accordance with such arrangements as may be made to that effect with the authorities of the sending State concerned.

3. Where custody rests with the authorities of a sending State in accordance with paragraph 2 of this Article, it shall remain with these authorities until release or acquittal by the German authorities or until commencement of the sentence. The authorities of the sending State shall make the arrested person available to the German authorities for investigation and criminal proceedings (Ermittlungs- und Strafverfahren) and shall take all appropriate measures to that end and to prevent any prejudice to the course of justice (Verdunkelungsgefahr). They shall take full account of any special request regarding custody made by the competent German authorities.

Dominica (1957)

Art. XII. Par. 2

2) Whenever military authorities of the United States of America may exercise jurisdiction over an alleged offender, the authorities of the Dominican Republic shall assist in the arrest and handing over to such authorities of such alleged offender, the collection of evidence, and the carrying out of all necessary investigations, including the issuing of citations and in proper cases the handing over of exhibits and all objects connected with the offense. All persons not subject to United States jurisdiction under this agreement who are charged with offenses committed on the sites or who are found on the site in connection with offenses

committed in the Dominican Republic shall be turned over to the Dominican authorities. In such cases the United States authorities shall assist in the collection of evidence and the carrying out of all necessary investigations and in proper cases the handing over of exhibits and all objects connected with the offense.

Greece (1956)

Art. III. Par. 1

1. In such cases where the Government of Greece may exercise criminal jurisdiction as provided for in Article II above, the United States authorities shall take custody of the accused pending completion of trial proceedings. Custody of the accused will be maintained in Greece. During the trial and pretrial proceedings the accused shall be entitled to have a representative of the United States Government present. The trial shall be public unless otherwise agreed.

Nicaragua (1958)

Ar. IX. Par. 4(c)

(c) The custody of an accused member of the United States Coast Guard over whom Nicaragua is to exercise jurisdiction shall be the responsibility of the United States of America pending completion of judicial proceedings. The United States authorities will make such an accused immediately available to the authorities of Nicaragua, upon their request, for purposes of investigation and trial.

0148

<u>Spain</u> (1953)

<u>Par. 3(d), (e) and (i)</u>

d. When United States authorities reasonably believe that the individual being detained or confined is a member of the United States Forces, the Chief, Joint United States Military Group, or his designated representative, will so certify to the Mixed Commission on Jurisdiction, (or a member thereof when the Mixed Commission on Jurisdiction is not in session) and will further request that the alleged offender be released into the custody of United States military authorities. The request will indicate the approximate time that the individual appointed to take the alleged offender into custody will present himself to the detaining authorities.

e. The Mixed Commission on Jurisdiction, or a member thereof, will honor the certification and request and will instruct the detaining or confining authority to release the alleged offender to the custody of United States military authorities.

i. If a member of the United States Forces is apprehended by United States authorities for the commission of an offense punished by Spanish laws, a report thereof and the aforementioned certifications will be submitted to the Mixed Commission on Jurisdiction immediately but the individual shall be retained in the custody of United States authorities.

8. (b) The custody of a member of the United States Forces over whom Spanish authorities are to exercise jurisdiction, because of waiver of jurisdiction by United States authorities or because the offense charged is not punishable under the Uniform Code of Military Justice, shall remain

0149

with the United States authorities until such time as the trial is concluded and the sentence pronounced. The United States authorities shall accept the responsibility of assuring the presence of the offender at the appointed time of trial.

United Kingdom (1957)
Art. VII.(1)

(1) No arrest of a person who is a member of the United States Forces or who is a national of the United States subject to the United States Uniform Code of Military Justice shall be made and no process, civil or criminal, shall be served on any such person within a Site except with the permission of the Commanding Officer in charge of the United States Forces in such Site; but should the Commanding Officer refuse to grant such permission he shall (except where, under Article V, jurisdiction is to be exercised by the United States or is not exercisable by the courts of the Bahama Islands) forthwith take the necessary steps to arrest the person charged and surrender him to the appropriate authority of the Bahama Islands or to serve such process, as the case may be, and to provide for the attendance of the server of such process before the appropriate court of the Bahama Islands or procure such server to make the necessary affidavit or declaration to prove such service.

Art. IX

Where a person charged with an offense which falls to be dealt with by the courts of the Bahama Islands is in a Site, or a person charged with an offense which falls under

0150

Article V to be dealt with by courts of the United States
in in the Bahama Isaldns but outside a Site, such person
shall be surrendered to the Government of the Bahama
Isaldns, or to the United States authorities, as the
case may be, in accordance with special arrangements
made between that Government and those authorities.

The West Indies (1961)

Art. IX. 5(c)

Unless otherwise agreed, the custody of an accused
member of the United States Forces over whom the authorities
of a Territory are to exercise jurisdiction shall, if he
is in the hands of the United States authorities, remain
with the United States authorities until he is charged.
In cases where the United States authorities may have the
responsibility for custody pending the completion of judicial
proceedings, the United States authorities shall, upon request,
make such a person immediately available to the authorities
of the Territory for purposes of investigation and trial
and shall give full consideration to any special views of
such authorities as to the way in which custody should be
maintained.

Netherlands (1951)

The U.S. assumes the responsibility for custody pending
Trial. The U.S. authorities will make these people immediately available to Netherlands authorities upon their request
for purposes of investigation and trial and will give full
attention to any other special wishes of the appropriate
Netherlands authorities as to the way in which custody
should be carried out.

0151

Japan (1960)

Same as NATO Provision (Text)

Agreed Minute Re Par. 5

1. In case the Japanese authorities have arrested an offender who is a member of the United States armed forces, the civilian component, or a dependent subject to the military law of the United States with respect to a case over which Japan has the primary right to exercise jurisdiction, the Japanese authorities will, unless they deem that there is adequate cause and necessity to retain such offender, release him to the custody of the United States military authorities provided that he shall, on request, be made available to the Japanese authorities, if such be the condition of his release. The United States authorities shall, on request, transfer his custody to the Japanese authorities at the time he is indicated by the latter.

2. The United States military authorities shall promptly notify the Japanese authorities of the arrest of any member of the United States armed forces, the civilian component or a dependent in any case in which Japan has the primary right to exercise jurisdiction.

0152

NATO (1953)

Art. VII. Par. 7(b)

(b) The authorities of the receiving State shall give sympathetic consideration to a request from the authorities of the sending State for assistance in carrying out a sentence of imprisonment pronounced by the authorities of the sending State under the provision of this Article within the territory of the receiving State.

Japan (1960)

Same as NATO Provision

Agreed Minute Re Par. 5

5. If the status of any person brought into Japan under paragraph 1 of this Article is altered so that he would no longer be entitled to such admission, the United States authorities shall notify the Japanese authorities and shall, if such person be required by the Japanese authorities to leave Japan, assure that transportation from Japan will be provided within a reasonable time at no cost to the Government of Japan.

Australia (1963)

Art. 8, Par. 7(b)

(b) The authorities of Australia shall give sympathetic consideration to a request from the military authorities of the United States for assistance in carrying out a sentence of imprisonment pronounced by the authorities of the United States under the provisions of this Article within Australia.

한·미국 간의 상호방위조약 제4조에 의한 시설과 구역 및 한국에서의 미국군대의 지위에 관한 협정(SOFA) 전59권. 1966.7.9 서울에서 서명 : 1967.2.9 발효(조약 232호) (V.56 형사재판관할권 관계자료) 345

Japan (1960)

Art. 17

10. (a) Regularly constituted military units or formations
of the United States armed forces shall have the right to
police any facilities or areas which they use under Article
II of this Agreement.

The military police of such forces may take all appropriate measure to ensure the maintenance of order and
security within such facilities and areas.

(b) Outside these facilities and areas such military
police shall be employed only subject to arrangements with
the authorities of Japan and in liaison with those authorities
and in so far as such employment is necessary to maintain
discipline and order among the members of the United States
armed forces.

Re Par. 10(a) and 10(b)

1. The United States military authorities will normally
make all arrests within facilities and areas in use by and
guarded under the authority of the United States armed forces.
This shall not preclude the Japanese authorities from making
arrests within facilities and areas in cases where the
competent authorities of the United States armed forces
have given consent, or in case of pursuit of a flagrant
offender who has committed a serious crime.

Where persons whose arrest is desired by the Japanese
authorities and who are not subject to the jurisdiction
of the United States armed forces are within facilities and
areas in use by the United States armed forces are within

0154

facilities and areas in use by the United States armed
forces, the United States military authorities will undertake,
upon request, to arrest such persons. All persons arrested
by the United States military authorities, who are not
subject to the jurisdiction of the United States armed
forces, shall immediately be turned over to the Japanese
authorities.

The United States military authorities may, under due
process of law, arrest in the vicinity of a facility or
area any person in the commission or attempted commission
of an offense against the security of that facility or area.
Any such person not subject to the jurisdiction of the
United States armed forces shall immediately be turned over
to the Japanese authorities.

2. The Japanese authorities will normally not exercise
the right of search, seizure, or inspection with respect
to any persons or property within facilities and areas
in use by and guarded under the authority of the United
States armed forces or with respect to property of the
United States armed forces wherever situated, except in
cases where the competent authorities of the United States
armed forces consent to such search, seizure, or inspection
by the Japanese authorities of such person or property.

Where search, seizure, or inspection with respect to
persons or property within facilities and areas in use by
the United States armed forces or with respect to property
of the United States armed forces in Japan is desired by
the Japanese authorities, the United States military
authorities will undertake, upon request, to make such
search, seizure, or inspection. In the event of judgment
concerning such property, except property owned or utilized

0155

by the United States Government or its instrumentalities,
the United States will turn over such property to the
Japanese authorities for disposition in accordance with
the judgment.

Germany (1959)

Art. 28

1. The military police of a force shall have the right
to patrol on public roads, on public transport, in restuarants
(Gasteatten) and in all other places to which the public
has access and to take such measures with respect to the
members of a force, of a civilian component or dependents
as are necessary to maintain order and discipline. Insofar
as it is necessary or expedient the details of the exercise
of this right shall be agreed upon between the German
authorities and the authorities of a force, who shall maintain
close mutual liaison.

2. If public order and safety are endangered or disturbed
by an incident in which members of a force or a civilian
component or dependents are involved, the military police
of a force shall, if so requested by the German authorities,
take appropriate measures with respect to such persons to
maintain or restore order and discipline.

Australia (1963)

Art. 20

1. Regularly constituted military units or formations
of the United States Forces shall have the right to police
any camps, establishments or other premises or areas of
which the United States Forces have exclusive occupation as
the result of arrangement with the Australian Government.

0156

United States military police may take all appropriate measures to ensure the maintenance of order and security in such premises or areas.

2. Outside such premises and areas, United States military police will be employed only subject to arrangements with the appropriate Australian authorities and in liaison with such appropriate Australian authorities and in so far as such employment:

a. is appropriate to provide for the protection of United States installations in premises or areas of which the United States Forces have the use, but not exclusive occupation; or

b. is necessary to maintain discipline and order among the members of the United States Forces and to ensure their security.

3. The United States Government may, after appropriate consultation in any case between the relevant authorities of the two Governments, designate areas comprising buildings or portions of buildings or installations in premises or areas of which the United States Forces have use or occupation to be areas into which only personnel authorised by the local United States Commander may enter. The United States Forces will be responsible for the internal security of areas so designated.

Dominican Rep. (1957)

Art. XIX

During the period for which this agreement remains in force, no law of the Dominican Republic which would derogate from or prejudice any of the rights conferred on the Government of the United States of America by this

한·미국 간의 상호방위조약 제4조에 의한 시설과 구역 및 한국에서의 미국군대의 지위에 관한 협정(SOFA) 전59권. 1966.7.9 서울에서 서명 : 1967.2.9 발효(조약 232호) (V.56 형사재판관할권 관계자료) 349

agreement shall be enforced within the site or other
installation except with the concurrence of the Government
of the United States of America.

Nicaragua (1958)
Art. IX

8. The United States Coast Guard shall have the right
to police any facilities or areas which it uses under the
terms of this Agreement. The authorities of the United
States Coast Guard may take all appropriate measures to
ensure the maintenance of order and security within the
Loran Site.

The West Indies (1961)
Art. IX

12. Regularly constituted military units or formation
of the United Forces shall have the right to police the
defence areas. The military police of the United States
Forces may take all appropriate measures to ensure the
maintenance of order and security within defence areas.

NATO (1953)
Art. VII.Par. 10(a)

(a) Regulary constituted military units or formations
of a force shall have the right to police any camps, establishments or other premises which they occupy as the result
of an arrangement with the receiving State. The military
police of the force may take all appropriate measures to
ensure the maintenance of order and security on such premises.

0158

(b) Outside these premises, such military police shall be employed only subject to arrangements with the authorities of the receiving State and in liaison with those authorities, and in so far as such employment is necessary to maintain discipline and order among the members of the force.

Ethiopia (1953)

Art. XVII

7. The Government of the United States shall have the right to police the Installations and to take all appropriate measures to assure the maintenance of discipline, order and security in such Installations.

8. Outside the Installations, members of the United States forces may be employed for police duties by arrangement with the appropriate authorities of the Imperial Ethiopian Government insofar as such employment is necessary to maintain discipline and order among the United States forces. In such cases, Ethiopian security forces with whom members of the United States forces may be serving on police duty shall have paramount authority with respect to the person or property of persons subject to Ethiopian jurisdiction.

Iceland (1951)

ANNEX ON THE STATUS OF UNITED STATES PERSONNEL AND PROPERTY

Art. 2 (10)

The United States forces shall have the right to police the agreed areas and to take all appropriate measures to insure the maintenance of discipline, order and security

0159

in such areas. Outside the agreed areas, military members
of the United States forces shall be employed in police
duties subject to arrangements with the authorities of Iceland
and jointly with those authorities, and insofar as such
employment is necessary to maintain discipline and order
among the members of the United States forces and the
dependents of members thereof.

The Icelandic authorities with whom members of the
United States forces may be so employed shall have paramount
authority with respect to the person or property of Icelandic
nationals and other persons of non-Icelandic nationality,
except members of the United States forces and their
dependents and non-Icelandic employees of contractors of
the United States, involved in any matter concerning the
maintenance of order and discipline referred to above
outside the agreed areas.

Libya (1954)

Art. XX. Par. (8) and (9)

(8) The Government of the United States of America will
have the right to police the agreed areas and to maintain
order therein and may arrest therein any alleged offenders
and, when they are triable by the Libyan courts, will
forthwith turn them over to the Libyan authorities for trial.

(9) Outside the agreed areas, members of the United
States forces may be employed on police duties by arrangement with the appropronte Libyan authorities. The Libyan
authorities shall be primarily responsible for the protection
of cables carrying light, power or communications to any
of the agreed areas, whether such cables are the property

0160

of the Government of the United States of America or otherwise, but they may make arrangements with the United
States authorities for the employment of members of the
United States forces for this purpose. In such cases,
the Libyan police with whom members of the United States
forces may be serving shall have paramount authority with
respect to the persons and property of persons who are
nationals of or ordinarily resident in Libya.

Philippines (1947)

Art. XIV. Par. 1

Arrest and Service of Process

1. No arrest shall be made and no process, civil or
criminal, shall be served within any base except with the
permission of the commanding officer of such base; but should
the commanding officer refuse to grant such permission
he shall (except in cases of arrest where the United States
has jurisdiction under Article XIII) forthwith take the
necessary steps to arrest the person charged and surrender
him to the appropriate authorities of the Philippines or
to serve such process, as the case may be, and to provide
the attendance of the server of such process before the
appropriate court in the Philippines or procure such server
to make the necessary affidavit or declaration to prove
such service as the case may require.

<u>German</u> (1959) .... (supplement)

<u>Art. 20</u>

1. The military authorities of a sending State may, without a warrant of arrest, take into temporary custody any person not subject to their jurisdiction.

   (a) if such person is caught or pursued in flagrante delicto and either

      (i) the identity of the person cannot be established immediately, or

      (ii) there is reason to believe that the person may flee from justice; or

   (b) if so requested by a German authority; or

   (c) if such person is a member of the force or of the civilian component of another sending State, or a dependent of any such member, upon request by an authority of that State.

2. If there is danger in delay and a German public prosecutor or German police officer cannot be called in time, the military authorities of a sending State may, without a warrant of arrest, take into temporary custody a person not subject to their jurisdiction if there are strong reasons to suspect (dringender Verdacht) that such person has committed or is making a punishable attempt to commit an offence within, or directed against, an installation of that State, or an offence punishable under Article 7 of the Fourth Law Amending the Criminal Law dated 11 June 1957 (Bundesgesetzblatt Teil 1, page 597) in conjunction with Sections 99, 100, 100c, 100d, 100e, 109f, 109g and 363, of the German Criminal Code, or under such legislation as may replace these provisions in future. This provision shall apply only if the person in question is a fugitive from

0162

justice or in hiding or if there are good reasons to fear that he is seeking to evade criminal proceedings consequent upon the commission of such offence or punishable attempt.

3. In cases falling within paragraph 1 or 2 of this Article the military authorities may, to such extent as may be necessary, disarm the person so taken into temporary custody, and may search him and seize any items in his possession which may serve as evidence for the purposes of the investigation of the suspected or alleged offence.

4. The military authorities shall, without delay, deliver any person taken into temporary custody in accordance with this Article, together with any weapons or other items so seized, to the nearest German public prosecutor or police officer or judge or to the military authorities of the sending State to whose force or civilian component the person belongs either as a member or as a dependent of such member.

5. The provisions of this Article shall not affect the constitutional immunities of the parliaments of the Federation and the Lander.

한·미국 간의 상호방위조약 제4조에 의한 시설과 구역 및 한국에서의 미국군대의 지위에 관한 협정(SOFA)
전59권. 1966.7.9 서울에서 서명 : 1967.2.9 발효(조약 232호) (V.56 형사재판관할권 관계자료) 355

<u>Custody of members of a Force, or a civilian component
or dependents.</u>

<u>Greece-U.S.</u> (Entered into force September 7, 1956)

Article 3.

(primary j.)

1. In such cases where the Government of Greece may exercise <u>criminal jurisdiction</u> as provided for in <u>Article 2</u> above, the United States authorities shall take custody of the accused pending completion of trial proceedings. Custody of the accused willlbermaintainedtinhGreece. During the trial and pretrial proceedings the accused shall be entitled to have a representative of the United States Government present. The trial shall be public unless otherwise agreed.

<u>Nicaragua-U.S. Argeement</u> for the establishment of a Loran Transmitting Station (1958)

Article 9, paragraph 4 (c)

The custody of an accused member of the United States Coast Guard over whom Nicaragua is to exercise jurisdiction shall be the responsibility of the United States of America pending completion of judicial proceedings. The United States authorities will make such an accused immediately availabæe to the authorities of Nicaragua, upon their request, for purposes of investigation and trial.

<u>West Indies—U.S. Agreement</u>

Article 9, paragraph 5 (c)

Unless oterwise agreed, the custody of an accused member of the United States Forces over whom the authorities of a Territory are to exercise jurisdiction shall, if he is in the hands of the United States authorities, remain with the United States authorities uhtil he is charged. In cases where the United States authorities may have the responsibility for custody pending the completion of judicial proceedings, the United States authorities shall, upon request, make such a person immediately available to the authorities of the Territory for purposes of investigation and trial and shall give full consideration to any special views of such authorities as to the way in which custody should be maintained.

0164

Waiver of the Primary Right

Greece-U.S. (Entered into force September 7, 1956)

Article 21

1. The Greek authorities, recognizing that it is the primary responsibility of the United States authorities to maintain good order and discipline where persons subject to United States military law are concerned, will, upon the request of the United States authorities, waive their primary right to exercise jurisdiction under Article V11, paragraph 3 (c) of that Agreement, except when they determine that it is of particular importance that jurisdiction be exercised by the Greed authorities.

2. In those cases where, in accordance with the foregoing paragraph, there is waiver of jurisdiction by the Greek authorities, the competent United States authorities shall inform the Greed Government of the disposition of each such case.

Nicaragua-U.S. Agreement for the establishment of a Loran Transmitting Station (1958)

Article 9, paragraph 3 (c)

. . . .

The authorities of Nicaragua, recognizing that it is the primary responsibility of the United States authorities to maintain good order and discipline when persons subjuect to United States military law are concerned, will, upon the request of the United States of America authorities, waive their primary right to exercise jurisdiction under this Article, except where they determine that it is of particular importance that jurisdiction be exercised bythe authorities of Nicaragua.

West Indies - U.S. Agreement conderning United States Defence Areas in the Federation of the West Indies (February 19, 1961)

Article 9, paragraph 3 (c)

. . . .

The authorities of the Territory will waive, upon request, their primary right to exercise jurisdiction under this Article, except where they in their discretion determine and notify the United States authorities that it is of particular importance that such jurisdiction be not waived.

0165

EXCLUSIVE JURISDICTION)& ITS CONCURRENCE

ICELAND (Annex)

Article 11

4. (c) If the United States or Iceland, whichever has the primary right, decides not to exercise jurisdiction, it shall notify the authorities of the United States or Iceland, as the case may be, as soon as practicable. The authorities of the United States or of Iceland, whichever has the primary right, shall give sympathetic consideration to a request from the authorities of the United States of Iceland, as the case may be, for a waiver of its rights in cases where the authorities of the other country considers such waiver to be of particular importance.

0166

JAPAN

Article XVI

3.　(c) If the State having the primary right decides not to exercise jurisdiction, it shall notify the authorities of the other State as soon as practicable. The authorities of the State having the primary right shall give sympathetic consideration to a request from the authorities of the other State for a waiver of its right in cases where that other State considers such waiver to be of particular importance.

(Agreed official minutes)

4.　Re paragraph 3 (c):

(a) Mutual procedures relating to waivers of the primary right to exercise jurisdiction shall be determined by the Joint Board. These procedures shall be similar to those adopted by the Joint Committee under the Administrative Agreement between the Government of Japan and the Government of the United States of America.

(b) Trials of cases in which the Japanese authorities have waived the primary right to exercise jurisdiction, and trials of cases involving of fences described in paragraph 3 (a) (ii) committed against the State or nationals of Japan shall be held promptly in Japan within a reasonable distance from the places where the offences are alleged to have taken place unless other arrangements are mutually agreed upon. Representatives of the Japanese authorities may be present at such trials.

0167

LIBYA

Article XX

2. In other cases the Libyan courts shall exercise jurisdiction unless the Government of the United Kingdom of Libya waives its right to exercise jurisdiction. The Government of the United Kingdom of Libya will give sympathetic consideration to any request from the United States authorities for a waiver of its right in cases where the United States authorities consider such waiver to be of particular importance, or where suitable punishment can be applied by disciplinary action without recourse to a court.

0168

Article VII

3. (c) If the State having the primary right decides not
to exercise jurisdiction, it shall notidy the
authorities of the other State as soon as
practicable. The authorities of the State having
the primary right shall give sympathetic consideration
to a request from the authorities of the State for
a waiver of its right in cases where that other State
considers such waiver to be of particular importance.

0169

AUSTRALIA

Article 8

3.   (c)   If the State having the primary right decides
not to exercise jurisdiction, it shall notify
the authorities of the other State as soon as
practicable. The authorities of the State
having the primary right shall give sympathetic
consideration to a request from the authorities
of the other state for a waiver of its right in
cases where that other state considers such waiver
to be of particular importance.

0170

DOMINICAN REPUBLIC

Article 12

(b) Except during a period of hostilities in which either Government is engaged, the Government of the United States of America and the Government of the Dominican Republic shall have concurrent jurisdiction over offenses committed outside the areas referred to in Article 11 by persons described in subparagraph (a) against a Dominican national or nationals of a third country. In each such case, the two Governments through the Mixed Military Commission provided for under Article XI shall decide which Government shall exercise jurisdiction and shall give consideration to whether the offense arose out of any act or omission done in the performance of official duties. During a period of hostilities in which either Government is engaged, the principle stated in subparagraph (a) shall apply.

0171

GREECE

Article 11

1. The Greek authorities, recognizing that it is the primary responsibility of the United States authorities to maintain good order and discipline where persons subject to United States military law are concerned, will, upon the request of the United States authorities, waive their primary right to exercise jurisdiction under Article VII, paragraph 3 (c) of that Agreement, except when they determine that it is of particular importance that jurisdiction be exercised by the Greek authorities.

0172

NICAGAGUA

Article 9

3.   (c) If the State having the primary right decides
not to exercise jurisdiction, it shall notify the
authorities of the other States as soon as practicable.
The authorities of Nicaragua, recognizing that it is the
primary responsibility of the United States authorities to
maintain good order and discipline when persons subject
to United States military law are concerned, will, upon
the request of the United States of America authorities,
waive their primary right to exercise jurisdiction under
this Article, except there they determine that it is of
particular importance that jurisdiction by exercised by the
authorities of Nicaragua.

0173

NORTH ATLANTIC TREATY

Article 7

3. (c) If the State having the primary right decides
not to exercise jurisdiction, it shall notify
the authorities of the other State as soon as
paracticable. The authorities of the State
having the primary right shall give sympathetic
consideration to a request from the authorities
of the other State for a waiver of its right
in cases where that other State considers such
waiver to be of particular importance.

0174

SPAIN

(Procedural Agreement)

8. a. In those cases where Spanish authorities desire
to prosecute a member of the United States Forces in
Spanish courts, a request for such jurisdiction, and the
reasons therefor, will be made to the Chief, Joint United
States Military Group, through the Mixed Commission on
Jurisdiction in Madrid, Spain. The Chief, Joint United
States Military Group, will give full consideration to
any request formulated by the competent Spanish authorities
and if he accedes to the request, he or his delegated
representative will execute a waiver of jurisdiction which
will confer upon Spanish authorities the right to proceed
to trial of the individual summoned.

0175

UNITED KINGDOM

Article 5

(4) In every case in which under this Article the Government of the United States of American has the right to exercise exclusive jurisdiction, the following provisions shall have effect:

(a) The United States authorities shall inform the Government of the Bahama Islands as soon as is practicable whether or not they elect to exercise subh jurisdiction over any alleged offenses which may be brought to their attention by the competent authorities of the Bahama Islands or in any other case in which the United States authorities are requested by the competent authorities of the Bahama Islands to furnish such information.

0176

WEST INDIES

Article 9

3. (c) If the authorities having the primary right
decide not to exercise jurisdiction, they shall
notify the other authorities as soon as
practicable. The United States authorities shall
give sympathetic consideration to a request from
the authorities of the Territory for a waiver of
their primary right in cases where the authorities
of the Territory consider such waiver to be of
particular importance. The authorities of the
Territory will waive, upon request, their primary
right to exercise jurisdiction under this Article,
except where they in their discretion determine
and notify the United States authorities that it
is of particular importance that such jurisdiction
be not waived.

0177

<u>Waiver of the Primary Right</u>

ICELAND (Annex)

Article 11

4.   (c) If the United States or Iceland, whichever has the :r primary right, decides not to exercise jurisdiction, it shall notify the authorities of the United States or Iceland, as the case may be, as soon as practicable. The authoritites of the United States or of Iceland, whichever has the primary right, shall give sympathetic consideration to a request from the authorities of the United States of Iceland, as the case may be, for a waiver of its rights in cases where the authorities of the other country considers such waiver to be of particular importance.

0178

Article XVI

3.   (c) If the State having the primary right decides not to exercise jurisdiction, it shall notify the authorities of the other State as soon as practicable. The authorities of the State having the primary right shall give sympathetic consideration to a request from the authorities of the other State for a waiver of its right in cases where that other State considers such waiver to be of particular importance.

(Agreed official minutes)

4.   Re paragraph 3 (c):

(a) Mutual procedures relating to waivers of the primary right to exercise jurisdiction shall be determined by the Joint Board. These procedures shall be similar to those adopted by the Joint Committee under the Administrative Agreement between the Government of Japan and the Government of the United States of America.

(b) Trials of cases in which the Japanese authorities have waived the primary right to exercise jurisdiction, and trials of cases involving offences described in paragraph 3 (a) (ii) committed against the State or nationals of Japan shall be held promptly in Japan within a reasonable distance from the places where the offences are alleged to have taken place unless other arrangements are mutually agreed upon. Representatives of the Japanese authorities may be present

0179

at such trials.

0180

LIBYA

Article XX

2. In other cases the Libyan courts shall exercise
jurisdiction unless the Government of the United Kingdom
of Libya waives its right to exercise jurisdiction. The
Government of the United Kingdom of Libya will give sympathetic
consideration to any request from the United States authorities
for a waiver of its right in cases where the United States
authorities consider such waiver to be of particular importance,
or where suitable punishment can be applied by disciplinary
action without recourse to a court.

0181

NATO

Article VII

3.   (c) If the State having the primary right decides not
to exercise jurisdiction, it shall notidy the
authorities of the other State as soon as
practicable. The authorities of the State having
the primary right shall give sympathetic consideration
to a request from the authorities of the State for
a waiver of its right in cases where that other State
considers such waiver to be of particular importance.

0182

AUSTRALIA

Article 8

3. (c) If the State having the primary right decides
    not to exercise jurisdiction, it shall notify
    the authorities of the other State as soon as
    practicable. The authorities of the State
    having the primary right shall give sympathetic
    consideration to a request from the authorities
    of the other state for a waiver of its right in
    cases where that other state considers such waiver to
    be of particular importance.

0183

DOMINICAN REPUBLIC

Article 12

(b) Except during a period of hostilities in which
either Government is engaged, the Government of
the United States of America and the Government
of the Dominican Republic shall have concurrent
jurisdiction over offenses committed outside the
areas referred to in Article 11 by persons described
in subparagraph (a) against a Dominican national or
nationals of a third country. In each such case, the
two Governments through the Mixed Military Commission
provided for under Article XI shall decide which
Government shall exercise jurisdiction and shall give
consideration to whether the offense arose out of any
act or omission done in the performance of official
duties. During a period of hostilities in which
either Government is engaged, the principle stated in
subparagraph (a) shall apply.

0184

GREECE

Article 11

1. The Greek authorities, recognizing that it is the primary responsibility of the United States authorities to maintain good order and discipline where persons subject to United States military law are concerned, will, upon the request of the United States authorities, waive their primary right to exercise jurisdiction under Article VII, paragraph 3 (c) of that Agreement, except when they determine that it is of particular importance that jurisdiction be exercised by the Greek authorities.

0185

NICAGAGUA

Article 9

3.   (c) If the State having the primary right decides
not to exercise jurisdiction, it shall notify the
authorities of the other States as soon as practicable.
The authorities of Nicaragua, recognizing that it is the
primary responsibility of the United States authorities to
maintain good order and discipline when persons subject
to United States military law are concerned, will, upon
the request of the United States of America authorities,
waive their primary right to exercise jurisdiction under
this Article, except there they determine that it is of
particular importance that jurisdiction by exercised by the
authorities of Nicaragua.

0186

NORTH ATLANTIC TREATY

Article 7

3.　(c) If the State having the primary right decides
not to exercise jurisdiction, it shall notify
the authorities of the other State as soon as
paracticable. The authorities of the State
having the primary right shall give sympathetic
consideration to a request from the authorities
of the other State for a waiver of its right
in cases where that other State considers such
waiver to be of particular importance.

0187

SPAIN

(Procedural Agreement)

8. a. In those cases where Spanish authorities desire to prosecute a member of the United States Forces in Spanish courts, a request for such jurisdiction, and the reasons therefor, will be made to the Chief, Joint United States Military Group, through the Mixed Commission on Jurisdiction in Madrid, Spain. The Chief, Joint United States Military Group, will give full consideration to any request formulated by the competent Spanish authorities and if he accedes to the request, he or his delegated representative will execute a waiver of jurisdiction which will confer upon Spanish authorities the right to proceed to trial of the individual summoned.

0188

UNITED KINGDOM

Article 5

(4) In every case in which under this Article the
Government of the United States of American has the right
to exercise exclusive jurisdiction, the following provisions
shall have effect:

(a) The United States authorities shall inform the
Government of the Bahama Islands as soon as is practicable
whether or not they elect to exercise such jurisdiction
over any alleged offenses which may be brought to their
attention by the competent authorities of the Bahama
Islands or in any other case in which the United States
authorities are requested by the competent authorities
of the Bahama Islands to furnish such information.

0189

Article XIII

JURISDICTION

1. The Philippines consents that the United States shall have the right to exercise jurisdiction over the following offenses:

(a) Any offense committed by any person within any base except where the offender and offended parties are both Philippine citizens (not members of the armed forces of the United States on active duty) or the offense is against the security of the Philippines;

(b) Any offense committed outside the bases by any member of the armed forces of the United States in which the offended party is also a member of the armed forces of the United States; and

(c) Any offense committed outside the bases by any member of the armed forces of the United States against the security of the United States.

2. The Philippines shall have the right to exercise jurisdiction over all other offenses committed outside the bases by any member of the armed forces of the United States.

3. Whenever for special reasons the United States may desire not to exercise the jurisdiction reserved to it in paragraphs 1 and 6 of this Article, the officer holding the offender in custody shall so notify the fiscal (prosecuting attorney) of the city or province in which the offense has been committed within ten days after his arrest, and in such a case the Philippines shall exercise jurisdiction.

4. Whenever for special reasons the Philippines may desire not to exercise the jurisdiction reserved to it in paragraph 2 of this Article, the fiscal (prosecuting attorney) of the city or province where the

- 1 -

offense has been committed shall so notify the officer holding the offender in custody within ten days after his arrest, and in such a case the United States shall be free to exercise jurisdiction. If any offense falling under paragraph 2 of this Article is committed by any member of the armed forces of the United States:

(a) while engaged in the actual performance of a specific military duty, or

(b) during a period of national emergency declared by either Government and the fiscal (prosecuting attorney) so finds from the evidence, he shall immediately notify the officer holding the offender in custody that the United States is free to exercise jurisdiction. In the event the fiscal (prosecuting attorney) finds that the offense was not committed in the actual performance of a specific military duty, the offender's commanding officer shall have the right to appeal from such finding to the Secretary of Justice within ten days from the receipt of the decision of the fiscal and the decision of the Secretary of Justice shall be final.

5. In all cases over which the Philippines exercises jurisdiction the custody of the accused, pending trial and final judgement, shall be entrusted without delay to the commanding officer of the nearest base, who shall acknowledge in writing that such accused has been delivered to him for custody pending trial in a competent court of the Philippines and that he will be held ready to appear and will be produced before said court when required by it. The commanding officer shall be furnished by the fiscal (prosecuting attorney) with a copy of the information against the accused upon the filing of the original in the competent court.

6. Notwithstanding the foregoing provisions, it is mutually agreed that in time of war the United States shall have the right to

- 2 -

exercise exclusive jurisdiction over any offenses which may be committed
by members of the armed forces of the United States in the Philippines.

7. The United States agrees that it will not grant asylum in
any of the bases to any person fleeing from the lawful jurisdiction
of the Philippines. Should any such person be found in any base, he
will be surrendered on demand to the competent authorities of the
Philippines.

8. In every case in which jurisdiction over an offense is
exercised by the United States, the offended party may institute a
separate civil action against the offender in the proper court to the
Philippines to enforce the civil liability which under the laws of
the Philippines may arise from the offense,

Article XIV
ARREST AND SERVICE OF PROCESS

1. No arrest shall be made and no process, civil or criminal,
shall be served within any base except with the permission of the
commanding officer refuse to grant such permission he shall (except
in cases of arrest where the United States has jurisdiction under
Article XIII) forthwith take the necessary steps to arrest the person
charged and surrender him to the appropriate authorities of the Philippines
or to serve such process, as the case may be, and to provide the attendance
of the server of such process before the appropriate court in the
Philippines or procure such server to make the necessary affidavit or
declaration to prove such service as the case may require.

2. In cases where the service courts of the United States have
jurisdiction under Article XIII, the appropriate authorities of the
Philippines will, on request, give reciprocal facilities as regards the
service of process and the arrest and surrender of alleged offenders.

- 3 -

0192

U.S.-ETHIOPIA

1953

Article XVII

1. Members of the United States forces shall respect the laws of Ethiopian and abstain from any activities inconsistent with the spirit of this Agreement. The Government of the United States shall take appropriate measures to this end.

2. The United States military authorities shall have the right to exercise within Ethiopia all jurisdiction and control over United States forces conferred on the United States military authorities by the laws and regulations of the United States, except as limited by this Article.

3. Members of the United States forces shall be immune from the criminal jurisdiction of Ethiopian courts, and, in matters arising from the performance of their official duties, from the civil jurisdiction of Ethiopian courts, provided that, in particular cases, the United States authorities may waive such immunity. In all other cases, Ethiopian courts shall have jurisdiction.

4. Whenever United States authorities exercise jurisdiction or control pursuant to paragraph 2 of this Article, the judicial proceedings shall be conducted within the Installations or outside of Ethiopia. In such cases the appropriate authorities of the Imperial Ethiopian Government shall, upon request, assist in the collection of evidence and in the carrying out of all necessary investigations. Necessary arrangements will be made by the appropriate authorities of Ethiopia to secure the presence of Ethiopian nationals and other persons in Ethiopia (except members of the United States forces) as witnesses for official investigations and for military tribunals, and, in appropriate cases,

- 4 -

0193

to seize and hand over evidence, exhibits and objects connected with the offense. The United States authorities shall, in like United States forces and assist the Ethiopian authorities in the case of an offense to be tried in the Ethiopian courts.

5. Ethiopian authorities may arrest members of the United States forces outside the Installations for the commission or attempted commission of an offense, but, in the event of such an arrest, the member or members shall be immediately turned over to the United States authorities. Except for Ethiopian nationals and other persons normally resident in Ethiopia, any person fleeing from the jurisdiction of the United States forces and found in any place outside the Installations may, on request, be arrested by the Ethiopian authorities and turned over to the United States authorities.

6. The United States authorities shall deliver to the Ethiopian authorities for trial and punishment all Ethiopian nationals and other persons normally resident in Ethiopia who have been charged by the Ethiopian or the United States authorities with having committed offenses within the limits of the Installations.

7. The Government of the United States shall have the right to police the Installations and to take all appropriate measures to assure the maintenance of discipline, order and security in such Installations.

8. Outside the Installations, members of the United States forces may be employed for police duties by arrangement with the appropriate authorities of the Imperial Ethiopian Government insofar as such employment is necessary to maintain discipline and other among the United States forces. In such cases, Ethiopian security forces with whom members of the United States forces may be serving on police duty shall have paramount authority with respect to the person or property of persons subject to Ethiopian jurisdiction.

- 5 -

0194

9. Each Government undertakes that persons subject to the jurisdiction of its courts who commit contempt or perjury in connection with courts-martial proceedings or proceedings of other military tribunals, shall be subjected to appropriate punitive action by its courts.

10. The Imperial Ethiopian Government undertakes to establish such measures of control or zones of access adjacent to such Installations as may, from time to time, in the opinion of the two Governments be essential for maintenance of the internal and external security of the Installations as well as the sanitation and health conditions of those Installations.

한·미국 간의 상호방위조약 제4조에 의한 시설과 구역 및 한국에서의 미국군대의 지위에 관한 협정(SOFA)
전59권. 1966.7.9 서울에서 서명 : 1967.2.9 발효(조약 232호) (V.56 형사재판관할권 관계자료) 387

Criminal Jurisdiction

Article XVII

1. Subject to the provisions of this Article,

(a) the military authorities of the United States shall have the right to exercise within Japan all criminal and disciplinary jurisdiction conferred on them by the law of the United States over all persons subject to the military law of the United States;

(b) the authorities of Japan shall have jurisdiction over the members of the United States armed forces, the civilian component, and their dependents with respect to offenses committed within the territory of Japan and punishable by the law of Japan.

2. (a) The military authorities of the United States shall have the right to exercise exclusive jurisdiction over persons subject to the military law of the United States with respect to offenses, including offenses relating to its security, punishable by the law of the United States, but not by the law of Japan.

(b) The authorities of Japan shall have the right to exercise exclusive jurisdiction over members of the United States armed forces, the civilian component, and their dependents with respect to offenses, including offenses relating to the security of Japan, punishable by its law but not by the law of the United States.

(c) For the purposes of this paragraph and of paragraph 3 of this Article a security offense against a State shall include

(i) treason against the State;

(ii) sabotage, espionage or violation of any law relating to official secrets of that State, or secrets relating

- 7 -

0196

to the national defense of that State.

3. In cases where the right to exercise jurisdiction is concurrent the following rules shall apply:

(a) The military authorities of the United States shall have the primary right to exercise jurisdiction over members of the United States armed forces or the civilian component in relation to

(i) offenses solely against the property or security of the United States, or offenses solely against the person or property of another member of the United States armed forces or the civilian component or of a dependent;

(ii) offenses arising out of any act or omission done in the performance of official duty.

(b) In the case of any other offense the authorities of Japan shall have the primary right to exercise jurisdiction.

(c) If the State having the primary right decides not to exercise jurisdiction, it shall notify the authorities of the other State as soon as practicable. The authorities of the State having the primary right shall give sympathetic consideration to a request from the authorities of the other State for a waiver of its right in cases where that other State considers such waiver to be of particular importance.

4. The foregoing provisions of this Article shall not imply any right for the military authorities of the United States to exercise jurisdiction over persons who are nationals of or ordinarily resident in Japan, unless they are members of the United States armed forces.

5. (a) The military authorities of the United States and the authorities of Japan shall assist each other in the arrest of members of the United States armed forces, the civilian component, or their

한·미국 간의 상호방위조약 제4조에 의한 시설과 구역 및 한국에서의 미국군대의 지위에 관한 협정(SOFA) 전59권. 1966.7.9 서울에서 서명 : 1967.2.9 발효(조약 232호) (V.56 형사재판관할권 관계자료) 389

dependents in the territory of Japan and in handing them over to the authority which is to exercise jurisdiction in accordance with the above provisions.

(b) The authorities of Japan shall notify promptly the military authorities of the United States of the arrest of any member of the United States armed forces, the civilian component, or a dependent.

(c) The custody of an accused member of the United States armed forces or the civilian component over whom Japan is to exercise jurisdiction shall, if he is in the hands of the United States, remain with the United States until he is charged by Japan.

6. (a) The military authorities of the United States and the authorities of Japan shall assist each other in the carrying out of all necessary investigations into offenses, and in the collection and production of evidence, including the seizure and, in proper cases, the handing over of objects connected with an offense. The handing over of such objects may, however, be made subject to their return within the time specified by the authority delivering them.

(b) The military authorities of the United States and the authorities of Japan shall notify each other of the disposition of all cases in which there are concurrent rights to exercise jurisdiction.

7. (a) A death sentence shall not be carried out in Japan by the military authorities of the United States if the legislation of Japan does not provide for such punishment in a similar case.

(b) The authorities of Japan shall give sympathetic consideration to a request from the military authorities of the United States for assistance in carrying out a sentence of imprisonment pronounced by the military authorities of the United States under the provisions of this Article within the territory of Japan.

8. Where an accused has been tried in accordance with the provisions

- 9 -

0198

of this Article either by the military authorities of the United
States or the authorities of Japan and has been acquitted, or has been
convicted and is serving, or has served, his sentence or has been
pardoned, he may not be tried again for the same offense within the
territory of Japan by the authorities of the other State. However, nothing
in this paragraph shall prevent the military authorities of the United
States from trying a member of its armed forces for any violation
of rules of discipline arising from an act or omission which constituted
an offense for which he was tried by the authorities of Japan.

9. Whenever a member of the United States armed forces, the
civilian component or a dependent is prosecuted under the jurisdiction
of Japan he shall be entitled:

(a) to a prompt and speedy trial,

(b) to be informed, in advance of trial, of the specific charge
or charges made against him,

(c) to be confronted with the witnesses against him,

(d) to have compulsory process for obtaining witnesses in his
favor, if they are within the jurisdiction of Japan,

(e) to have legal representation of his own choice for his
defense or to have free or assisted legal representation under the
conditions prevailing for the time being in Japan;

(f) if he considers it necessary, to have the services of
a competent interpreter, and

(g) to communicate with a representative of the Government
of the United States and to have such a representative present at his
trial.

10. (a) Regularly constituted military units or formations of the
United States armed forces shall have the right to police any facilities
or areas which they use under Article II of this Agreement.

- 10 -

0199

The military police of such forces may take all appropriate measu
to ensure the maintenance of order and security within such facilities
and areas.

(b) Outside these facilities and areas such military police
shall be employed only subject to arrangements with the authorities
of Japan and in liaison with those authorities and in so far as such
employment is necessary to maintain discipline and order among the
members of the United States armed forces.

11. In the event of hostilities to which the provisions of Article
V of the Treaty of Mutual Cooperation and Security apply, either the
Government of the United States or the Government of Japan shall have
the right, by giving sixty days notice to the other, to suspend the
application of any of the provisions of this Article. If this right is
exercised, the Governments of the United States and Japan shall
immediately consult with a view to agreeing on suitable provisions to r
place the provisions suspended.

12. The provisions of this Article shall not apply to any offenses
committed before the entry into force of this Agreement. Such cases
shall be governed by the provisions of Article XVII of the Administrative Agreement under Article III of the Security Treaty between the
United States of America and Japan, as it existed at the relevant time.

Agreed Minutes

Article XVII

Re paragraph 1 (a) and paragraph 2(a)
The scope of persons subject to the military laws of the United
States shall be communicated, through the Joint Committee, to the
Government of Japan by the Government of the United States.

- 11 -

0200

Re paragraph 2(c)

Both Governments shall inform each other of the details of all security offenses mentioned in this subparagraph and the provisions ing such offenses in the existing laws of their respective countries

Re paragraph 3 (a) (ii):

Where a member of the United States armed forces or the civilian component is charged with an offense, a certificate issued by or on behalf of his commanding officer stating that the alleged offense, if committed by him, arose out of an act or omission done in the performance of official duty, shall, in any judicial proceedings, be sufficient evidence of the fact unless the contrary is proved.

The above statement shall not be interpreted to prejudice in any way Article 318 of the Japanese Code of Criminal Procedure.

Re paragraph 3(c)

1. Mutual procedures relating to waivers of the primary right to exercise jurisdiction shall be determined by the Joint Committee.

2. Trials of cases in which the Japanese authorities have waived the primary right to exercise jurisdiction, and trials of cases involving offenses described in paragraph 3 (a) (ii) committed against the State or nationals of Japan shall be held primly in Japan within a reasonable distance from the places where the offenses a alleged to have taken place unless other arrangements are mutually agre upon. Representatives of the Japanese authorities may be present at suc trials.

Re paragraph 4

Dual nationals, United States and Japanese, who are subject to the military law of the United States and are brought to Japan by the United States shall not be considered as nationals of Japan, but shall be considered as United States nationals for the purpose of this paragraph.

- 12 -

0201

Re paragraph 5

1. In case the Japanese authorities have arrested an offender who is a member of the United States armed forces, the civilian component, or a dependent subject to the military law of the United States with respect to a case over which Japan has the primary right to exercise jurisdiction, the Japanese authorities will, unless they deem that there is adequate cause and necessity to retain such offender, release him to the custody of the United States military authorities provided that he shall, on request, be made availabl to the Japanese authorities, if such be the condition of his release. The United States authorities shall, on request, transfer his custody to the Japanese authorities at the time he is indicated by the latter.

2. The United States military authorities shall promptly notify the Japanese authorities of the arrest of any member of the United States armed forces, the civilian component or a dependent in any case in which Japan has the primary right to exercise jurisdiction.

Re paragraph 9

1. The rights enumerated in items (a) through (e) of this paragraph are guaranteed to all persons on trial in Japanese courts by the provisions of the Japanese Constitution. In addition to these rights, a member of the United States armed forces, the civilian component or a dependent who is prosecuted under the jurisdiction of Japan shall have such other rights as are guaranteed under the laws of Japan to all persons on trial in Japanese courts. Such additional rights include the following which are guaranteed under the Japanese Constitution:

(a) He shall not be arrested or detained without being at once informed of the charge against him or without the immediate privilege of counsel; nor shall he be detained without adequate cause; and upon demand of any person such cause must be immediately shown in open court in his presence and the presence of his counsel;

- 13 -

0202

(b) He shall enjoy the right to a public trial by an impartial tribunal;

(c) He shall not be compelled to testify against himself;

(d) He shall be permitted full opportunity to examine all witnesses;

(e) No cruel punishments shall be imposed upon him.

2. The United States authorities shall have the right upon request to have access at any time to members of the United States armed forces, the civilian component, or their dependents who are confined or detained under Japanese authority.

3. Nothing in the provisions of paragraph 9(g) concerning the presence of a representative of the United States Government at the trial of a member of the United States armed forces, the civilian component or a dependent prosecuted under the jurisdiction of Japan, shall be so constructed as to prejudice the provisions of the Japanese Constitution with respect to public trials.

Re paragraphs 10(a) and 10(b)

1. The United States military authorities will normally make all arrests within facilities and areas in use by and guarded under the authority of the United States armed forces. This shall not preclude the Japanese authorities from making arrests within facilities and areas in cases where the competent authorities of the United States armed forces have given consent, or in case of pursuit of a flagrant offender who has committed a serious crime.

Where persons whose arrest is desired by the Japanese authorities and who are not subject to the jurisdiction of the United States armed forces are within facilities and areas in use by the United States armed forces are within facilities and areas in use by the United States armed forces, the United States military authorities will undertake, upon request, to arrest such persons. All persons arrested by the United

0203

States military authorities, who are not subject to the jurisdiction of the United States armed forces, shall immediately be turned over to the Japanese authorities.

The United States military authorities may, under due process of law, arrest in the vicinity of a facility or area any person in the commission or attempted commission of an offense against the security of that facility or area. Any such person not subject to the jurisdiction of the United States States armed forces shall immediately be turned over to the Japanese authorities.

2. The Japanese authorities will normally not exercise the right of search, seizure, or inspection with respect to any persons or property within facilities and areas in use by and guarded under the authority of the United States armed forces or with respect to property of the United States armed forces wherever situated, except in cases where the competent authorities of the United States armed forces consent to such search, seizure, or inspection by the Japanese authorities of such person or property.

Where search, seizure, or inspection with respect to persons or property within facilities and areas in use by the United States armed forces or with respect to property of the United States armed forces in Japan is desired by the Japanese authorities, the United States military authorities will undertake, upon request, to make such search, seizure, or inspection. In the event of judgment concerning such property, except property owned or utilized by the United States Government or its instrumentalities, the United States will turn over such property to the Japanese authorities for disposition in accordance with the judgment.

- 15 -

N A T O

August 23, 1953

Criminal Jurisdiction

Article VII

1. Subject to the provisions of this Article,

(a) the military authorities of the sending State shall have the right to exercise within the receiving State all criminal and disciplinary jurisdiction conferred on them by the law of the sending State over all persons subject to the military law of the State;

(b) the authorities of the receiving State shall have jurisdiction over the members of a force or civilian component and their dependents with respect to offences committed within the territory of the receiving State and punishable by the law of that State.

2 (a) The military authorities of the sending State shall have the right to exercise exclusive jurisdiction over persons subject to offences, including offences relating to its security, punishable by the law of the sending State, but not by the law of the receiving State.

(b) The authorities of the receiving State shall have the right to exercise exclusive jurisdiction over a members of a force or civilian component and their dependents with respect to offences, including offences relating to the security of that State, punishable by its law but not by the law of the sending State.

(c) For the purposes of this paragraph and of paragraph 3 of this Article a security offence against a State shall include

(i) treason against the State;

(ii) sabotage, espionage or violation or any relating to official secrets of that State, or secrets relating to the national defence of that State.

한·미국 간의 상호방위조약 제4조에 의한 시설과 구역 및 한국에서의 미국군대의 지위에 관한 협정(SOFA)
전59권. 1966.7.9 서울에서 서명 : 1967.2.9 발효(조약 232호) (V.56 형사재판관할권 관계자료) 397

3. In cases where the right to exercise jurisdiction is concurrent the following rules shall apply:

(a) The military authorities of the sending State shall have the primary right to exercise jurisdiction over a member of a force or of a civilian component in relation to

(i) offences solely against the property or security of that State, or offences solely against the person or property of another member of the force or civilian component of that State or of a dependent;

(ii) offences arising out of any act or omission done in the performance of official duty.

(b) In the case of any other offence the authorities of the receiving State shall have the primary right to exercise jurisdiction.

(c) If the State having the primary right decides not to exercise jurisdiction, it shall notify the authorities of the other State as soon as practicable. The authorities of the State having the primary right shall give sympathetic consideration to a request from the authorities of the State for a waiver of its right in cases where that other State considers such waiver to be of particular importance.

4. The foregoing provisions of this Article shall not imply any right for the military authorities of the sending State to exercise jurisdiction over persons who are nationals of or ordinarily resident in the receiving State, unless they are members of the force of the sending State.

5. (a) The authorities of the receiving and sending States shall assist each other in the arrest of members of a force or civilian component or their dependents in the territory of the receiving State and in handing them over to the authority which is to exercise jurisdiction in accordance with the above provisions.

7

0206

(b) The authorities of the receiving State shall notify promptly the military authorities of the sending State of the arrest of any member of a force or civilian component or a dependent.

(c) The custody of an accused member of a force or civilian component over whom the receiving State is to exercise jurisdiction shall, if he is in the hands of the sending State, remain with that State until he is charged by the receiving State.

6. (a) The authorities of the receiving and sending State shall assist each other in the carrying out of all necessary investigation into offences, and in the collection and production of evidence, including the seizure and, in proper cases, the handing over of objects connected with an offence. The handing over of such objects may, however, be made subject to their return within the time specified by the authority delivering them.

(b) The authorities of the Contracting Parties shall notify one another of the disposition of all cases in which they are concurrent rights to exercise jurisdiction.

7. (a) A death sentence shall not be carried out in the receiving State by the authorities of the sending State if the legislation of the receiving State does not provide for such punishment in a similar case.

(b) The authorities of the receiving State shall give sympathetic consideration to a request from the authorities of the sending State for assistance in carrying out a sentence of imprisenment pronounced by the authorities of the sending State under the provision of this Article within the territory of the receiving State.

8. Where an accused has been tried in accordance with the previsions of this Article by the authorities of one Contracting Party and has been acquitted, or has been convicted and is serving, or has serve, his sentence or has been pardoned, he may not be tried again for the same offence within the same territory by the authorities of another

- 18 -

0207

Contracting Party. However, nothing in this paragraph shall prevent the military authorities of the sending State from trying a member of its force for any violation of rules of discipline arising from an act or omission which constituted an offence for which he has tried by the authorities of another Contracting Party.

9. Whenever a member of a force or civilian component or a dependent is prosecuted under the jurisdiction of a receiving State he shall be entitled--

(a) to a prompt and speedy trial

(b) to be informed, in advance c or charges made against him;

(c) to be confronted with the witnesses against him;

(d) to have compulsory process for obtaining witnesses in his favour, if they are within the jurisdiction of the receiving State;

(e) to have legal representation of his own choice for his defence or to have free or assisted legal representation under the conditions prevailing for the time being in the receiving State;

(f) if he considers it necessary, to have the services of a competent interpreter; and

(g) to communicate with a representative of the Government of the sending State and, when the rules of the court permit, to have such a representative present at his trial.

10. (a) Regulary constituted military units or formations of a force shall have the right to police any camps, establishments or other premises which they occupy as the result of an arrangement with the receiving State. The military police of the force may take all appropriate measures to ensure the maintenance of order and security on such premises.

(b) Outside these premises, such military police shall be employed only subject to arrangements with the authorities of the receiving State and in liaison with those authorities, and in so far as such employment is necessary to maintain discipline and order among the members of the force.

11. Each Contracting Party shall seek such legislation as it deems necessary to ensure the adequate security and protection within its territory of installations, equipment, property, records and official information of other Contracting Parties, and the punishment of persons who may contravene laws enacted for that purpose.

한·미국 간의 상호방위조약 제4조에 의한 시설과 구역 및 한국에서의 미국군대의 지위에 관한 협정(SOFA)
전59권. 1966.7.9 서울에서 서명 : 1967.2.9 발효(조약 232호) (V.56 형사재판관할권 관계자료) 401

ARTICLE 17

Criminal Jurisdiction

1. Where, in order to decide upon the authority
competent to exercise jurisdiction with respect to an
offence, it is necessary to determine whether an act is
punishable by the law of a sending State, the German court
or authority dealing with the case shall suspend the
proceedings and shall notify the competent authority of
the sending State. The appropriate authority of the sending
State may, within twenty-one days after receipt of the
notification, or at any time if such notification has
not yet been made, submit to the German court or authority
a certificate stating whether or not the act is punishable
by the law of the sending State. If the certificate is
affirmative on this point, it shall specify the provision
or legal basis under which the act is punishable, as well
as the penalty prescribed.

2. The German court or authority shall make its
decision in conformity with the certificate. In exceptional
cases, however, such certificate may, at the request of
the German court or authority, be made the subject of
review through discussions between the Federal Government
and the diplomatic mission in the Federal Republic of
the sending State.

3. If it is to be determined whether an offence is
punishable under German law, the procedure provided in

- 1 -

0210

paragraphs 1 and 2 of this Article shall apply mutatis mutandis with respect to the offence, the certificate being then issued by the supreme competent administrative authority of the Federal Republic or of the German Land concerned.

4. The provisions of paragraph 1, 2 and 3 of this Article shall not apply as between the Federal Republic and any sending State which informs the Federal Republic that it does not intend to avail itself of these provisions or to extend the benefits thereof to the Federal Republic.

ARTICLE 18

1. Whenever, in the course of criminal proceedings against a member of a force or of a civilian component, it becomes necessary to determine whether an offence has arisen out of any act or omission done in the performance of official duty, such determination shall be made in accordance with the law of the sending State Concerned. The highest appropriate authority of such sending State may submit to the German court or authority dealing with the case a certificate thereon.

2. The German court or authority shall make its decision in conformity with the certificate. In exceptional cases, however, such certificate may, at the request of the German court or authority, be made the subject of review through discussions between the Federal Government and the diplomatic mission in the Federal Republic of the sending State.

- 2 -

ARTICLE 19

1. At the request of a sending State, the Federal Republic shall, within the framework of sub-paragraph (c) of paragraph 3 of Article VII of the NATO Status of Forces Agreement, waive in favour of that State the primary right granted to the German authorities under sub-paragraph (b) of paragraph 3 of that Article in cases of concurrent jurisdiction, in accordance with paragraph 2, 3, 4, and 7 of this Article.

2. Subject to any particular arrangements which may be made under paragraph 7 of this Article, the military authorities of the sending States shall notify the competent German authorities of individual cases falling under the waiver provided in paragraph 1.

3. Where the competent German authorities hold the view that, by reason of special circumstances in a specific case, major interests of German administration of justice make imperative the exercise of German jurisdiction, they may recall the waiver granted under paragraph 1 of this Article by a statement to the competent military authorities within a period of twenty-one days after receipt of the notification envisaged in paragraph 2 or any shorter period which may be provided in arrangements made under paragraph 7. The German authorities may also submit the statement prior to receipt of such notification.

4. If, pursuant to paragraph 3 of this Article, the competent German authorities have recalled the waiver in a specific case and in such case an understanding cannot be reached in discussions between the authorities concerned,

-- 3 --

0212

the diplomatic mission in the Federal Republic of the sending State concerned may make representations to the Federal Government. The Federal Government, giving due consideration to the interests of German administration of justice and to the interests of the sending State, shall resolve the disagreement in the exercise of its authority in the field of foreign affairs.

5. (a) With the consent of the German authorities, the military authorities of a sending State which has requested the waiver under paragraph 1 of this Article may transfer to the German courts or authorities for investigation, trial and decision, particular criminal cases in which jurisdiction rests with that State.

(b) With consent of the military authorities of a sending State which has requested the waiver under paragraph 1 of this Article, the German authorities may transfer to the military authorities of that State for investigation, trial and decision, particular criminal cases in which jurisdiction rests with the Federal Republic.

6. (a) Where a German court or authority exercise exclusive jurisdiction under sub-paragraph (b) of paragraph 2 of Article VII of the NATO Status of Forces Agreement, a copy of any document served on the accused shall be delivered, upon special or general request of the sending State concerned, to the liaison agency referred to in Article 32 of the present Agreement.

(b) The liaison Agency shall lend its assistance to the German courts and authorities to facilitate service of process in criminal matters.

- 4 -

0213

7. In the implementation of the provisions of this Article and to facilitate the expeditious disposal of offences of minor importance, arrangements may be made between the military authorities of a sending State or States and the competent German authorities. These arrangements may also extend to dispensing with notification and to the period of time referred to in paragraph 3 of this Article within which the waiver may be recalled.

ARTICLE 20

1. The military authorities of a sending State may, without a warrant of arrest, take into temporary custody any person not subject to their jurisdiction.

(a) if such person is caught or pursued in flagrante delicto and either

(i) the identity of the person cannot be established immediately, or

(ii) there is reason to believe that the person may flee from justice; or

(b) if so requested by a German authority; or

(c) if such person is a member of the force or of the civilian component of another sending State, or a dependent of any such member, upon request by an authority of that State.

2. If there is danger in delay and a German public prosecutor or German police officer cannot be called in time, the military authorities of a sending State may, without a warrant of arrest, take into temporary custody a person not subject to their jurisdiction if there are

- 5 -

0214

strong reasons to suspect (dringender Verdacht) that such person has committed or is making a punishable attempt to commit an offence within, or directed against, an installation of that State, or an offence punishable under Article 7 of the Fourth Law Amending the Criminal Law dated 11 June 1957 (Bundesgesetzblatt Teil I, page 597) in conjunction with Sections 99,100, 100c, 100d, 100e, 100f, 109g and 363, of the German Criminal Code, or under such legislation as may replace these provisions in future. This provision shall apply only if the person in question is a fugitive from justice or in hiding or if there are good reason to fear that he is seeking to evade criminal proceedings consequent upon the commission of such offence or punishable attempt.

3. In cases falling within paragraph 1 or 2 of this Article the military authorities may, to such extent as may be necessary, disarm the person so taken into temporary custody, and may search him and seize any items in his possession which may serve as evidence for the purpose of the investigation of the suspected or alleged offence.

4. The military authorities shall, without delay, deliver any person taken into temporary custody in accordance with this Article, together with any weapons or other items so seized, to the nearest German public prosecutor or police officer or judge or to the military authorities of the sending State to whose force or civilian component the person belongs either as a member or as a dependent of such member.

- 6 -

5. The provisions of this Article shall not affect the constitutional immunities of the parliaments of the Federation and the Laender.

ARTICLE 21

1. Where an investigation is initialed or an arrest made by a German authority in respect of an act punishable under Article 7 of the Fourth Law Amending the Criminal Law dated 11 June 1957 (Bundesgesetzblatt Teil I, page 597) or under such legislation as may replace that Article in future, the German authority conducting the investigations shall notify the military authorities of the sending State concerned without delay. The same shall apply if a German authority initiates an investigation or makes an arrest in respect of an act otherwise directed against the security of a sending State or of its force.

2. Where an investigation is initiated or an arrest made in the Federal territory by a competent authority of a sending State in respect of an act committed in the Federal territory and relating to the matters affecting the security of the Federal Republic, this authority shall inform the German authorities without delay.

ARTICLE 22

1. (a) Where jurisdiction is exercised by the authorities of a sending State, custody of members of the force, of the civilian component, or dependents shall rest with the authorities of that State.

- 7 -

0216

(b) Where jurisdiction is exercised by the German authorities, custody of members of a force, of a civilian component, or dependents shall rest with the authorities of the sending State in accordance with paragraphs 2 and 3 of this article.

2. (a) Where the arrest has been made by the German authorities, the arrested person shall be handed over to the authorities of the sending State concerned if such authorities so request.

(b) Where the arrest has been made by the authorities of a sending State, or where the arrested person has been handed over to them under subparagraph (a) of this paragraph, they

(i) may transfer custody to the German authorities at any time;

(ii) shall give sympathetic consideration to any request for the transfer of custody which may be made by the German authorities in specific cases.

(c) In respect of offences solely against the security of the Federal Republic, custody shall rest with the German authorities in accordance with such arrangements as may be made to that effect with the authorities of the sending State concerned.

3. Where custody rests with the authorities of a sending State in accordance with paragraph 2 of this Article, it shall remain with these authorities until release or acquittal by the German authorities or until commencement of the sentence. The authorities of the sending State shall make the arrested person available

- 5 -

한·미국 간의 상호방위조약 제4조에 의한 시설과 구역 및 한국에서의 미국군대의 지위에 관한 협정(SOFA) 전59권. 1966.7.9 서울에서 서명 : 1967.2.9 발효(조약 232호) (V.56 형사재판관할권 관계자료) 409

to the German authorities for investigation and criminal proceedings (Ermittlungs - und Strafverfahren) and shall take all appropriate measures to that end and to prevent any prejudice to the course of justice (Verdunkelungsgefahr). They shall take full account of any special request regarding custody made by the competent German authorities.

ARTICLE 23

Where a person is arrested in any case referred to in paragraph 1 of Article 21 of the present Agreement, a represxntative of the sending State concerned shall have access to that person. Where a person arrested in any case referred to in paragraph 2 of that Article is held in custody by the authorities of a force, a German representative shall have a corresponding right to the extent to which the sending State avails itself of the right of access afforded by the first sentence of this Article. The German authorities and the military authorities of the sending State shall conclude such arrangements as may be required for the implementation of this Article. A representative of the State which has custody may be present when the right of access is exercised.

ARTICLE 24

At the request of the Federal Republic or of a sending State, the German authorities and the authorities of that State shall conclude arrangements to facilitate the fulfilment of the obligations of mutual assistance provided for in sub-paragraph 5 and sub-paragraph (a) of paragraph 6 of Article VII of the NATO Status of Forces Agreement.

- 9 -

ARTICLE 25

1. (a) Where criminal jurisdiction over a member of a force or of a civilian component or a dependent is exercised by a German court or a German authority, a representative of the sending State concerned shall have the right to attend the trial. Where an offence is solely directed against the security of the Federal Republic, or against any property within the Federal Republic, or against a German or a person present in the Federal territory, and jurisdiction is exercised in the Federal Republic by a court or authority of a sending State, a German representative shall have the right to attend the trial.

(b) For the purpose of the provision set forth in sub-paragraph (a) of this paragraph

　　(i) the expression "property within the Federal Republic" shall not include property belonging either to a force or a civilian component or to a member of a force or of a civilian component or to a dependent;

　　(ii) the expression "a person present in the Federal territory" shall not include a member of a force or of a civilian component or a dependent.

(c) The provision set forth in sub-paragraph (a) of this paragraph shall not apply if the attendance of a national representative is incompatible with the security requirements of the State exercising jurisdiction which are not at the same time security requirements of the other State.

- 10 -

(d) German courts and authorities on the one
hand, and the courts and authorities of the sending State
on the other hand, shall give each other timely notification
of the place and time of the trial.

2. Under the conditions stated in paragraph 1 of this
Article a representative of the sending State shall also
have a right to attend interrogations and other pre-trial
investigations to such extent as may be agreed between
the authorities of that State and those of the Federal
Republic. If such arrangements are concluded, the
shall, under the conditions stated in paragraph 1, give to
a German representative, a right corresponding to that of
the representative of the sending State, and shall provide
procedures for reciprocal notification.

ARTICLE 26

1. Where a member of a force or of a civilian component
or a dependent is arraigned before a court of a sending
State for an offence committed in the Federal territory
against German interests, the trial shall be held in that
territory.

(a) except where the law of the sending State requires
otherwise, or

(b) except where, in cases of military exigency or
in the interests of justice, the authorities of the sending
State intend to hold the trial outside the Federal territory.
In this event they shall afford the German authorities timely
opportunity to comment on such intention and shall give due
consideration to any comments the latter may make.

- 11 -

2. Where the trial is held outside the Federal territory, the authorities of the sending State shall inform the German authorities of the place and date of the trial. A German representative shall be entitled to be present at the trial, except where his presence is incompatible with the rules of the court of the sending State or with the security requirements of that State, which are not at the same time security requirements of the Federal Republic. The authorities of the sending State shall inform the German authorities of the judgement and of the final outcome of the proceedings.

ARTICLE 27

Section 212 to 212 (b) of the German Code of Criminal Procedure, relating to expedited procedure, shall not be applicable in criminal proceedings against members of a force, of a civilian component, or against dependents.

ARTICLE 28

1. The military police of a force shall have the right to patrol on public roads, on public transport. in restuarants (Gastaetten) and in all other places to which the public has access and to take such measures with respect to the members of a force, of a civilian component or dependents as are necessary to maintain order and discipline. Insofar as it is necessary or expedient the details of the exercise of this right shall be agreed upon between the German authorities and the authorities of a force, who shall maintain close mutual liaison.

- 12 -

한·미국 간의 상호방위조약 제4조에 의한 시설과 구역 및 한국에서의 미국군대의 지위에 관한 협정(SOFA)
전59권. 1966.7.9 서울에서 서명 : 1967.2.9 발효(조약 232호) (V.56 형사재판관할권 관계자료) 413

2. If public order and safety are endangered or disturbed by an incident in which members of a force or a civilian component or dependents are involved, the military police of a force shall, if so requested by the German authorities, take appropriate measures with respect to such persons to maintain or restore order and discipline.

ARTICLE 29

1. The Federal Republic shall bring about such legislative measures as it deems necessary to ensure the adequate security and protection within its territory of the forces, of the civilian components and of their members. This shall also apply to the Armed Forces of a sending State stationed in Berlin, to the civilian component thereof and their members with regard to offences committed within the Federal territory.

2. To implement paragraph 11 of Article VII of the NATO Status of Forces Agreement and paragraph 1 of this Article the Federal Republic shall, in particular,

(a) ensure, in accordance with the provisions of German criminal law on treason, the protection of military secrets of the sending States;

(b) ensure, by way of criminal law, the protection of a force, a civilian component and their members to an extent not inferior to the protection which is or will be afforded to the German Armed Forces in the following fields:

(i) influencing the force, the civilian component or their members with intent to undermine their willingness to serve;

- 13 -

(ii) exposing the force to contempt;

(iii) inducement to disobedience;

(iv) inducement to desertion;

(v) facilitation of desertion;

(vi) sabotage;

(vii) collection of information concerning military matters;

(viii) operation of a military intelligence service;

(ix) reproduction or description of military equipment, military installations or facilities, or of military activities;

(x) taking of aerial photographs.

3. For the purposes of sub-paragraph (a) of paragraph 2 of this Article, the term "military secrets" shall mean such facts, objects, conclusions and discoveries, in particular writings, drawings, models, formulae, or information about them, as concern defence and are kept secret by an agency of a sending State located on Federal territory or in Berlin out of consideration for the security of that State or of its force, or its Armed Forces stationed in Berlin. The term shall not include objects in respect of which the decision about keeping them secret is a matter for the Federal Republic, or information concerning such objects.

ARTICLE 30

To facilitate the implementation of Article VII of the NATO Status of Forces Agreement and the provisions of the present Agreement supplementary thereto, and ensure their uniform application, Mixed Commissions composed of a

- 14 -

0223

German representative to be appointed by the Federal Government and a representative of the sending State concerned shall be constituted at the request of either party. The task of these Mixed Commissions shall be to discuss questions submitted to them by the Federal Government or the highest authority of the force concerned with respect to the application of the provisions referred to in this Article. The German authorities and the authorities of the sending State shall give sympathetic consideration to any joint recommendation made by a Mixed Commission.

ARTICLE 31

With respect to the right to free judicial assistance and the exemption from the obligation to post security for costs, members of a force or of a civilian component shall enjoy the rights determined in agreements in force in these fields between the Federal Republic and the sending State concerned. The presence on duty of such persons in the Federal territory shall, in the application of such agreements, be deemed to be residence therein.

ARTICLE 32

1. (a) Service upon members of a force, of a civilian component, or on dependents of a plaint or other document or court order initiating non-criminal proceedings before a German court or authority shall be made through a liaison agency to be established or designated by each of the sending States. The German courts or authorities may request the liaison agency to ensure service of other documents arising in such proceedings.

- 15 -

0224

(b) Receipt of an application submitted by a German court or authority for service shall be acknowledged by the liaison agency without delay. Service shall be effective when the document to be served is delivered to the addressee by his unit commander or by a representative of the liaison agency. Notification in writing that service has been effected shall be given without delay to the German court or authority.

(c) (i) If, upon the expiry of a period of twenty-one days from the date of acknowledgement of receipt by the liaison agency, the German court or authority has received neither unification in writing that service has been effected in accordance with sub-paragraph (b) of this paragraph nor any communication stating that it has not been possible to effect service, the court or authority shall forward to the liaison agency another copy of the application for service with notice that seven days after receipt by the liaison agency service shall be deemed to have been effected. At the expiry of this seven-day period, service shall be deemed to have been effected.

(ii) Service shall not, however, be deemed to have been effected if the liaison agency notifies the German court or authority prior to the expiry of the period of twenty-one days or seven days, as the case may be, that it has not been able to effect service. The liaison agency shall inform the German court or authority of the reasons for its inability to do so.

(iii) In the case specified in item (ii) of this sub-paragraph, the liaison agency may also request

- 16 -

the German court or authority to extend the period stating
in such request the reasons thereof. If this request for
extension is accepted by the German court or authority,
items (i) and (ii) shall be applicable mutatis mutandis to
the period so extended.

2. Where a German court or authority serves a judgement
or a document in appellate proceedings (Rechtsmittelschrift),
a copy thereof shall, upon special or general request of the
sending State concerned, be delivered to liaison agency
of that State without delay, except where the liaison
agency itself is, in accordance with the second sentence
of sub-paragraph (a) of paragraph I of this Article, requested
to effect such service.

ARTICLE 33

Members of a force, of a civilian component or dependents
shall not suffer prejudice to their interests when official
duties or duly authorized absence temporarily prevents their
attendance at non-criminal proceedings to which they are
parties.

ARTICLE 34

1. The military authorities shall render all assistance
in their power to secure compliance with judgments, decisions,
orders and settlements (vollstreckbare Titel) in non-criminal
proceedings of German courts and authorities.

2. A member of a force or of a civilian component or
a dependent shall not be deprived of his personal liberty
by a German court or authority whether to enforce a judgment,

- 17 -

0226

decision, order and settlement, to compel an oath of disclosure (Offenbarungseid) or for any other reason resulting from non-criminal proceedings.

3. A payment due to a member of a force or of a civilian component from his Government shall be subject to attachment, garnishment or other form of execution ordered by a German court or authority only to the extent permitted by the applicable in the territory of the sending State.

4. Where the enforcement of a judgment, decision, order and settlement in non-criminal proceedings of a German court or authority is to take place within an installation of a force, such enforcement shall be effected by a German enforcement officer in the presence of a representative of the force.

ARTICLE 35

Where a judgment, decision, order and settlement (vollstreckbarer Titel) of a German court or authority is to be enforced against a debtor to whom a payment is due in respect of employment with a force or civilian component in accordance with the provisions of Article 56 of the present Agreement or in respect of direct deliveries or services to a force or a civilian component, the following provisions shall apply:

(a) Where such a payment is made through a German authority and that authority has been requested by an enforcing agency to make the payment to the judgement creditor instead of to the debtor, that authority shall be entitled to comply with such request within the scope of

- 18 -

0227

419

the provisions of German law.

(b) (i) Where such a payment is not made through a German authority, the authorities of the force or of the civilian component shall, upon request by an enforcing agency and insofar as the law of the sending State concerned permits, deposit with the competent agency out of the sum admitted to be owing to the debtor the sum specified in the request. Such deposit shall operate as a discharge of the force or the civilian component from its obligation to the debtor the extent of the amount deposited.

(ii) Insofar as the law of the sending State concerned does not permit the procedure prescribed in item (i) of this sub-paragraph, the authorities of the force or of the civilian component shall take all appropriate measures to assist the enforcing agency in the execution of the judgment, decision, order and settlement in question.

ARTICLE 36

1. Service by German courts and authorities upon members of a force, of a civilian component or on dependents shall not be effected by publication or advertisement.

2. Where service of any document is to be effected by a German process server upon any person who is inside an installation of a force, the authority of the force responsible for the administration of the installation shall take all measures necessary to enable the German process server to effect such service.

- 19 -

0228

ARTICLE 37

1. (a) Where a member of a force or of a civilian component is summened to appear before a German court or authority, the military authorities, unless military exigency requires otherwise, shall secure his attendance provided that such attencance is compulsory under German law. The liaison agency shall be requested to ensure execution of such summons.

(b) The provisions of sub-paragraph (a) of this paragraph shall apply mutatis mutandis to dependents insofar as the military authorities are able to secure their attenddance otherwise dependents will be summoned in accordance with German law.

2. Where persons whose attendance cannot be secured by the military authorities are required as witnesses or experts by a court or a military authority of a sending State, the German courts and authorities shall, in accordance with German law, secure the attendance of such persons before the court or military authority of that State.

ARTICLE 38

1. If the course of criminal or non-criminal proceedings or hearings before a court or authority of a force or of the Federal Republic it appears that the disclosure of an official secret of either of the States concerned, or the disclosure of any information which could prejudice the security of either of them might result, the court or the authority shall, prior to taking further action, seek the written consent of the appropriate authority to the disclosure

- 20 -

한·미국 간의 상호방위조약 제4조에 의한 시설과 구역 및 한국에서의 미국군대의 지위에 관한 협정(SOFA) 전59권. 1966.7.9 서울에서 서명 : 1967.2.9 발효(조약 232호) (V.56 형사재판관할권 관계자료) 421

of the official secret or information. In the event that
the appropriate authority advances considerations against
disclosure, the court or authority shall take all steps in
its power, including those to which paragraph 2 of this
article relates, to prevent such disclosure, provided no
constitutional right of any party to the proceedings is thereby
impaired.

2. The provisions of Sections 172 to 175 of the
German Judicature Act (Gerichtsverfassungsgesetz) on the
exclusion of the public from hearings in criminal and non-
criminal proceedings, and of Section 15 of the German
Code of Criminal Procedure the transfer of criminal proceedings
to a court in a different district, shall be applied mutatis
mutandis in cases before German court and authorities where
there is a threat to the security of a force or of a civilian
component.

ARTICLE 39

Privileges and immunities of witnesses and experts shall
be those accorded by the law of the court or authority before
which they appear. The court or authority shall however,
give appropriate consideration to the privileges and immunities which witnesses and experts, if they are members of a
force or of a civilian component or dependents, would
have before a court of the sending State or, if they do not
belong to these categories of persons, would have before a
German court.

- 21 -

0230

A Review on the NATO Status of Forces Agreement
by Dr. Edward D. Re, Professor of law at St. John's
University.

0231

A Review on the NATO Status of Forces Agreement by
Dr. Edward D. Re, professor of law at St. John's
University.

I

Since, as part of our country's collective defense efforts
under the North Atlantic Treaty, American servicemen are
stationed in other countries, it has become necessary to determine
the rights and duties of these Americans while they are stationed
in the territory of another NATO country. Hence, the NATO Status
of Forces Agreement. It may be added that the agreement is not
limited to servicemen, but includes civilian employees and dependents.

It should be noted at the outset that the NATO Status of
Forces Agreement is not, as one might infer from its title,
an executive agreement or some informal understanding among the
heads of states or military commanders of the NATO countries.
Rather, it is a solemn treaty signed at London on June 19, 1951,
and duly ratified by the Senate of the United States on July 15,
1953, by a vote of 72 to 15. From a legal standpoint it is a
multilateral reciprocal treaty designed to implement the provisions
of the North Atlantic Treaty. Its exact title is "Agreement
between the Parties to the North Atlantic Treaty Regarding the
Status of Their Forces." Its express purpose is to establish

-1-

0232

<del>0231</del>

and setforth the terms and conditions which will determine the rights, duties, privileges, and immunities of the forces of one country that is a party to the agreement setnt or stationed in the territory of another country that is also a party to the agreement.

Before discussing the relevant portions of international law and the specific jurisdictional provisions of the agreement that have been subjected to severe criticism, a few preliminary observations should be made to place the specific topic to be treated in its accurate factual and legal framework.

First, since the treaty is reciprocal in nature, whatever duties and rights are spelled out for the troops and personnel of nation A stationed in the territory of nation B will also determine the legal status of the troops and personnel of nation B stationed in the territory of nation A. The tenor of the agreement, therefore, is clearly one of partnership and equality whereby one party to the agreement does not exact or expect what it does not itself concede or grant.

Secondly, the agreement is not limited to what has traditionally been referred to as passage of troops going from nation A to nation C and passing through the territory of nation B. The agreement, rather, is designed to give effect to what is actually

- 2 -

0233

a more or less permanent stationing of the troops and personnel of one country in the territory of another.

Thirdly, the NATO status of forces agreement, for the first time in our history, permits the stationing of American troops on foreign territory in times of peace. The agreement is not a watime agreement between Allies. It expressly provides for modification and suspension of the jurisdictional provisions in the event of hostilities.

These preliminary matters are of particular importance in determining the principles of international law that would govern such a situation because most of the precedents and authorities that have been urged in all discussions of this topic dealt with either the privileges and immunities of troops passing through a neutral country, invasion of enemy territory, or military occupation of enemy soil.

The provisions of the agreement that have been subjected to the severest criticism deal with the jurisdiction of a receiving state to try and to punish offenders for criminal offenses committed by personnel of a sending state within the territory of the receiving state. The agreement defines "sending" state as "the contracting party to which the force belongs." By "receiving" state is meant "the contracting party in the territory of which the force or civilian component is located, whether it be stationed there or passing in transit."

- 3 -

0234

Article VII of the agreement prescribes the circumstance under which the sending or receiving state will have either exclusive or concurrent jurisdiction to try offenders. In those situations where both states have concurrent jurisdiction article VII prescribes which state shall have the "primary" jurisdiction. Exclusive jurisdiction implies that only one State has the right to try an offender as in a case, for example, of security offenses which are against the laws of one country but not of another. If an offense violates the laws of both states, both states may have jurisdiction. However, the state that has the right to try the offender in the first instance, and in this sense may be said to have the prior or superior right to try the offender, is deemed to be the state having the "primary" jurisdiction. This does not imply, however, that in the ordinary case a person may twice be in jeopardy. Paragraph 8 of article VII expressly provides: "Where an accused has been tried in accordance with the provisions of this article by the authorities of one contracting party and has been acquitted or has been convicted and is serving, or has served, his sentence or has been pardoned, he may not be tried again for the same offense within the same territory by the authorities of another contracting party". This section safeguards an accused against double jeopardy. This,

- 4 -

0235

however, is subject to what may be deemed a military exception to double jeopardy which does not prevent the military authorities of sending state from trying a member of its force for a violation of rules of discipline arising from an act or omission which constituted an offense for which he was tried by the receiving state.

Article VII gives the sending state primary jurisdiction of the sending and receiving states. Paragraph 2 of article VII, which deals with exclusive jurisdiction, in effect, provides that each state shall have the sole right to try offenders for "security offenses such as treason, sabotage, and espionage which are punishable by the law of the state having exclusive jurisdiction and not by the law of the state." As can be imagined, problems involving the exclusive jurisdiction of a state will not be numerous and hence have not evoked undue criticism.

Article VII gives the sending state primary jurisdiction over two types of offenses committed by its armed forces. The first relates to offenses solely against the property or security of the sending state, or against the person or property of personnel of the sending state. The second relates to offenses arising out of any act or omission done in the performance of official duty. An American solider in France, therefore, who commits an offense against another American soldier or his property comes within the primary jurisdiction of the American military authorities. If the

- 5 -

0236

American soldier were to commit an offense while in the line of
duty, such an offense also would come within the primary jurisdiction of the American authorities.

Most of the criticisms that have been heaped upon the NATO
Status of Forces Agreement stem from that provision of article VII
that "in the case of any other offense the authorities of the
receiving state shall have the primary right to exercise jurisdiction." This includes the greater majority of the off-duty
offenses. It includes, for example, the case of the American
soldier in France, who may commit an assault upon a Frenchman, or
who may be driving an automobile while under the influence of
intoxicants and all of the other offenses that are usually
punishable by a civilian community.

A provision that is very important from the standpoint of
the practical administration of the agreement deals with the
waiver of jurisdiction by the state having the primary jurisdiction.
First, in the event that the state having the primary jurisdiction
does not desire to exercise jurisdiction, it shall notify the
authorities of the other state for a waiver of its right in cases
where that other state considers such waiver to be of particular
importance.

Pursuant to this provision, when the giving of sympathetic
consideration to a request for a waiver of a state's jurisdiction

- 6 -

results in a waiver of its jurisdiction, many problems are neatly avoided. Actually, experience indicates that it is only in the exceptional case that the receiving state will wish to exercise its primary jurisdiction to try a member of the force of the sending state and not grant the request for a waiver of its jurisdiction. It is unquestionably true that "the experience of the Armed Forces has been that the countries in which the United States forces are stationed give waivers of the jurisdiction in the great majority of cases."

III

The question, nevertheless, remains whether under international law the receiving state would have the right to try members of a force that it has invited or which has otherwise entered its territory with its consent. Certain cases where the receiving state has actually tried American soldiers for off-duty offenses committed on the territory of the receiving state have received a great deal of publicity and as a result the question may very well be asked why under the agreement the United States has agreed to subject American soldier to the criminal jurisdiction of the foreign country where he may be stationed. Based upon the firm belief that the rule of international law as laid down by Chief Justice John Marshall and many other later authorities

- 7 -

0238

is that troops of a friendly nation stationed within the territory of another are not subject to the local laws of the other country, but are subject only to their own country's laws and regulations for the government of the armed services, many patriotic Americans have vehemently objected to the approval of the NATO Status of Forces Agreement.

The view that the receiving state under international law would have no jurisdiction to try American soldiers for off-duty offenses has led Senator Bricker to state that to approve the criminal jurisdiction provisions of this treaty would amount to penalizing the American soldier in an effort to please our NATO allies. In the sincere belief that this unprecedented agreement reflects a callous disregard of the rights of American Armed Forces personnel, Senator Bricker proposed a reservation to the agreement intended to withhold from the receiving state all jurisdiction over criminal offenses committed by members of the United States forces. At the same time the reservation would have had the result of depriving the United States of jurisdiction over offenses by foreign forces in United States territory if the foreign state requested a waiver of American jurisdiction. The end result of such a reservation, had it been adopted, would have been to deprive the receiving state of jurisdiction over all offenses committed within its territory regardless of whether

- 8 -

0239

in the line of duty or the nature of offense. Thus, an American soldier while off duty in Paris could not be tried by the French authorities for an assault and battery upon a Frenchman, or for any other crime. Under the agreement, since its provisions are applicable to the political subdivisions of contracting parties, a French soldier who commits a crime while off duty in New York City can be tried by the appropriate court of the city or State of New York. If the reservation proposed by Senator Bricker would have been effective, such a French soldier could not be tried by local authorities, if a request were made by the French authorities for a waiver of jurisdiction. The Bricker reservation, together with the criminal jurisdiction provisions of the agreement, were thoroughly considered by Senate.

IV

If a member of the force of sending state is to be tried by receiving state for a criminal offense committed within the receiving state, the offender, naturally, will be tried according to the law of the receiving state and, hence, will receive whatever benefits and protections are afforded by that law. However, apart from rights existing under local national law, paragraph 9 of article VII of the agreement sets forth certain

- 9 -

0240

specific rights that must be accorded to an offender.

In addition to these safeguards, prior to the ratification of the agreement, the Senate adopted a statement or reservation proposed by its Committee on Foreign Relations. This statement declared that it was the understanding of the Senate which was inherent in its advice and consent to the ratification of the agreement that nothing in the agreement diminished or otherwise altered the right of the United States to safeguard its security by excluding or removing from the United States persons whose presence is deemed prejudicial to its safety and security. This statement was amended so as to include additional matters which expressed the sense of the Senate that:

1. The criminal jurisdiction provisions of article VII of the agreement were not to be deemed a precedent for future agreements.

2. Where a member of the Armed Forces of the United States is to be tried by a receiving state, his commanding officer shall examine the laws of such state with particular reference to the procedural safeguards contained in the Constitution of the United States.

3. If the commanding officer is of the opinion that there is danger that the accused will not be protected because of the

- 10 -

0241

absence or denial of constitutional rights he would enjoy in the United States, the commanding officer shall request a waiver of jurisdiction in accordance with the provisions of the agreement. If the receiving state refuses to waive its jurisdiction, the commanding officer shall request the Department of State to press such request through diplomatic channels.

4. When a member of the Armed Forces is tried by the receiving state a representative of the United States "will attend the trial" and will report any noncompliance with the procedural safeguards enumerated in paragraph 9 of article VII of the agreement to the commanding officer of the Armed Forces of the United States in the receiving state who, in turn, will request the Department of State to take appropriate action to protect the rights of the accused.

The late Senator McCarran, who opposed the reatification of the agreement, chiefly because in his opinion it was "violative of the rights of American nationals," indicated that, although paragraph 9 of article VII "looks like a pretty good list," upon analysis "it becomes apparent that some of the most important guaranties under our own Bill of Rights have been omitted from this list." He observed, among other thing, that there were no provisions guaranteeing a public trial, the privilege against self-incrimination, freedom from cruel and unusual punishments, the right to appeal or review a decision, freedom of religion, freedom of speech and of the press, right of free assembly and petition,

- 11 -

freedom from unreasonalbe searches and seizure, and the right to
trial by jury. Apart from the wisdom of inserting a Bill of
Rights in an international treaty of this nature, it should be noted
that some of the rights referred to, such as the one that there is
no presumption of innocence under the law of France and other
European nations, are fatually incorrect. Actually, the more
valid answer to Senator McCarran's criticism would probably
not be one dealing with technical principles of constitutional law
and the administration of criminal justice, but rather, would
deal with the highly developed system of jurisprudence that
prevails in the NATO countries. This fact was pointed out by
Senator Wiley, who added that "our experience with these countries
with respect to this problem has been good." Of course, the Senator
referred to our experience under the temporary bilateral arrangements that existed subsequent to World War II and prior to the
NATO Status of Forces Agreement. Senator McCarran, however, was
fully justified in observing that the accused's right "to communicate
with a representative of the government of the sending state"
differed from the right "to have such a representative present at
his trial," and this latter right, according to subdivision(g) of
paragraph 9 or article VII, would only exist "when the rules of
the court permit." To be deprived of the right to have a representative of the government of the sending state present at the trial

- 12 -

might very well be more important than a so-called public trial.
Furthermore, this limitation upon the right of an accused is
contrary to one of the requirements enumerated in the statement
of the Committee on Foreign Relations that a representative of the
United States attend the trial of an American serviceman being
tried in the courts of a receiving state. Although the statement
does not have legal effect, it does, nevertheless, declare and
make known to the commanding officer in the foreign country, and
through the Department of State to the foreign country itself,
the policy of the United States.

V

It is entirely justified to regard the case of the schooner
Exchange as the convenient and authoritative point of beginning
in a discussion of this subject. This celebrated case involved
a libel filed in the United States District Court for the District
of Pennsylvania by American citizens who claimed to be the former
owners of the schooner Exchange. They alleged that the vessel had
been seized outside the United States by orders of the Emperor
of France, and was subsequently commissioned as a man-of-war
by the French Government. After referring to the "perfect
equality and absolute independence of sovereigns" Chief Justice
Marshall stated that the "common interest impelling them to mutual

- 13 -

0244

intercourse, and an interchange of good offices with each other ***
have given rise to a class of cases in which every sovereign is
understood to waive the exercise of a part of that complete
exclusive territorial jurisdiction, which has been stated to be
the attribute of every nation." In enumerating this class of cases,
Mr. Chief Justice Marshall first mentioned "the exemption of the
person of the sovereign from arrest or detention within a foreign
territory"; secondly "the immunity which all civilized nations
allow to foreign minister" and then added: "A third case in which
a sovereign is understood to cede a portion of his territorial
jurisdiction is, where he allows the troops of a foreign prince
to pass through his dominions."

The celebrated jurist stated that the consent for foreign
troops to enter a friendly country is not presumed but must be
expressed. In relation to vessels, however, he stated that
the situation was different in that unless a particular part was
closed to a foreign naval vessel and notice of such fact was given
"the ports of a friendly nation are considered as open to the public
ships of all powers with whom it is at peace." The libel was therefore
dismissed and the vessel was released.

Even if it be assumed that a judicial decision of a national
tribunal can authoritatively expound principles of international

- 14 -

0245

law, and that concepts analogous to stare decisis are also applicable to international law, it is manifest that the remarks of Chief Justice Marshall dealing with the immunity of troops were dicta. These remarks, 67 years later, again in dicta were expanded to read as follows in Coleman v. Tennessee:

"It is well settled that a foreign army, permitted to search through friendly country or to be stationed in it, by permission of its government or sovereign, is exempt from the civil and criminal jurisdiction of the place."

The Coleman case dealt with a criminal offense committed on enemy territory. It involved a military occupation of "hostile country," and consequently "soldiers of the Army of the United States in Tennessee during the war — were not subject to the laws nor amenable to the tribunals of the hostile country." Henece the defendant was to be "delivered up to the military authorities of the United States to be dealt with as required by law."

Although the Coleman case dealt with a criminal offense committed by a member of an occupying force over enemy territory, the Court spoke of an exemption from the "civil and criminal jurisdiction of the place."

The dictum of the Coleman case became the holding of Dow v. Johnson decided the following year by the Supreme Court of the

- 15 -

0246

United States. In this case, General Dow was sued in a State
court of Louisiana for certain property that he, in his military
capacity, had ordered to be taken from a plantation owned by the
plaintiff Johnson. Judgment was given against the general by
default and an action was brought upon the Louisiana judgement in
the Circuit Court of the United States for the District of Maine.
Mr. Justice Field, who wrote the majority opinion for the Supreme
Court of the United States, held that General Dow was not to render
the judgment upon which the plaintiff brought suit.

The three cases just discussed are the American judicial
decisions principally relied upon to establish the immunity or
exemption of troops from the jurisdiction of the territorial
sovereign.

Another Supreme Court decision also relied upon is Tucker v.
Alexandroff. In the Tucker case, a detachment of the Russian
Navy with the consent of the United States entered the United
States for the purpose of manning a vessel that had been built
in this country for the Russian Navy. Pursuant to the specific
provisions of a treaty between the United States and Russia, the
Supreme Court held that the commanding officer of the Russian detachment was entitled to have deserter arrested and returned to his
control. The Tucker case is generally cited for its statement
concerning the holding of schooner Exchange case. It reads:

- 16 -

0247

"This case, the schooner Exchange, however, only holds that the public armed vessels of a foreign nation may, upon principles of comity, enter our harbors with the presumed license of the Government, and while there are exempt from the jurisdiction of the local courts; and by parity of reasoning, that if foreign troops are permitted to enter or cross our territory, they are still subject to the control of their officers and exempt from local jurisdiction." Although the preceding cases are not the only ones decided by American courts that had some bearing on the subject, they are the most relevant and the most cited precedents. Yet as can be gleaned even from the terse factual discussions contained herein, they fall far short of the mark surrounding the stationing of troops abroad pursuant to the North Atlantic Treaty.

VI

The true foundation and basis of the case of the schooner Exchange, however, is not found in its discussion of the three classes of cases "in which every sovereign is understood to waive the exercise of a part of that complete exclusive territorial jurisdiction," which has been stated to be "the attribute of every nation," but in the statement that declares categorically:

"The jurisdiction of the nation within its own territory is necessarily exclusive and absolute. It is susceptible of no limitation not imposed by itself. *** All exceptions therefore,

- 17 -

0248

to the full and complete power of a nation within its own territories must be traced up to the consent of the nation itself. They can flow from no other legitimate service."

Clearly, therefore, the rule is one of territorial supremacy and all exceptions thereto must be traced to the consent of the territorial sovereign. The exceptions involve situations where the territorial sovereign has involve situations where the territorial sovereign has waived the jurisdiction that would normally attach. These situations do not involve any extraterritoriality but are referred to as exemptions from the territorial jurisdiction. In such cases the person or thing is exempt or immune from the jurisdiction. The important question that persists deals with the scope or extent of the/munity or exemption.
im-

As indicated in Cheng Chi Cheung v. The King, some immunities are well settled while others are more uncertain. The immunity of the sovereign himself, his envoy, and his property, including his public armed ships, from the local or territorial jurisdiction is clear. The applicability and extent of the immunity over friendly foreign armed forces is not clear. Although it is clear that a certain immunity exists, it is equally clear that such an immunity is not unlimited and complete. As to troops, as distinguished from naval vessels, there does not even exist a presumed or implied consent to enter a friendly country. The

- 18 -

consent must be expressed, and as indicated by many of the writers the conditions of the movement are arranged *** in a preliminary treaty or agreement. In other words, the permission to enter the territory will also contain the conditions, privileges, and limitations upon which the permission is granted. Clearly, therefore, the matter of entry or passage of a force through foreign friendly territory is strictly a matter of consent.

A survey of the sources examined reveals that the granting of consent does not imso facto imply a complete exemption or immunity from the jurisdiction of the territorial sovereign. Even those authors who favor the existence of such an exemption indicate that in the absence of a special agreement the immunity is subject to limitations. Following the lead of Mr. Chief Justice Marshall, most authors concede that the immunity is limited to the passage of troops. The limitations are expressed in varying language. Lawrence speaks of the limitation within their own lines or were away on duty. Oppenheim similarly limits the immunity to the rayon of the fortress and to offenses committed on duty.

The most extensive discussion of this subject is found in an article written by an English scholar, G.P. Barton. After a treatment of the international agreements concluded in World War I, the interwar period, World War II, the relevant municipal legislation, and the existing judicial decisions, the author concludes that even though the military courts of a foreign friendly force

- 19 -

0250

are entitled to exercise jurisdiction over its members, which
includes the right to try a member for offenses against the local
law, "it has not yet been established that this right carries
with it the right to exercise exclusive jurisdiction over members
of these forces who commit offenses against the local law." He adds:

"On the contrary, it has been shown that there exists a rule
of international law according to which members of visiting forces
are, in principle, subject to the exercise of criminal jurisdiction
by the local courts and that any exceptions to that general and
far-reaching principle must be traced to express privilege or
concession."

It cannot be seriously questioned or disputed that all authors
recognize and agree that the scope and extent of the immunity is
really a matter of agreement between the interested States. This
view is fully justified by a survey of the practice of States.
The various bilaterial conventions, agreements, and arrangements
actually entered into reflect the particular needs of the parties
with regard to a sepcific situation to be dealt with. Some granted
complete immunity whereas others granted none. Not only was no
single type of agreement used, but those agreements granting a
complete exemption from the local jurisdiction were wartime agreements
considered to be temporary and exceptional and dictated by the conditions of war. The only existing multilateral treaties on the
subject do not recognize any unqualified immunity.

- 20 -

0251

Moreover those who insist that there exists a principle of complete exemption in the absence of agreement can find no support in the decided cases apart from the dictum in the Schooner Exchange case which, again in dicta, was expanded in the Coeman and Dow cases. The oft-cited Cheng Chi Cheung case involved the commission of a crime committed on board a naval vessel and the other cases were decided pursuant to a specific agreement.

Sound legal analysis, therefore, would require the conclusion that although a certain immunity exists for foreign visiting forces, the extent of the immunity is strictly a matter of agreement. It is for the territorial sovereign to determine the extent to which he wishes to waive the exercise of his jurisdiction. The agreements actually entered into by the nations of the world, and the decided cases clearly demonstrate that the problem has always involved reconciling "the practical necessities of the situation with a proper respect for national sovereignty."

Predicated upon the foregoing legal analysis, it is apparent that the contention that, in the absence of the agreement, the NATO countries would have no jurisdiction over American forces stationed there is completely untenable. The agreement not only concedes the primary jurisdiction to the sending state in offenses arising out of the performance of official duty, but also in offenses

- 21 -

0252

solely against the property or security of the sending state or against the person or property of the personnel of the sending state. In the remaining cases when the receiving state shall have the primary right to exercise jurisdiction, the agreement expressly provides for the giving of sympathetic consideration to a request for a waiver of such jurisdiction. It is in this area that a great deal can be done in the actual implementation of the agreement. Surely, if an American serviceman about to be tried by an American cout martial everything diplomatically possible should be done by the American authorities to see to it that the receiving state waive its primary jurisdiction. In this connection one is in accord with certain statements of Senator Bricker, that *** judge advocates should try to obtain a waiver of jurisdiction for every American serviceman in foreign custody." This seems to be in line with the resolution made by the Committee of Military Justice of the New York County Lawyers' Association pursuant to which the Defense Department was requested "to adopt a procedure whereby in all cases of United States Military Personnel involved with the civil authorities in Japan as well as in the NATO countries, efforts be made to have the personnel returned to United States military custody for appropriate disciplinary action by the military authorities." This resolution would also strengthen the procedural safeguards provided

- 22 -

0253

by paragraph 9 of article VII of the NATO agreement in those cases where the receiving state refuses to honor the request for a waiver of jurisdiction, by guaranteeing to every American serviceman "adequate legal representation not only by local counsel versed in local procedures, but in addition *** military counsel to aid in the defense of such person."

These suggestions seem to posses great merit and would justify legilsation to authorize marking available the necessary funds to engage the personnel required to achieve the desired purpose. They are sound suggestions, since they impliedly admit the wisdom of the American collective security plan. The alternative of abandonig NATO or the agreement is hardly a solution that warrants, in the view of our military leaders, serious consideration at this time. In view of the fact that the agreement is reciprocal, it seems difficult to speak of its terms as being unfair or unjust. Rather they tend to prove a statement made by Chief Justice Marshall in another famous case that "no principle of general law is more universally adknowledged than the perfect equality of nations." As indicated at the very beginning of the article, America is dealing with partners and Allies, not with conquered nations. After such deliberation the NATO Status of Forces Agreement represents the solemn compact that has been agreed to by sovereign nations.

- 23 -

0254

If it is to be changed or modified, it must be done so freely and willingly. It is earnestly hoped that the modification or supervision of its terms will not be made necessary by those provisions dealing with the dreaded "event of hostilities."

1. Exercise of criminal jurisdiction by foreign tribunals over persons subject to United States military law: During the period January 1, 1954, through November 30, 1954, 7,416 (3,987) persons subject to the United States military law were accused of offenses subject to the jurisdiction of foreign courts throughout the world. Jurisdiction was waived by foreign courts in 5,424 cases, and trial was had in 1,475 (793) cases. Charges were dropped as to 255 individuals, and 123 were acquitted. Confinement was imposed in 173 (38) cases but was suspended in all but 77 (16) cases. In 1,164 (693) cases, fines only were imposed. These figures include statistics under the North Atlantic Treaty Organization status of forces agreement, which is applicable to United States forces in Belgium, Canada, France, Greece, Luxembourg, The Netherlands, Norway, the United Kingdom, and Turkey. Of the 1,475 cases tried by foreign courts, 815 (452) were subject to the status of forces agreement.

Partial statistics of cases tried by countries include:
France 283 (117), The United Kingdom 271 (208), Canada 249 (125),

- 24 -

Panama 216 (104), Iceland 116 (25), and Japan 107 (36).

As of February 10, 1955, 58 United States citizens subject to military law were serving sentences to confinement in foreign institutions pursuant to sentences of foreign courts. Of course, 32 were for robbery and larceny, 15 for rape and related offenses, 6 for assault-type offenses, 4 for murder, and 1 for negligent homicide.

0256

독일 연방공화국의 주권 회복과 보충협정의 체결

1. 독일의 주권 회복

독일이 주권을 회복한 것은 미·영·불·독 4개국에 의하여 1954년 10월 23일 서명되고 1955년 5월 5일 발효된 "독일 연방 공화국에 있어서의 점령 정권의 철폐에 관한 의정서" (Protocol on the Termination of the Occupation Regime in the Federal Republic of Germany)   및

동 부속서류에 의한 것이다. 즉, 동 의정서의 부속서류의 하나인 "독일 연방공화국과 미·영·불, 3개국간의 관계에 관한 협약" (Convention on the Rights and Obligation of Foreign Forces and their Members in the Federal 제 1 조
Republic of Germany

1항에서 미·영·불, 3개국은 독일의 점령상태를 철폐할 것을 선언하였으며 동 제 2 항에서 "연방 공화국은 국내외 문제에 관하여 주권 국가로서의 전권을 갖는다" 라고 명백히 하였다.

2. 보충협정 체결교섭의 근거

한편, "독일 연방공화국과 미·영·불 3개국간의 관계에 관한 협약" 제 8 조 제 1 항 (B) 세항은 1952년 5월 26일 서명되고 의정서의 부속서류에 의하여 수정된 "독일 연방공화국에 주둔하고 있는 외국군대와 그 구성원의 권리와 의무에 관한 협약" 및 "외국 군대와 그 구성원에 대한 과세에 관한 협정" 및 "재정 협약" (Convention on the Rights and Obligation of Foreign Forces and their Members in the Federal Republic of Germany, Agreement on the Tax Treatment of the Forces and their Members, and Finance Convention, signed at Bonn on 26 May, 1962)

등 제 협정은 독일국에 주둔하고 있는 미·영·불 3개국과 기타 외국 군대의 권리와 의무를 규정하는 새로운 약정에 의하여 대치될때 까지 기속 유효하다고 선언하였다.

3. 체결될 지위협정의 성격

독일과 3 개국간의 관계에 관한 협약은 또한 앞으로 체결될 약정은 1951년 6월 19일 "나토" 회원국 간에 서명되고 1953년 8월 23일 발효된 "나토" 주둔군 지위협정에

0257

입각하여야 할 것과 독일국에 주둔하고 있는 외국 군대에 관련된 특수성에 감하여
필요한 규정에 의하여 보충될 것이라고 규정하였다. 환언하면, 동 의정서는
상기한바와 같이 첫째. 독일이 완전 자주독립 국가임을 선언하는 동시에
둘째로, 주권을 회복한 후에도 새로운 지위협정이 체결될 때 까지 점령하에서
적용된 군대의 군대 의무관계 각종 협약을 주권회복에 따라 수정하여 시행할 것을
규정하는 한편, 셋째로. 독일국이 완전한 주권국가로서 열강 회원국과 대등한
입장에서 "나토" 군대 지위협정에 입각한 새로운 지위협정의 체결을 교섭할수 있는
근거와 방향을 명시한 것이다.

4. 주독 외국 군대의 특수성

다만 독일국을 포함한 각 서명국은 독일국이 상금 동서로 국토가 양단되어 있어서
독일국 단독으로서는 동독 공산군으로 부터 국토를 방위할수 없는 입장에 있으므로
점령상태의 폐지에도 불구하고 많은 외국 군대를 계속 주둔시키지 않을수 없었다는
실정과 아울러 주둔군이 예측할수 없는 공산군과의 습격에 대비하여 항시 임전태세
를 갖추어야 하는 요청등 주둔군을 둘러싸고 있는 제반 특수 사정을 그려에 넣어
거기 "나토" 군대 지위협정을 그러한 실정에 알맞도록 보충 채택할 것에 합의하였던 것이다

5. 지위협정의 체결교섭과 서명 및 비준 발효

독일은 주권을 회복한후 이와같은 의정서와 그 부속서류의 제 규정에 입각하여
관계 각 파견국과 더불어 주독 외국 군대의 지위에 관한 협정체결교섭을 시작하여
1959년 8월 3일 소위 "독일 보충협정" 을 서명하는데 성공하였으며 동 협정은
다음과 같이 각 서명당사국의 비준동의를 거쳐 1963년 7월 1일 발효되었다.

협정 체결 당사국	비준서 또는 동의서 기탁 일자
1. United States of America	1961. 7. 28.
2. Canada	1961. 12.11.
3. France	1962. 1. 11.
4. United Kingdom	1962. 7. 9.
5. Netherlands	1962. 9. 10.
6. Belgium	1963. 5. 15.
7. Federal Republic of Germany	1963. 6. 1.

0258

상기와 같이 모든 서명각국이 비준서 또는 동의서를 기탁한후 30일이 경과한 다음 보충협정은 발효하였으며 그와 동시에 적용되어 오던 외국 군대의 권리와 의무에 관한 전기 제 협약은 폐기되었다.

6. **결 언**

따라서 독일 보충협정 특히 그중에서도 형사 재판권의 제 1 차 재판권의 포기에 관한 형태가 패전국에 강요된 형태가 아니라는 것은 상술한바와 같이 독일이 이 협정의 체결을 위한 교섭을 시작한 것이 완전한 주권을 회복한후 였을뿐만 아니라 "나토" 조약기구의 회원국의 자격으로 대등한 입장에서 교섭을 시작한 사실을 상기할때 자명하다 할수 있다.

다만, 동 포기조항이 다소 파견군 당국에 관대하게 보일수 있는 점이 있다면 그것은 주독 외국 군대가 수행하고 있는 군사 사명이 기타 "나토" 제국이나 일본에 주둔하고 있는 주둔군의 사명보다 중대하다는 현실에 기인하고 있다고 보아야 하며 또한 동 형태가 패전국의 형태가 아니라는 것은 금년 8월 31일 제 2 차 대전의 전승국의 일원인 자유중국이 미국과 체결한 중·미간 주둔군 지위협정에서 도 동일한 형태가 채택되었다는 사실이 이를 입증하고 있다.

일언지 폐하면 독일 보충협정은 상기 제 사실로 보아 결코 패전국에 강요된 형태라고 할수는 없으며 주둔군의 사명의 특수성과 접수국의 국가적 요청이 가져온 주둔군 지위협정의 하나의 유형이라고 보아야 할 것이다.

한·미국 간의 상호방위조약 제4조에 의한 시설과 구역 및 한국에서의 미국군대의 지위에 관한 협정(SOFA) 전59권. 1966.7.9 서울에서 서명 : 1967.2.9 발효(조약 232호) (V.56 형사재판관할권 관계자료) 451

Establishment of Communications Unit

Agreement effected by exchange of
notes Signed at Karachi July 18, 1959;
Entered into force July 18, 1959.
With munute of understanding and
exchange of notes.

The Pakistani Minister of Foreign Affairs and
Commonwealth Relations to the American Ambassador

Ministry of Foreign Affairs
and Commonwealth Relations
Karachi, the 18th July, 1959.

No. 40-SSP/59.

Your Excellency:

I refer to our recent discussions regarding the desire
of the United States to station a Communications Unit in
Pakistan. I have the honour to inform you that the Government
of Pakistan agrees to the stationing of such a Unit on the
following basis:

1. The Government of Pakistan will make available to the
United States the land areas and rights-of-way required for
the establishment and operation of the Communications Unit and
will provide protection for such Unit. The agreed areas
and rights-of-way are set forth in Annex A. (1).

2. The Communications Unit and personnel assigned to it
may install and use communications equipment, including antennas;
use continuously agreed radio frequencies and agreed wire
communications facilities; purchase locally goods and services
including construction materials, electrical power and
transportation services; make arrangements for the internal
security of those small areas, within the agreed areas,
designated for the exclusive use of the Communications Unit
(only authorized personnel may enter these latter areas);
carry arms in connection with official duties within the areas
designated for the exclusive use of the Communications Unit
and in connection with the courier duties outside the agreed
areas; move freely within, into and out of and between the
agreed areas; and may engage in such other activities as
may be necessary for the effective operation of the Unit
and the health and welfare of its personnel.

0260

3. The Communications Unit and personnel assigned to
it shall respect the laws of Pakistan and shall abstain from
any activity which would adversely affect the interests
of the people or the Government of Pakistan. The Government
of the United States will take necessary measures to prevent
abuse of the privileges granted by the Government of
Pakistan under the present Agreement.

4. The Government of Pakistan will, upon request,
assist the Communications Unit in the local procurement of
goods, materials, supplies and services required for the
establishment, operation and support of the Unit. The
Unit shall enjoy any preferential rates, charges, or
priorities which are available to the Armed Forces of
Pakistan for goods or services purchased locally in connection
with the operation of the Unit.

5. (a) (1) The personnel of the Communications Unit
shall receive exemption from payment of all duties and
taxes, including export duties, on their personal and
household goods brought into the country for their own
use within six months of their arrival.

Goods imported under this section will
not ordinarily be sold or disposed of in Pakistan by the
owner, except to other persons enjoying comparable privileges.
In the event of their sale or disposal to a person who does not
enjoy comparable privileges, the duty and taxes thereon
will be paid.

The Pakistan Customs Department will issue
appropriate regulations regarding the provisions of this
section.

(b) The temporary presence in Pakistan of a
member of the Unit shall constitute neither residence nor
domicile therein and shall not of itself subject him to
taxation in Pakistan, either on his income or on his
property, the presence of which in Pakistan is due to his
temporary presence there, nor, in the event of his death,
shall it subject his estate to a levy of death duties.

6. No tax, duty or other charge will be levied or
assessed on activities of the Unit or on material, equipment,
supplies or goods brought into or procured in Pakistan by
the United States authorities for the use of the Unit, its

- 2 -

0261

agencies or personnel assigned to the Unit.

7. The United States Government may construct
within the agreed areas the facilities required for support
of the Communications Unit under the terms and conditions set
forth in Article II through VII of the Military Defense
Construction Agreement signed at Karachi on May 28, 1956.(2)

8. Title to removable materials, equipment or property
brought into or acquired in Pakistan by or on behalf of the
Communications Unit will remain in the United States
Government. Such material, equipment or property may be
brought into or removed tax and duty free at any time from
Pakistan by the United States Government.

The materials, equipment and property of the Unit
and its official papers will be exempt from inspection,
search and seizure and may be removed freely by the
United States Government at any time.

9. Jurisdiction over personnel of the Unit shall be
exercised in accordance with the provisions of Annex B,
(1) an integral part hereof.

10. Arrangements required to give effect to this
Agreement will be the subject of agreement between the
Commanding Officer of the Communications Unit and Senior
Military Officer of the Pakistan Forces in the area.

11. In this Agreement the expressions "personnel
assigned to the Unit", "personnel of the Unit", and "member
of the Unit" include persons who are in Pakistan in
connection with the Agreement and who are (a) members of the
United States armed forces; (b) civilian personnel employed
by, serving with, or accompanying the United States armed
forces (except persons who are nationals of Pakistan or
ordinarily resident therein); or (c) dependents of the
persons defined in (a) and (b) above.

12. This Agreement shall remain in force for a period
of ten years and for a second period of ten years thereafter
unless either party gives written notice to the other at least
twelve months before the end of the first ten year period
of its desire to terminate this Agreement.

If the foregoing arrangements are acceptable to Your
Excellency's Government, I have the honour to propose that
this note and Your Excellency's note in reply to that effect

- 3 -

0262

shall constitute an Agreement between our two Governments on
this matter which shall enter into force on the date of your
note in reply.

I avail myself of this opportunity to renew to
Your Excellency the assurance of my highest consideration.

Manzur Qadir

(Manzur Qadir)
Minister of Foreign Affairs and
Commonwealth Relations

Enclosures; (2)
1. Annex A-Agreed Areas
and Rights of Way
2. Annex B-Jurisdiction

His Excellency Mr. James M. Langley,
The Ambassador of the United States of America
in Pakistan,
Karachi.

The American Ambassador to the Pakistani Minister
of Foreign Affairs and Commonwealth Relations

Embassy of the
United States of America
No. 32   Karachi, July 18, 1959.

Excellency:

I have the honor to acknowledge the receipt of your
note of today's date, together with Annex A and Annex B
attached thereto, the texts of which read as follows:
"I refer to our recent discussions regarding the
desire of the United States to station a Communications Unit
in Pakistan. I have the honour to inform you that the
Government of Pakistan agrees to the stationing of such a Unit
on the following basis:
"1. The Government of Pakistan will make available
to the United States the land areas and rights-of-way required
for the establishment and operation of the Communications
Unit and will provide protection for such Unit. The agreed
areas and rights-of-way are set forth in Annex A.

0263

- 4 -

"2.   The Communications Unit and personnel assigned
to it may install and use communications equipment,
including antennas; use continuously agreed radio
frequencies and agreed wire communications facilities;
purchase locally goods and services including construction
materials, electrical power and transportation services;
make arrangements for the internal security of those small
areas, within the agreed areas, designated for the
exclusive use of the Communications Unit (only authorized
personnel may enter these latter areas); carry arms in
connection with official duties within the areas designated
for the exclusive use of the Communications Unit and in
connection with the courier duties outside the agreed
areas; and may engage in such other activities as may be
necessary for the effective operation of the Unit and the
health and welfare of its personnel.

"3.   The Communications Unit and personnel assigned
to it shall respect the laws of Pakistan and shall abstain
from any activity which would adversely affect the interests
of the people or the Government of Pakistan.   The Government
of the United States will take necessary measures to prevent
abuse of the privileges granted by the Government of
Pakistan   under the present Agreement.

"4.   The Government of Pakistan will, upon request,
assist the Communications Unit in the local procurement of
goods, materials, supplies and services required for the
establishment, operation and support of the Unit.   The
Unit shall enjoy any preferential rates, charges, or
priorities which are available to the Armed Forces of
Pakistan for goods or services purchased locally in
connection with the operation of the Unit.

"5.   (a) (1) The personnel of the Communications
Unit shall receive exemption from payment of all duties and
taxes, including export duties, on their personal and
household goods brought into the country for their own use
within six months of their arrival.

Goods imported under this section will
not ordinarily be sold or disposed of in Pakistan by the
owner, except to other persons enjoying comparable privileges.
In the event of their sale or disposal to a person who does not
enjoy comparable privileges, the duty and taxes thereon
will be paid.

The Pakistan Customs Department will
issue appropriate regulations regarding the provisions of this
section.

(b). The temporary presence in Pakistan of a
member of the Unit shall constitute neither residence nor
domicile therein and shall not of itself subject him to
taxation in Pakistan, either on his income or on his
property, the presence of which in Pakistan is due
to his temporary presence there, nor, in the event of his
death, shall it subject his estate to a levy of death duties.

"6. No tax, duty or other charge will be levied or
assessed on activities of the Unit or on material, equipment,
supplies or goods brought into or procured in Pakistan by
the United States authorities for the use of the Unit,
its agencies or personnel assigned to the Unit.

"7. The United States Government may construct
within the agreed areas the facilities required for support
of the Communications Unit under the terms and conditions set
forth in Articles II through VII of the Military Defense
Construction Agreement signed at Karachi on May 28, 1956.

"8. Title to removable materials, equipment or property
brought into or acquired in Pakistan by or on behalf of the
Communications Unit will remain in the United States Government.
Such material, equipment or property may be brought into or
removed tax and duty free at any time from Pakistan by the
United States Government.

The materials, equipment and property of the Unit
and its official papers will be exempt from inspection, search
and seizure and may be removed freely by the United States
Government at any time.

"9. Jurisdiction over personnel of the Unit shall
be exercised in accordance with the provisions of Annex B,
an integral part hereof.

"10. Arrangements required to give effect to this
Agreement will be the subject of agreement between the
Commanding Officer of the Communications Unit and Senior
Military Officer of the Pakistan Forces in the area.

"11. In this Agreement the expressions "personnel
assigned to the Unit", "personnel of the Unit", and "member
of the Unit" include persons who are in Pakistan in connection
with the Agreement and who are (a) members of the United States
armed forces; (b) civilian personnel employed by, serving
with, or accompanying the United States armed forces (except

- 6 -

0265

persons who are nationals of Pakistan or ordinarily resident therein); or (c) dependents of the persons defined in (a) and (b) above.

"12. This Agreement shall remain in force for a period of ten years and for a second period of ten years thereafter unless either party gives written notice to the other at least twelve months before the end of the first ten year period of its desire to terminate this Agreement.

"If the foregoing arrangements are acceptable to Your Excellency's Government, I have the honour to propose that this note and Your Excellency's note in reply to that effect shall constitute an Agreement between our two Governments on this matter which shall enter into force on the date of your note in reply.

"I avail myself of this opportunity to renew to Your Excellency the assurance of my highest consideration.

" ANNEX A

AAgreed Areas and Rights of Way

" The United States may use the land areas and rights-of-way described herein in accordance with the provisions of this Annex and the Agreement on the United States Communications Unit of July 18, 1959, of which this Annex is a part.

"Site I

"Site I is located on the Chumkani Road which runs eastward from the Peshawar-Kohat Road approximately three miles south of Peshawar.

"1. Parcel Number 1. A parcel of land enclosed by boundaries established as follows: Base Point--- 50.5 feet northward from the one-mile marker on the Chumkani Road on a line running perpendicular to the road. From this base point a line running in a westerly direction and parallel to the road with bearing South 89 degrees 30 minutes 00 seconds West, a distance of 2,500.00 feet to the southwest corner; thence North 0 degrees 30 minutes 00 seconds West, a distance of 5,000.00 feet to the northwest corner; thence North 89 degrees 30 minutes 00 seconds East,

0266

- 7 -

a distance of 5,000.00 feet to the northeast corner;
thence South 0 degrees 30 minutes 00 seconds East,
a distance of 5,086.69 feet to the southeast corner;
thence a line running parallel to the road bearing
North 83 degrees 07 minutes 40 seconds West, a distance
of 675.58 feet to a point on the southern boundary line;
thence South 89 degrees 30 minutes 00 seconds West,
a distance of 1,830.00 feet to the point of beginning.
All bearings magnetic.

        "2. Parcel Number 2. A parcel of land that
lies within the boundaries of Parcel Number 1 described in
paragraph 1, with boundaries established as follows:
Base Point--- the base point for Parcel Number 2 is the same
as the base point for Parcel Number 1, described in
paragraph 1. The southern boundary runs for 425.00 feet
along the southern boundary of Parcel Number 1. The
southeast corner of Parcel Number 2 is 225.00 feet to the
east of the base point. The southwest corner is 200.00
feet to the west of the base point. The western boundary is a
line running from the southwest corner on a bearing of
North 0 degrees 30 minutes 00 seconds West, a distance
of 600.00 feet to the northwest corner. The northern
boundary is a line running from the northwest corner on a
bearing North 89 degrees 30 minutes 00 seconds East,
a distance of 425.00 feet to the northeast corner. The
eastern boundary is a line running from the northeast corner
on a bearing South 0 degrees 30 minutes 00 seconds East,
a distance of 600.00 feet to the southeast corner. All
bearings magnetic.

        "3. Parcel Number 3. A parcel of land enclosed
by boundaries established as follows: Base Point----
a point 14.5 feet southward on a line starting at the
one-mile marker on the Chumkani road and running perpendicular
to the road. From this base point a line running in an
easterly direction parallel to the road, bearing North
89 degrees 30 minutes 00 seconds East, a distance of
1,070.00 feet to the northeast corner; thence South
51 degrees 12 minutes 35 seconds West, a distance of
2,420.74 feet to the southeast corner; thence South
89 degrees 30 minutes 00 seconds West, a distance of

- 8 -

0267

200.00 feet to the southwest corner; thence North O
degrees 30 minutes OO seconds West, a distance of 1,500.00
feet to the northwest corner; thence North 89 degrees
30 minutes OO seconds East, a distance of 1,030.00 feet
to the point of beginning. All bearings magnetic.

"4. Parcel Number 4. A parcel of land located
west of and adjacent to Parcel Number 3 above, enclosed by
boundaries established as follows: Base Point---
a point on the northwest corner of Parcel Number 3 of Site
I, said point being 14.5 feet south and 1.030.00 feet west
of the one mile marker on the Chumkani Road; thence
in a westerly direction with the bearing South 89 degrees
30 minutes OO seconds West, and along the south line of
said Chumkani Road, a distance of 1,742.4 feet; thence in
a southerly direction with bearing South O degrees 30
minutes OO seconds East, and parallel to the west boundary
line of said Parcel No. 3, a distance of 1,500.00 feet;
thence in an easterly direction with bearing North 89 degrees
30 minutes OO seconds East, a distance of 1,742,4 feet to
a point on the southwest corner of said Parcel Number 3;
thence in a northerly direction with bearing North O degrees
30,minutes OO seconds West, and along the west boundary
line of said Parcel Number 3, a distance of 1,500.00 feet
to the point of beginning; said tract containing 60 acres,
more or less. All bearings magnetic.

"Parcels Number 2, Number 3 and Number 4 are for the
exclusive use of the Communications Unit.

"In order to provide utility services in Parcels
Number 2, Number 3 and Number 4, the Communications Unit
may install, use,operate and maintain utility systems, to
include water, power, communications, and sewage, over,
across and under the Chumkani Road adjoining these parcels.

"In that part of Parcel Number 1 which is outside
Parcel Number 2, the Communications Unit may lay cables and
erect antennas, poles, connecting lines, power lines, and
support wires; and personnel assigned to the Unit may enter
and move within the area freely at any time for purposes
related to the operation of the Communications Unit.

It is understood that the land in Parcel Number 1 which
is outside Parcel Number 2 may be used by the land owners
for agricultural purposes under conditions which will not
interfere with the operations of the Communications Unit.

Authorities of the Government of Pakistan will, upon
request, make arrangements necessary to insure that the
landowners are informed of such conditions and comply with them.

"Site II

"Site II is located south of Peshawar approximately
seven miles, and east of the Peshawar-Kohat road approximately
43 miles.

"1. Parcel Number 5.   A parcel of land enclosed by
boundaries established as follows: Base Point--- a point
on the south edge of the road running eastward from the
seven-mile marker on the Peshawar-Kohat road, at a distance
approximately 4 miles east of the Peshawar-Kohat road,
and approximately 2,200.00 feet west of the intersection at
which the east-west road intersects a road that loops to
the south around a high earth mound and also branches to
the north. The base point is 20.00 feet south of the center
line of the east-west road and is marked by concrete monument
with a nail embedded on the top. From this base point a
line running parallel to the road in an easterly direction,
bearing South 72 degrees 50 minutes 00 seconds East, a distance
of 1,200.00 feet to the northeast corner; thence South
17 degrees 10 minutes 00 seconds West, a distance of 2,400.00
feet to the southeast corner; thence North 72 degrees 50
minutes 00 seconds West, a distance of 2,400.00 feet to
the southwest corner; thence North 17 degrees 10 minutes
00 seconds East, a distance of 2,400.00 feet to the northwest
corner; thence South 72 degrees 50 minutes 00 seconds East,
a distance of 1,200.00 feet to the point of beginning.
All bearings magnetic.

"2. Parcel Number 6.   A square parcel of land each
side of which is 660.00 feet long, located approximately at
the center of Parcel Number 5.

"3. Access Road.   A strip of land thirth feet wide
connecting the northern boundary of parcel Number 6 with
the east-west road for use by the Communications Unit as an
access road.

"Parcel Number 6 is for the exclusive use of the
Communications Unit.

"In that part of Parcel Number 5 which is outside
Parcel Number 6, the Communications Unit may lay cables and
erect antennas, poles, connecting lines, power lines, and

0269

- 10 -

한·미국 간의 상호방위조약 제4조에 의한 시설과 구역 및 한국에서의 미국군대의 지위에 관한 협정(SOFA)
전59권. 1966.7.9 서울에서 서명 : 1967.2.9 발효(조약 232호) (V.56 형사재판관할권 관계자료)   461

support wires; and personnel assigned to the Unit may enter
and move within the area freely at any time for purposes related
to the operation of the Communications Unit.

"It is understood that the land in Parcel Number 5
which is outside Parcel Number 6 and the road may be used
by the landowners for agricultural purposes under conditions
which will not interfere with the operations of the
Communications Unit. Authorities of the Government of
Pakistan will, upon request, make arrangements necessary
to insure that the landowners are informed of such conditions
and comply with them.

"Site III

"Site III is located approsimately 13 miles south
of Peshawar on the east side of the Peshawar-Kohat road.

"1. <u>Parcel Number 7</u>. A parcel of land enclosed by
boundaries established as follows: Base Point-- a point
marked by a brick monument buried 40.00 feet east of the
center line of the Peshawar-Kohat road opposite the 13mile
marker. From this base point a line running on a northerly
direction, parallel to the road, on a bearing North 02
degrees 30 minutes 00 seconds East, a distance of 494.45
feet; thence a distance of 652.3 feet on a bearing North 08
degrees 02 minutes 00 seconds East; and thence a distance of
59.10 feet on a bearing North 20 degrees 15 minutes 00 seconds
East to the northwest corner; thence South 87 degrees 30
minutes 00 seconds East, a distance of 2,319.09 feet to the
northeast corner; thence South 02 degrees 30 minutes 00
seconds West, a distance of 2,400.00 feet to the southeast
corner; thence North 87 degrees 30 minutes 00 seconds West,
a distance of 2,400.00 feet to the southwest corner;
thence North 02 degrees 30 minutes 00 seconds East, a distance
of 1,200.00 feet to the point of beginning. All bearings
magnetic.

"2. <u>Parcel Number 8</u>. A square parcel of land each
side ofwhich is 660.00 feet long, located approximately
at the center of Parcel Number 7.

"3. <u>Access Road.</u> A strip of land thirty feet wide
connecting the center of the western boundary of Parcel
Number 8 with the Peshawar-Kohat road for use by the
Communications Unit as an access road. Parcel Number 8 is

0270

for the exclusive use of the Communications Unit.

"In that part of Parcel Number 7 which is outside Parcel Number 8, the Communications Unit may lay cables and erect antennas, poles, connecting lines, power lines, and support wires; and personnel assigned to the Unit may enter and move within the area freely at any time for purposes related to the operations of the Communications Unit.

"It is understood that the land in Parcel Number 7 which is outside Parcel Number 8 and the road may be used by the landowners for agricultural purposes under conditions which will not interfere with the operations of the Communications Unit. Authorities of the Government of Pakistan will, upon request, make arrangements necessary to insure that the landowners are informed of such conditions and comply with them.

"ANNEX B(1)

"Jurisdiction

"Recognizing the responsibility of the courts of Pakistan for the administration of justice in Pakistan, and also the responsibility of the United States military authorities for maintaining good order and discipline among personnel of the Unit, it is agreed that jurisdiction over such personnel shall be exercised in accordance with the provisions of this Annex.

"1. Subject to the provisions of this Annex,

(a) the civil authorities of Pakistan shall have jurisdiction over the personnel of the Unit with respect to offenses committed within the territory of Pakistan and punishable by the law of Pakistan;

(b) the military authorities of the United States shall have the right to exercise within Pakistan all criminal and disciplinary jurisdiction conferred on them by the laws of the United States over the personnel of the Unit.

"2. (a) The authorities of Pakistan shall have the right to exercise exclusive jurisdiction over the personnel of the Unit with respect to offenses, including offences relating to the security of Pakistan, punishable by the law of Pakistan, but not by the law of the United States.

(b) The military authorities of the United States shall have the right to exercise exclusive jurisdiction over

0271

- 12 -

the personnel of the Unit with respect to offences, including offences relating to the security of the United States, punishable by the law of the United States, but not by the law of Pakistan.

(c) For the purposes of this paragraph and the paragraph next following, a security offence against the State shall include

(i) treason against the State;

(ii) sabotage, espionage or violation of any law relating to the official secrets of that State, or
secrets relating to the national defence of that State.

"3. In cases where the right to exercise jurisdiction is concurrent the following rules shall apply:

(a) The military authorities of the United States shall have the primary right to exercise jurisdiction over the personnel of the Unit in relation to

(i) offences solely against the property or security of the United States, or offences solely against the person or property of another member of the Unit;

(ii) offences arising out of any act or ômission done in the performance of official duty; and

(iii) subject to the provision of paragraph 1(b), offences committed solely within those parts of the agreed areas which are designated for the exclusive use of the Ĝommunications Unit.

(b) In the case of any other offence the authorities of Pakistan shall have the primary right to exercise jurisdiction.

(c) If the State having the primary right decides not to exercise jurisdictinn, it shall notify the authorities of the other State as soon as practicable. The authorities of Pakistan, recognizing that it is the primary responsibility of the United States authorities to maintain good order and discipline where persons subject to United States military law are concerned, will, upon the request of the United States authorities, waive their primary right to exercise jurisdiction pursuant to this Annex, except where the Government of Pakistan determines that it is of particular importance that jurisdiction be exercised by the Pakistan authorities.

"4.   The foregoing provisions of this Annex shall
not imply any right for the military authorities of the
United States to exercise jurisdiction over persons who
are nationals of or ordinarily resident in Pakistan, unless
they are members of the Unit.

"5. (a)   The authorities of Pakistan and the
United States shall assist each other in the arrest of
members of the Unit and in handing them over to the authority
which is to exercise jurisdiction in accordance with the
above provisions.

(b)   The authorities of Pakistan shall notify
promptly the military authorities of the United States of
the arrest of any member of the Unit.

(c)   The custody of an accused member of the
Unit, over whom Pakistan is to exercise jurisdiction,
shall remain with the United States. The United States
assumes the responsibility for custody pending conclusion
of judicial proceedings. The United States authorities
will make any member of the Unit immediately available to
Pakistan authorities upon their request for purposes of
investigation and trial.

"6. (a)   The authorities of Pakistan and the United
States shall assist each other in the carrying out of all
necessary investigations into offences and in the collection
and production of evidence, including the seizure and, in
proper cases, the handing over of objects connected with the
offence. The handing over of such objects may, however,
be made subject to their return within the time specified by
the authority delivering them.

(b)   The authorities of Pakistan and the
United States shall notify each other of the disposition of
all cases in which there are concurrent rights to exercise
jurisdiction.

"7.   The authorities of Pakistan shall give sympathetic
consideration to a request by the United States for
assistance in carrying out a sentence of imprisonment
pronounced by the authorities of the United States under the
provisions of this Annex within the terriotry of Pakistan.

- 14 -

0273

"8. If a case against a member of the Unit has been tried or disposed of in accordance with the provisions of this Annex by the authorities of one State, he shall not be prosecuted in Pakistan for the same offence by the authorities of the other State.

"9. Whenever a member of the Unit is prosecuted in Pakistan Courts, he shall be entitled

    (a) to a prompt and speedy trial;

    (b) to be informed in advance of trial of the specific charge or charges made against him;

    (c) to be confronted with the witnesses against him;

    (d) to have compulsory process for obtaining witnesses in his favor, if they are within the jurisdiction of Pakistan;

    (e) to have legal representation of his own choice for his defence at all stages of the proceedings;

    (f) if he considers necessary, to have the services of an interpreter; and

    (g) to communicate with a representative of the United States and to have such a representative present at all stages of the proceedings.

"10. If a member of the Unit is acquitted after trial by a court in Pakistan, no appeal against his acquittal shall be presented by the prosecution. In cases other than acquittal, no appeal shall be taken by the prosecution except on grounds of legal error.

"11. The authorities of Pakistan will have jurisdiction with respect to civil suits or claims involving injury or death or loss or damage to property arising out of acts or omissions of members of the Unit provided that if the act or omission is in the performance of official duty, the authorities in Pakistan shall not exercise their jurisdiction.

"12. The determination whether an act or omission is or is not in the performance of official duty for the purposes of paragraph 3(a)(ii) or paragraph 11 shall, in the first instance, be made by the United States military authorities after appropriate consultation with the Pakistan authorities. If the authorities of Pakistan and the United States hold divergent views on this point, the matter shall be decided between the diplomatic authorities of the United States and the appropriate authorities of the Government of Pakistan."

- 15 -

0274

I have the honor to inform Your Excellency that the Government of the United States of America accepts the arrangements contained in your note, together with Annex A and Annex B attached thereto, and regards your note and this reply as constituting an Agreement between our two Governnents, the Agreement to enter into force on this day.

Accept, Excellency, the renewed assurances of my highest consideration.

James M. Langley

His Excellency

Manzur Qadir,
Minister of Foreign Affairs
and Commonwealth Relations,
Karachi.

MINUTE OF UNDERSTANDING

It is agreed that the following conditions shall apply to the privileges extended to personnel of the Communications Unit in paragraph 5(a) of the Agreement on the United States Communications Unit of July 18, 1959:

1. The exemption applies to direct imports only and not to lo al purchase or clearances from bond.

2. No Pakistan foreign exchange is involved in such imports.

3. The number of motor cars imported under this section by each person assigned to the Unit shall not exceed one.

James M. Langley

James M. Langley
United States Ambassador

Manzur Qadir

Manzur Qadir
Minister of Foreign Affairs
and Commonwealth Relations

Karachi
July 18, 1959.

In Duplicate Originals.

- 16 -

0275

Embassy of the
United States of America
Karachi, July 18, 1959.

Dear Mr. Minister:

Today the Governments of the United States of
America and Pakistan exchanged notes formalizing our
Agreement on the United States Communications Unit and the
status of the members of the Unit who enter Pakistan in
connection therewith.

Annex B of that Agreement provides for the exercise
of jurisdiction over such members. In this regard, I would
be grateful for your confirmation of the following
understandings:

1. That no cruel or unusual punishment would be
   inflicted upon any person over whom the Pakistani
   authorities might exercise jurisdiction prusuant
   to Annex B;

2. That should any person over whom the Pakistani
   authorities exercise such jurisdiction subsequently
   be confined by those authorities, the United States
   military authorities would be permitted to visit
   such person periodically at the place of confinement;

3. That in implementation of the provisions of
   paragraph 3(c) of Annex B, it shall not be necessary
   for the United States to make a request for waiver
   in each particular case, and it shall be taken for
   granted that Pakistan has waived its primary right
   to exercise jurisdiction thereunder except where
   the Government of Pakistan determines in a specific
   case that it is of particular importance that
   jurisdiction be exercised therein by the authorities
   of Pakistan;

4. That with reference to paragraph 5(c) of Annex
   B, concerning custody of an accused member of the
   Unit, the United States authorities will give full
   consideration to the special wishes of the
   appropriate Pakistan authorities as to the manner
   in which the custody of an accused member of the Unit

0276

shall be carried into effect;

5. That with respect to paragraph 11 of Annex B, concerning civil suits or claims arising out of any act or omission done in the performance of official duty over which the authorities of Pakistan shall not exercise their jurisdiction, meritorious claims thereunder will be settled by the United States Military authorities in accordance with procedures which enable them to make expeditious settlement of such claims.

      Sincerely yours,

                      James M. Langley

                      James M. Langley
                          Ambassador

Mr. Manzur Qadir,
    Minister of Foreign Affairs
      and Commonwealth Relations,
      Karachi.

The Pakistani Minister of Foreign Affairs and
Commonwealth Relations to the American Ambassador

                  Minister for Foreign Affairs
                  and Commonwealth Relations
                  Karachi.
                  July 18th, 1959.

Dear Mr. Ambassador:

    As requested in your letter of July 18th, 1959, I am pleased to confirm our understandings:

1. That no cruel or unusual punishment would be inflicted upon any person over whom the Pakistani authorities might exercise jurisdiction pursuant to Annex B;

2. That should any person over whom the Pakistani authorities exercise such jurisdiction subsequently be confined by those authorities, the United States military authorities would be permitted to visit such person periodically at the place of confinement;

3. That in implementation of the provisions of paragraph 3 (c) of Annex B, it shall not be necessary for the United States to make a request for waiver in each particular case, and it shall be taken for granted that Pakistan had waived its primary right to exercise jurisdiction thereunder

0277

except where the Government of Pakistan determines
in a specific case that it is of particular
importance that jurisdiction be exercised therein
by the authorities of Pakistan;

4. That with reference to paragraph 5(c) of Annex
B, concerning custody of an accused member of the
Unit, the United States authorities will give full
consideration to the special wishes of the appropriate
Pakistan authorities as to the manner in which the
custody of an accused member of the Unit shall be
carried into effect;

5. That with respect to paragraph 11 of Annex B,
concerning civil suits or claims arising out of any
act or omission done in the performance of official
duty over which the authorities of Pakistan shall
not exercise their jurisdiction, meritorious claims
thereunder will be settled by the United States
military authorities in accordance with procedures
which enable them to make expeditious settlement of
such claims.

Sincerely yours,

Manzur Qadir

(Manzur Qadir)
Minister of Foreign Affairs
and Commonwealth Relations

His Excellency Mr. James M. Langley,
The Ambassador of the United States of America
in Pakistan,
Karachi.

0278

외교문서 비밀해제: 주한미군지위협정(SOFA) 23
주한미군지위협정(SOFA) 서명 및 발효 23

초판인쇄 2024년 03월 15일
초판발행 2024년 03월 15일

지은이 한국학술정보(주)
펴낸이 채종준
펴낸곳 한국학술정보(주)
주 소 경기도 파주시 회동길 230(문발동)
전 화 031-908-3181(대표)
팩 스 031-908-3189
홈페이지 http://ebook.kstudy.com
E-mail 출판사업부 publish@kstudy.com
등 록 제일산-115호(2000. 6. 19)

ISBN   979-11-7217-034-9 94340
        979-11-7217-011-0 94340 (set)